TOM

COX G3

THE WORLD'S
WORST AIRCRAFT

THE WORLD'S
WORST AIRCRAFT
FROM PIONEERING FAILURES TO MULTIMILLION DOLLAR DISASTERS

JIM WINCHESTER

Grange
BOOKS

This edition first published in 2005 for Grange Books
An imprint of Grange Books plc
The Grange
Kingsnorth Industrial Estate
Hoo, nr Rochester
Kent ME3 9ND
www.grangebooks.co.uk

Reprinted in 2006

ISBN-10: 1-84013-752-5
ISBN-13: 978-1-84013-752-1

Editorial and design by
Amber Books Ltd
Bradley's Close
74–77 White Lion Street
London N1 9PF
www.amberbooks.co.uk

Project Editor: James Bennett
Picture Research: James Hollingworth
Design: EQ Media

Printed in Singapore

CONTENTS

INTRODUCTION

The choice of the 150 'worst' aircraft contained in this volume is the author's own, although friends offered many suggestions. As such it should not be regarded as definitive in any way. Strictly speaking, a number of these entries could be considered more as 'flops' than 'worst' in the sense of having many inherent faults.

Most of the aircraft here have some redeeming features. Many were arguably not bad at all. Some were commercially unsuccessful, others no longer met military requirements or followed them too rigidly. Some definitely should never have left the drawing board. One or two barely did – only making it as far as a mock-up or partly completed prototype.

A few manufacturers appear again and again in this book. Generally speaking a few bad aircraft will appear from time to time in any company's stable – if the company keeps going long enough and is willing to try new things. A number of the planemakers featured here are of course still in business. Nothing written here is meant as a slur on these companies and their current products. After all, if they are still making aircraft (and only a handful of the manufacturers mentioned in this book still are) they must be doing something right.

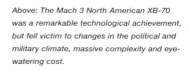

Above: The Mach 3 North American XB-70 was a remarkable technological achievement, but fell victim to changes in the political and military climate, massive complexity and eye-watering cost.

Above: At the other end of the scale, the Hiller VZ-1 was a man-size contraption that allowed a soldier to hover several metres off the ground making a very loud noise as he did so. No practical use was found for the aircraft.

Until the 1920s, it can be argued that aircraft design was in its infancy and there was still much to learn, so it is perhaps unfair to be too harsh on some of the designs from this era. What seems blindingly obvious as a disaster waiting to happen today must have looked like the next great advance in aeronautics. Nonetheless, plenty of designers fell into the 'should have known better' category. Some inventors persisted with attempts to prove that the Wright Brothers, Louis Blériot and other great pioneers had it all wrong, and built multiplanes, ornithopters and other devices that largely vibrated themselves to bits before putting their pilots in too much danger, but, at least, not from a high fall.

Fewer aircraft which qualify as 'bad' are made these days. Extensive computer modelling and simulation allows the bugs to be ironed out before metal (or carbon fibre) is cut. The small number of major aircraft projects and their great cost make aerospace companies somewhat risk averse, as failure can easily 'cost the farm'.

All the aircraft contained in here were somebody's labour of love and all represent someone's dream, costing a lot of money and effort in their day. A number saw the wasting of large fortunes, the careers of many talented people and the lives of their crews. It is easy to take cheap shots at someone who has tried and failed, but the author (who has not designed any flying machines to date) hopes he has been able to find the humour in some of these stories of aircraft that never quite took off.

BAD TIMING

Most of the aircraft in this section could have been great successes, but appeared too late and were immediately obsolescent, or conversely were initially successful but past their sell-by date when most needed. Some of these embodied notable firsts, but either the times changed or they didn't.

Unfortunately for military aircraft the consequence of obsolescence has usually been measured in young men's lives. Failed combat aircraft were usually shunted to training or second-line units as soon as possible, but in many cases not before they had suffered heavy attrition, as with the Douglas TBD and the Fairey Battle.

Military requirements move on, particularly in wartime. The Boeing Sea Ranger was obsolete by the time it was built, but only because the US Navy had changed its strategy following the opening battles of the Pacific War. The Douglas Mixmaster would have been marvellous if it had appeared a year or two earlier than it did. Conversely, the proposed attack variant would have been useful in Korea if the USAF had persisted with it.

In the civil field, the attempt to produce a replacement for the DC-3 led to many false starts, including the Saab Scandia and the Aviation Traders Accountant.

Left: The giant Bristol Brabazon. Building an airliner larger than a 747 proved beyond the resources of Britain's postwar aircraft industry.

The Accountant (named for its supposed good economics) was another attempt to replace the DC-3 in the postwar airlines and air forces. Aviation Traders, a small British company mainly involved in converting passenger aircraft to freighters, decided to enter the market in 1952 with a modern-technology turboprop.

The company changed its mind a lot over construction methods and configuration and promised that the production aircraft would differ greatly from the prototype, perhaps not the wisest marketing strategy. If the company had won big orders they had no suitable facilities in which to produce them. Eventually the company's own accountants were heeded and it was realized that the sensible decision was to not proceed further. The ATL-90 was stored in 1958 after a very short flying career, and broken up in 1960.

SPECIFICATIONS

CREW:	2–3 and 28 passengers
POWERPLANT:	two 1291kW (1730hp) Rolls-Royce Dart R.Da.6 turboprops
CRUISING SPEED:	470km/h (295mph)
SPAN:	25.15m (82ft 6in)
LENGTH:	18.93m (62ft 1in)
HEIGHT:	7.70m (25ft 3in)
WEIGHT:	maximum 14,512kg (32,000lb)

Left: Aviation Traders was a small company trying to replace an established design in a competitive market. Not surprisingly it failed to sell any examples of the Accountant and quit while it was ahead.

The Rolls-Royce Dart turboprop was the engine of choice of the day, powering the Fokker Friendship and Handley Page Dart Herald, both of which were built by large manufacturers on the basis of sound economics.

Standard accommodation would be 28 passengers, although a 42-seat ATL-91 version was planned, as was a 14-seat executive transport.

The unusual shape of the forward fuselage was due to the swing nose arrangement proposed for production freighter aircraft. The passenger version would have had a different shape.

G-ATEL

11

BLOHM UND VOSS BV 238 *(1944)*

Originally designed as a passenger flying boat for the postwar Lufthansa, the BV 238 design was adapted in 1941 for military use as a maritime patrol and transport aircraft. When completed in 1944 it was the largest aircraft since the Maxim Gorkii (q.v.) and the heaviest built to that time. A quarter-scale testbed called the FGP 227 was deemed necessary to test the aerodynamics and water handling, but it completely failed to take off when tested on wheels and was then damaged by saboteurs. All the engines seized on its first flight from water – months after the first full-scale BV 238 flew. The sole complete BV 238 was caught on a lake by P-51 Mustangs and sunk by machine-gun fire in September 1944. Although three further BV 238s and three BV 250 landplane bombers were under construction, the loss of the only flying example caused the Luftwaffe to give up on the idea.

SPECIFICATIONS

CREW:	12
POWERPLANT:	six 1417kW (1900hp) Daimler-Benz DB 603G inline piston engines
MAX SPEED:	425km/h (264mph)
SPAN:	60.17m (197ft 5in)
LENGTH:	43.36m (142ft 3in)
HEIGHT:	12.80m (42ft)
WEIGHT:	maximum 100,000kg (220,460lb)

Left: Development of the BV 238 started so late and took so long that air superiority was lost by the time it flew. It proved as vulnerable on the water as it would have in the air.

If it had entered service, the BV 238 would have had machine guns in nose and tail turrets, at the rear of the wings and in fuselage beam stations. A dorsal turret would have had two 20mm (0.79in) cannon.

The BV 238 was the world's heaviest aircraft in 1944. Fully loaded it would have needed rocket assistance to get airborne.

The original powerplant choice was four 24-cylinder Jumo 223 engines, but when these were not available, Blohm und Voss had to settle for six 12-cylinder Daimler-Benz motors.

BOEING XPBB-1 SEA RANGER (1942)

In 1940 the solution to German U-boats off the US east coast was deemed to be giant long-range flying-boat bombers. Boeing was the obvious builder with its track record of the prewar 'Clipper' airliners and the Navy ordered 57 to start with. Boeing built a whole new plant at Renton by Lake Washington to build the Sea Ranger. The XPBB-1 prototype flew in July 1942 and was the largest twin-engined aircraft built to date, but the experiences of the Pacific War saw the War Department completely revise its strategy in favour of land-based bombers. The Sea Ranger programme was cancelled and the Renton plant was swapped with the army for one in Kansas. Renton subsequently built over 1000 B-29s and later C-135 jet tanker/transports and 707 airliners. The solitary Sea Ranger never flew a combat mission before it was mothballed and scrapped.

SPECIFICATIONS

CREW:	10
POWERPLANT:	two 1715kW (2300hp) Wright R-3350-8 piston engines
MAX SPEED:	348km/h (215mph)
SPAN:	42.58m (139ft 9in)
LENGTH:	28.88m (94ft 9in)
HEIGHT:	10.40m (34ft 2in)
WEIGHT:	45,872kg (101,130lb)

Left: Only the single example of the Sea Ranger was built and it inevitably became known as the Lone Ranger. When the XPBB flew away from the factory built for it, it marked the end of a long history of Boeing flying boats.

Surprisingly for such a large flying boat, the XPBB was twin-engined. Defensive armament was only four machine guns but the bomb load was greater than a B-29's.

The XPBB-1's wing was based on that of the B-29 Superfortress. Some of the aerodynamics were inherited from Boeing's Model 314 Clipper.

There was a plan to use special barges to catapult launch the Sea Ranger so as to increase the already long range, but this was never tested.

BOULTON PAUL DEFIANT (1937)

Alongside the Spitfire and Hurricane in the Battle of Britain was the Defiant, a fighter of a completely different concept, one which proved fatally flawed. In its first few combats, the Defiant achieved tactical surprise on the Luftwaffe, whose fighters approached from behind thinking they had an unwary Hurricane in their sights, only to be met by the concentrated fire of four machine guns. The Me 109 pilots soon learned that the Defiant was a sluggish performer and that its guns were hard to bring to bear in the forward quarter. In one July 1940 engagement, No.141 Squadron lost all nine airborne Defiants. Disasters like this saw the Defiant quickly withdrawn from the day fighter squadrons. The Defiant was more effective as a night-fighter, being the most successful British aircraft during the winter of 1940–41.

SPECIFICATIONS (Defiant II)

CREW:	2
POWERPLANT:	one 954kW (1280hp) Rolls-Royce Merlin XX piston engine
MAX SPEED:	504km/h (313mph)
SPAN:	11.98m (39ft 4in)
LENGTH:	10.77m (35ft 4in)
HEIGHT:	3.45m (11ft 4in)
WEIGHT:	loaded 3821kg (8424lb)

Left: The heavy four-gun turret severely affected the Defiant's performance and manoeuvrability. The Luftwaffe discovered its weak spots and several squadrons were decimated in the Battle of Britain.

The Defiant Mk I was powered by the same Merlin engine as the contemporary Spitfire and Hurricane models, but was larger and considerably heavier.

All the Defiant's weapons were in the charge of the gunner, it being thought the pilot could better fly the aircraft without having to concentrate on aiming at a target.

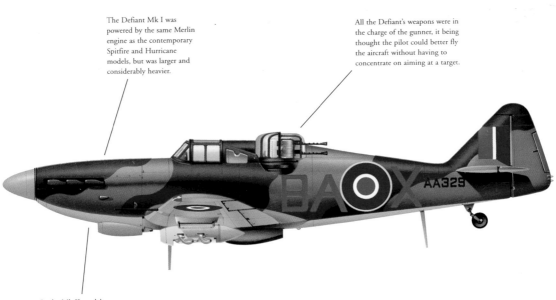

In the Mk II model, a more powerful Merlin was fitted, as was a larger rudder. Many were converted to target tugs and others were used for air-sea rescue work.

BRISTOL BRABAZON (1949)

In the middle of the war a committee headed by Lord Brabazon drew up a plan for Britain's postwar civil aviation needs. In his honour the largest landplane ever designed in Britain was named when it was completed after three years construction. Designed for four Proteus turboprop engines, the unavailability of these resulted in the use of eight Centaurus piston engines geared to drive four contra-rotating propellers, which were really not enough for adequate performance.

The structure was built too lightly so as to get the maximum range and payload from the design. Skin and frame cracks were detected, but the Brabazon didn't fly long enough for these to prove critical. However, they contributed to officialdom's failure to certify the Brabazon for unrestricted operations. This and the increasing cost of the project saw its scrapping in 1952.

SPECIFICATIONS

CREW:	6 flight deck, 8 cabin and 100 passengers
POWERPLANT:	eight 1977kW (2650hp) Bristol Centaurus 20 radial piston engines
MAX SPEED:	483km/h (300mph)
SPAN:	70.10m (230ft)
LENGTH:	53.95m (177ft)
HEIGHT:	15.24m (50ft)
WEIGHT:	loaded 131,542kg (290,000lb)

Left: Larger than a 747, the Brabazon transatlantic airliner proved a giant white elephant. There was too much space and too much weight but not enough power to carry its 100 passengers, ensuring uneconomic operation.

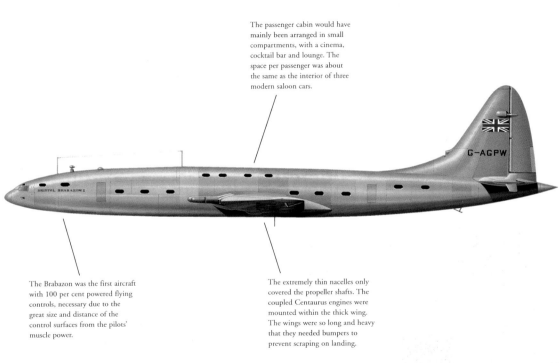

The passenger cabin would have mainly been arranged in small compartments, with a cinema, cocktail bar and lounge. The space per passenger was about the same as the interior of three modern saloon cars.

The Brabazon was the first aircraft with 100 per cent powered flying controls, necessary due to the great size and distance of the control surfaces from the pilots' muscle power.

The extremely thin nacelles only covered the propeller shafts. The coupled Centaurus engines were mounted within the thick wing. The wings were so long and heavy that they needed bumpers to prevent scraping on landing.

CONVAIR 880/990 (1959 and 1961)

As the controlling shareholder in TWA, Howard Hughes had enormous clout and was behind Convair's belated entry into the jet airliner market. Unfortunately, by the late 1950s his mind was well and truly going, and his requirements continually changed. Hughes wanted five-abreast seating, other airlines demanded six seats across, and he wouldn't let Convair sell any jetliners to airlines that competed directly with TWA. Finally, after 18 of the CV-880s were under construction, TWA said they couldn't pay for them. Eventually 65 were sold for less than the bought-in parts, such as engines and radio equipment, cost. The totally new CV-990 was an even bigger flop, and only 37 were built. In all, the fiasco cost General Dynamics (Convair's parent company) over $450 million or a quarter of its total value.

SPECIFICATIONS (CV-880)

CREW:	4–5 and 149 passengers
POWERPLANT:	four 73.40kN (16,500lb) thrust General Electric CJ805 turbojets
MAX SPEED:	1006km/h (625mph)
SPAN:	36.58m (120ft)
LENGTH:	42.49m (139ft 5in)
HEIGHT:	12.04m (39ft 6in)
WEIGHT:	maximum 115,688kg (255,000lb)

Left: The CV-880 was named for its speed of 880 feet per second and was faster than its competitors. Unfortunately it was less capacious and shorter ranged as well.

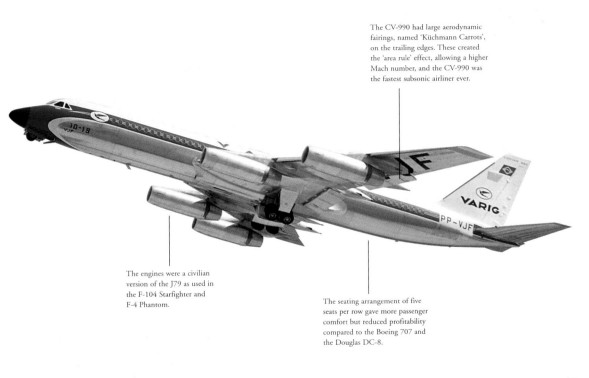

The CV-990 had large aerodynamic fairings, named 'Küchmann Carrots', on the trailing edges. These created the 'area rule' effect, allowing a higher Mach number, and the CV-990 was the fastest subsonic airliner ever.

The engines were a civilian version of the J79 as used in the F-104 Starfighter and F-4 Phantom.

The seating arrangement of five seats per row gave more passenger comfort but reduced profitability compared to the Boeing 707 and the Douglas DC-8.

CONVAIR B-32 DOMINATOR (1942)

Although it flew two weeks before its competitor, the B-29, and had the same engines, the Dominator was even more trouble-prone than the Superfortress and production B-32s were only delivered eight months after B-29s had entered combat. To achieve even these late deliveries, the sophisticated remote-controlled gun barbettes were deleted, as was the cabin pressurization system. The project was nearly cancelled several times. A total of 118 B-32s were built, but only 15 of these reached an operational unit, which flew just six combat missions from Okinawa before the war ended. One B-32 was lost on operations. After a few more reconnaissance missions the B-32 programme was cancelled, although production continued for some months. Then completed examples were flown off for scrapping. The others were scrapped at the factory.

SPECIFICATIONS

CREW:	8
POWERPLANT:	four 1641kW (2200hp) Wright R-3350-23 Cyclone radial piston engines
MAX SPEED:	575km/h (357mph)
SPAN:	41.15m (135ft)
LENGTH:	25.02m (82ft 1in)
HEIGHT:	9.80m (32ft 2in)
WEIGHT:	loaded 55,906kg (123,250lb)

Left: The little-known Dominator was produced as a backup in case the B-29 project failed and was designed to the same specification, but was inferior in every way.

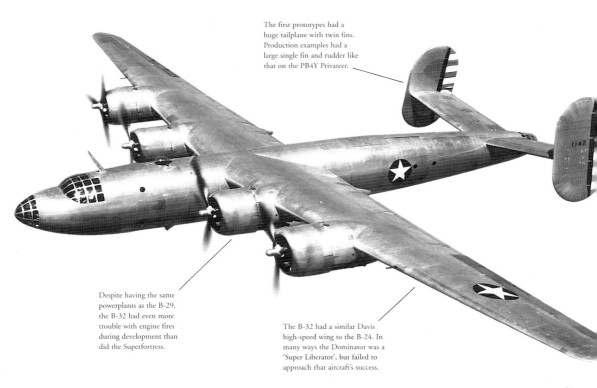

The first prototypes had a huge tailplane with twin fins. Production examples had a large single fin and rudder like that on the PB4Y Privateer.

Despite having the same powerplants as the B-29, the B-32 had even more trouble with engine fires during development than did the Superfortress.

The B-32 had a similar Davis high-speed wing to the B-24. In many ways the Dominator was a 'Super Liberator', but failed to approach that aircraft's success.

23

DOUGLAS TBD DEVASTATOR *(1935)*

The TBD Devastator was the US Navy's first monoplane torpedo-bomber and embodied many new features. Combat tactics changed little from the biplane era, however. An effective torpedo attack requires a slow and steady approach, making the Devastators easy targets. Once the TBD had braved fighters and ships' guns of all calibres, the success of its attack depended on whether the torpedo ran true and if it actually exploded against the target. US wartime torpedoes were notoriously ineffective. Although Devastators sank one Japanese carrier at Coral Sea, the Battle of Midway in June 1942 saw the TBD force wiped out without inflicting damage on the Japanese.

Only five of the 41 TBDs involved in the battle made it back and the battle left fewer than 20 TBDs in the inventory. By August 1942 they were withdrawn from the front line.

SPECIFICATIONS

CREW:	3
POWERPLANT:	one 671kW (900hp) Pratt & Whitney R-1830-64 Twin Wasp radial piston engine
MAX SPEED:	332km/h (208mph)
SPAN:	15.24m (50ft)
LENGTH:	10.67m (35ft)
HEIGHT:	4.60m (15ft 1in)
WEIGHT:	maximum 4624kg (10,194lb)

Left: At the Battle of Midway the lumbering Devastator's main achievement was to distract the Japanese from the dive-bomber attacks. The cost included an entire Devastator squadron and all but one of its aviators.

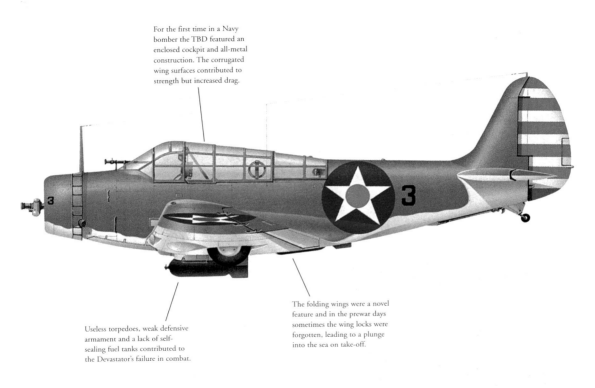

For the first time in a Navy bomber the TBD featured an enclosed cockpit and all-metal construction. The corrugated wing surfaces contributed to strength but increased drag.

Useless torpedoes, weak defensive armament and a lack of self-sealing fuel tanks contributed to the Devastator's failure in combat.

The folding wings were a novel feature and in the prewar days sometimes the wing locks were forgotten, leading to a plunge into the sea on take-off.

DOUGLAS XB-42 MIXMASTER (1942)

The XB-42 was designed to get the greatest performance out of a twin-engined airframe by mounting the engines internally and having a very clean wing. Flight testing discovered propeller vibration and inefficient engine cooling. The handling was tricky, there being particular problems with excessive yaw. One of the two XB-42s crashed near Washington D.C. Douglas was making good progress with fixing the various problems, but the end of the war reduced the urgency for all the exciting projects then underway and the USAAF decided it could afford to wait for jets. Trying their best, Douglas added two 7.1kN (1600lb) thrust auxiliary jets under the wings to create the XB-42A. It provided some data on the interaction of jets and propellers during its short flying career, but the chance of a production contract was long gone.

SPECIFICATIONS (XB-42)

CREW:	3
POWERPLANT:	two 988kW (1325hp) Allison V-1710-25 inline piston engines
MAX SPEED:	660km/h (410mph)
SPAN:	21.51m (70ft 6in)
LENGTH:	16.41m (53ft 10in)
HEIGHT:	5.74m (18ft 10in)
WEIGHT:	maximum 16,194kg (35,702lb)

Left: Named after a kitchen appliance, the Mixmaster had the usual teething troubles, but met or exceeded its performance targets. It had the misfortune to appear just as jets promised to transform combat aircraft.

Opening the bomb doors in flight interrupted the airflow to the propeller and caused excessive vibrations.

The bomber version had six machine guns. The four on the wing trailing edge were aimed by the copilot, whose seat could turn to face aft. An attack version armed with 16 machine guns or a 75mm (3in) cannon and two machine guns, or two 37mm (1.5in) cannon was proposed.

The XB-42A was retired in 1949 and is now in storage for the National Air and Space Museum. Somewhere along the way its wings were removed for transport and haven't been seen since.

The XB-42 originally had a separate bubble canopy for each pilot so as to minimize drag. Unfortunately this arrangement made communication very difficult and was greatly disliked.

350224

FAIREY ALBACORE *(1938)*

The archaic-looking Fairey Swordfish of 1934 was one of the most successful Allied carrier-borne aircraft of World War II. Its intended replacement, the more powerful, enclosed-cockpit Albacore flew as early as 1938, but despite all its supposed advantages, it never supplanted the 'Stringbag'. Tests proved the cabin was too hot in the front and too draughty in the back. The controls were too heavy, particularly in comparison with the Swordfish, and the stalling characteristics were bad. In general, all the endearing qualities of the Swordfish were ruthlessly eliminated in the new model. Although the Albacore was reasonably successful in combat, crews preferred the Swordfish, and production of the latter continued for a year after its 'successor' was phased out. The Swordfish served on until the end of the European war, but the last Albacores had gone 18 months earlier.

SPECIFICATIONS

CREW:	3
POWERPLANT:	one 843kW (1130hp) Bristol Taurus XII radial engine
MAX SPEED:	259km/h (161mph)
SPAN:	15.24m (50ft)
LENGTH:	12.14m (39ft 10in)
HEIGHT:	4.32m (14ft 2in)
WEIGHT:	maximum 4745kg (10,460lb)

Left: There were three times as many examples of the Swordfish built as there were of the uninspired Albacore. The Albacore complemented rather than supplanted the faithful 'Stringbag'.

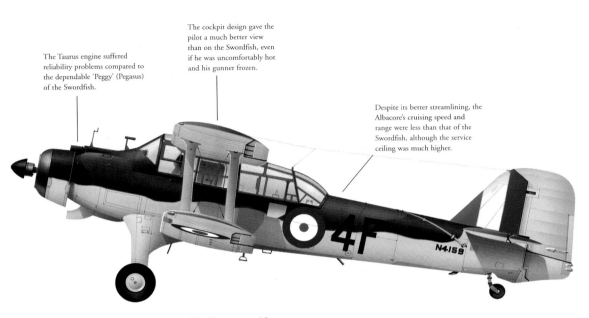

The Taurus engine suffered reliability problems compared to the dependable 'Peggy' (Pegasus) of the Swordfish.

The cockpit design gave the pilot a much better view than on the Swordfish, even if he was uncomfortably hot and his gunner frozen.

Despite its better streamlining, the Albacore's cruising speed and range were less than that of the Swordfish, although the service ceiling was much higher.

The Albacore was used for torpedo attacks, bombing, flare dropping and training Swordfish crews.

FAIREY BATTLE (1936)

Designed in 1932–33, the Battle, with its metal skin and streamlined monoplane layout, was the height of modernity when it appeared in 1936, but by the outbreak of war was too unmanoeuvrable and slow to avoid modern fighters and too lightly armed to cause much damage.

On 10 May 1940 the Battles were thrown into action against the German advance into the Low Countries, making low-level raids against convoys, troops and bridges. All attacking aircraft were shot down or damaged on the first day. An attack on bridges over the Albert Canal resulted in total losses and the awarding of two (posthumous) Victoria Crosses. Belgium's small force of Battles was expended in the same attack. Battles were soon relegated to roles such as target tugs and, with a particularly ugly two-cockpit version, training.

SPECIFICATIONS (Mk I)

CREW:	3
POWERPLANT:	one 768kW (1030hp) Rolls-Royce Merlin IV-12 piston engine
MAX SPEED:	414km/h (257mph)
SPAN:	16.46m (54ft)
LENGTH:	12.90m (42ft 4in)
HEIGHT:	4.72m (15ft 6in)
WEIGHT:	maximum 4895kg (10,792lb)

Left: Nearly 2200 Battles were built for the RAF and friendly air forces. After a spectacularly short combat career, they were found uses away from the front line, in places like South Africa and Canada.

The Battle had the same Merlin engine as the Spitfire Mk I, but when loaded weighed nearly half as much again, giving it a top speed over 160km/h (100mph) less than the Spitfire.

The Battle was designed as a two-seater with crew of pilot and observer, but provision was later made for a gunner, armed with a single World War I-vintage Vickers machine gun.

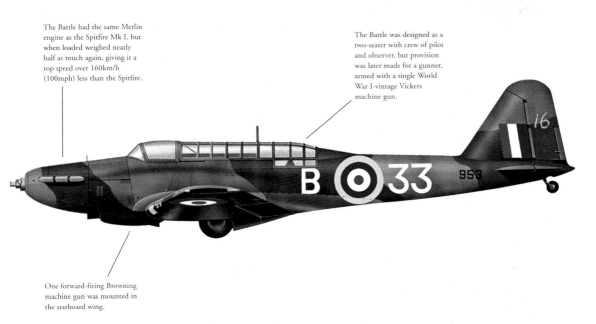

One forward-firing Browning machine gun was mounted in the starboard wing.

FAIREY FULMAR (1937)

A naval relative of the Battle, the Fulmar was intended as a long-range carrier fighter to replace such types as the Blackburn Roc, which perhaps was not aiming particularly high. Despite having a slightly more powerful engine than the Battle I and being smaller in all dimensions, the Fulmar's empty weight was over 909kg (2000lb) greater and so speed and altitude capability was less. Partly this was because of the Admiralty's prewar insistence that all shipboard aircraft carry a navigator to keep the pilot from getting lost. The Fulmar was designed without any rearwards-facing armament, operational crews resorted to Tommy guns, flare pistols and in desperation, bundles of toilet paper thrown into the slipstream to confuse a pursuer. Nevertheless, against unescorted bombers, the Fulmar did quite well in protecting Mediterranean convoys, although the best Axis bombers were usually fast enough to escape the plodding fighter.

SPECIFICATIONS (Mk I)

CREW:	2
POWERPLANT:	one 805kW (1080hp) Rolls-Royce Merlin VIII V-12 piston engine
MAX SPEED:	398km/h (247mph)
SPAN:	14.15m (46ft 5in)
LENGTH:	12.24m (40ft 2in)
HEIGHT:	4.27m (14ft)
WEIGHT:	maximum 4853kg (10,700lb)

Left: Something of a makeshift solution, the Fulmar could not compete with contemporary land-based fighters, but held the line until 1942 when better types became available.

The Fulmar had essentially the same engine and armament as the early Spitfires, although it was a lot heavier and carried an extra crewman.

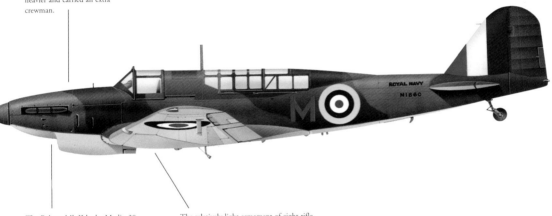

The Fulmar Mk II had a Merlin 30 engine with nearly 300 more horsepower. Despite this, it was only 16km/h (10mph) faster than the Mk I.

The relatively light armament of eight rifle-calibre machine guns and the slow top speed of the Fulmar allowed many German and Italian bombers to get away with limited damage.

FARMAN JABIRU *(1923)*

Perhaps not the least successful of the many airliner types that struggled to establish European air routes in the 1920s, the Farman F.121 Jabiru (Stork) scores extra points for sheer ugliness. Winning a safety prize on its 1923 debut, the Jabiru did not enter service for three years, largely due to problems with cooling the rear (pusher) pair of engines, which were generally World War I surplus. Running four worn-out engines for nine passengers was uneconomic and the aircraft's career was short. If the F-3X wasn't enough of a horror, Farman followed it with the F-4X, powered by three uncowled 224kW (300hp) Salmson engines, one of which was mounted at the top of the forward fuselage. Apart from removing cooling problems, all this achieved was to reduce capacity by two seats to achieve the same performance. Of the four F-4Xs built, two were lost within a year.

SPECIFICATIONS (F-3X)

CREW:	1–2 and 9 passengers
POWERPLANT:	four 132kW (180hp) Hispano-Suiza 8AC piston engines
CRUISING SPEED:	175km/h (109mph)
SPAN:	19.00m (62ft 4in)
LENGTH:	13.68m (44ft 11in)
HEIGHT:	4.50m (14ft 8in)
WEIGHT:	loaded 5000kg (11,023lb)

Left: Farman's own airline was one of only two users of the Jabiru, flying them between Paris, Brussels and Amsterdam for a few years.

At least three different radiator arrangements were tried in attempts to cure the Jabiru's chronic cooling problems.

Perched atop the airframe in an open cockpit, the Jabiru's pilot had great difficulty taxiing accurately.

Passengers sat in wicker chairs angled towards the centre, and had a superb view from the continuous row of windows around the cabin.

REPUBLIC XF-12 RAINBOW (1946)

Designated XF-12, when F stood for 'photo' in the pre-1947 system, and later XR-12, the Rainbow was a high-speed high-altitude reconnaissance aircraft, intended to scout targets over Japan for the B-29s. This may have happened if the programme had started earlier, because when the war ended with the atomic bombings, the first aircraft was only partly complete. Republic still hoped to make the Rainbow into a 46-seat airliner, which they called the RC-2. Their selling point was speed, for which customers would pay a premium. Unfortunately, the expected postwar boom was not immediate and the airlines bought the slower but roomier DC-4 and Boeing 377 instead. An XR-12 was not delivered to the Air Force until late 1948, but crashed on its second test flight. The other Rainbow was sent to a gunnery range.

SPECIFICATIONS

CREW:	5–7
POWERPLANT:	four 2238kW (3000hp) Pratt & Whitney R-4360 piston engines
MAX SPEED:	729km/h (450mph)
SPAN:	39.35m (129ft 2in)
LENGTH:	30.11m (98ft 9in)
HEIGHT:	unknown
WEIGHT:	maximum 51,411kg (113,240lb)

Left: The Republic Rainbow met all its performance targets but suffered from bad timing both as a reconnaissance platform and as an airliner. Republic went back to making single-seat fighter-bombers.

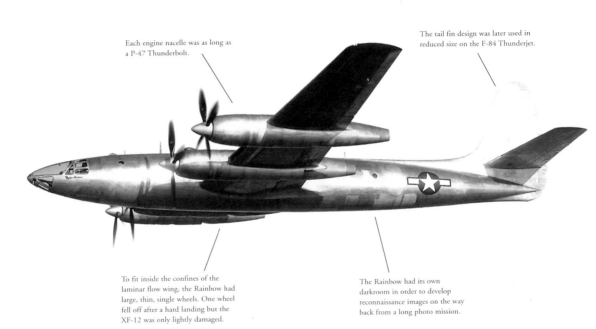

Each engine nacelle was as long as a P-47 Thunderbolt.

The tail fin design was later used in reduced size on the F-84 Thunderjet.

To fit inside the confines of the laminar flow wing, the Rainbow had large, thin, single wheels. One wheel fell off after a hard landing but the XF-12 was only lightly damaged.

The Rainbow had its own darkroom in order to develop reconnaissance images on the way back from a long photo mission.

37

ROYAL AIRCRAFT FACTORY B.E.2 (1912)

The B.E.2 was designed with emphasis on stability, which made it particularly suitable for reconnaissance for the British Army on the Western Front. In mid-1915 the nature of air war changed with the arrival of the agile Fokker Eindecker with its forward-firing guns. Reconnaissance and bomber aircraft were shot from the skies, with the B.E.2s suffering the worst losses. Reconnaissance aircraft soon needed large escorts, but if a B.E.2 was caught by a fighter, usually all it had to defend itself was pistols or rifles fired by the observer. With the observer in the front, no effective machine-gun arrangement was possible. Continued employment (and production) of B.E.2s in an increasingly dangerous environment led to claims in Parliament that young men were being sent out to be murdered. By 1917 most B.E.2s were found more suitable employment as trainers.

SPECIFICATIONS (B.E.2c)

CREW:	2
POWERPLANT:	one 67kW (90hp) RAF 1a V-8 piston engine
MAX SPEED:	116km/h (72mph)
SPAN:	11.23m (36ft 10in)
LENGTH:	8.30m (27ft 3in)
HEIGHT:	3.45m (11ft 4in)
WEIGHT:	maximum 972kg (2142lb)

Left: The sedate, stable and very slow B.E.2 made a fine photographic platform in conditions of air superiority, but when Germany fielded the first fighting scouts, the RFC's crews were slaughtered.

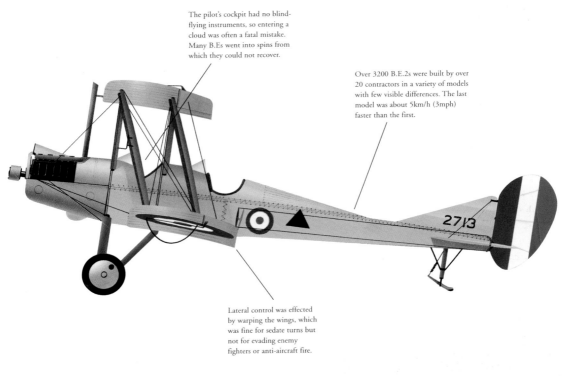

The pilot's cockpit had no blind-flying instruments, so entering a cloud was often a fatal mistake. Many B.Es went into spins from which they could not recover.

Over 3200 B.E.2s were built by over 20 contractors in a variety of models with few visible differences. The last model was about 5km/h (3mph) faster than the first.

Lateral control was effected by warping the wings, which was fine for sedate turns but not for evading enemy fighters or anti-aircraft fire.

SAAB SCANDIA 90A (1946)

A part from the nosewheel layout and more powerful engines, any description of Sweden's Scandia would apply to the DC-3 of 1935. A lot had happened in the intervening decade, and even at its inception some considered that it 'was only a Dakota with its tail in the air'. Pratt & Whitney developed a new engine for the Scandia, the R-2180, giving better speed and payload characteristics than the DC-3, although its 32 seats and its external dimensions closely matched the 'Dak'. SAS bought 11 Scandias for their domestic and short European routes, while Aerovias Brasil (later VASP) bought six and later took all the SAS aircraft, operating them up to 1969. Five were written off in Brazil between 1958 and 1964 and today the sole survivor is in a Brazilian museum.

SPECIFICATIONS

CREW:	4 and 32 passengers
POWERPLANT:	two 1231kW (1650hp) Pratt & Whitney R-2180-E1 radial piston engines
MAX SPEED:	450km/h (280mph)
SPAN:	28.00m (91ft 10in)
LENGTH:	21.30m (69ft 10in)
HEIGHT:	7.10m (23ft 4in)
WEIGHT:	take-off 16,500kg (36,366lb)

Left: At a time when American and British planemakers were moving to four-engined airliners with supercharged engines, Saab tried to reinvent the DC-3, although they were not alone in this regard.

Pilots considered the cockpit glazing to be inadequate, with most panels too small and the sills too high. Looking across the cockpit, the pilot on the opposite side could see very little.

Two versions were proposed, one with 24 seats in one double row and one single row, and a 32-seat model with two double rows. The pressurized Saab 90B version was never built.

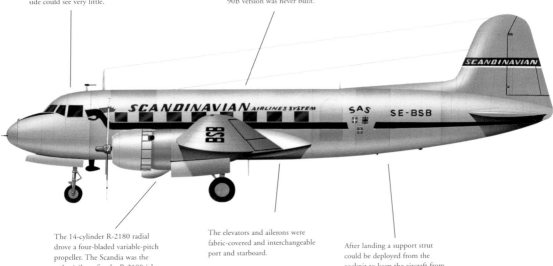

The 14-cylinder R-2180 radial drove a four-bladed variable-pitch propeller. The Scandia was the only civil use for the R-2180 (also known as the Twin Wasp E1) engine, although a military version was used in the prototype Piasecki H-16 helicopter.

The elevators and ailerons were fabric-covered and interchangeable port and starboard.

After landing a support strut could be deployed from the cockpit to keep the aircraft from tipping backwards during passenger and baggage loading and unloading.

SAUNDERS-ROE PRINCESS *(1952)*

Designed to combine Britain's lead in large flying-boat design with innovations in turbine engine technology, the Princess proved to be a giant white elephant. In 1945 long runways for civil aircraft were still scarce and the Princess seemed like the answer for transatlantic and Empire services. No one really asked what BOAC, the state-owned airline, wanted. Technical problems with the coupled Proteus engines contributed to delays and cost overruns. The first flight date slipped from 1949 to 1952. Costs quadrupled and by 1953 only one small operator was still using flying boats on services out of the UK, BOAC and others having moved on to the new generation of landplanes such as the Boeing Stratocruiser. With no customer, the three prototypes were stored and broken up in 1967.

SPECIFICATIONS

CREW:	6 flight deck and 105 passengers
POWERPLANT:	ten 2819kW (3780hp) Bristol Proteus 2 turboprops arranged as four coupled and two single units
MAX SPEED:	612km/h (380mph)
SPAN:	66.90m (219ft 6in)
LENGTH:	45.11m (148ft)
HEIGHT:	17.37m (57ft)
WEIGHT:	maximum 156,457kg (345,000lb)

Left: The second-biggest flying boat after the 'Spruce Goose', the Princess arrived just as large landplanes were coming into their own. Only one prototype of the Princess was completed to fly.

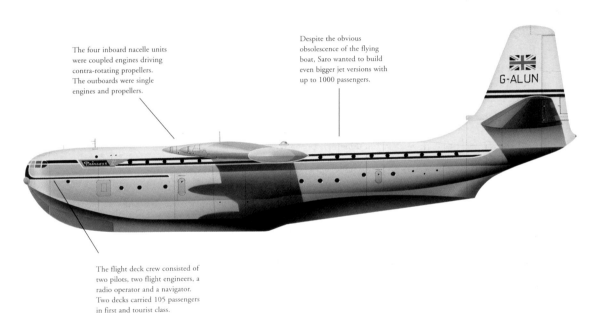

The four inboard nacelle units were coupled engines driving contra-rotating propellers. The outboards were single engines and propellers.

Despite the obvious obsolescence of the flying boat, Saro wanted to build even bigger jet versions with up to 1000 passengers.

G-ALUN

The flight deck crew consisted of two pilots, two flight engineers, a radio operator and a navigator. Two decks carried 105 passengers in first and tourist class.

SHENYANG J-8 'FINBACK' *(1969)*

W ork began in 1967 on China's first indigenous combat aircraft, the J-8 (J=Jian or fighter) based on MiG-21 technology and aerodynamics, and by 1969 a prototype had flown. Unfortunately the Cultural Revolution then intervened and development was suspended for eight years. The improved J-8-I was ready to fly in 1980 but was somehow lost before flight tests began.

A prototype J-8-I finally flew in 1981 and limited production was authorized in 1985. By the time production was completed in 1988 with only 75–80 aircraft produced, China had a fighter representing the very best of 1950s technology. Illustrating the glacial pace of Chinese fighter development, which even today takes a long time to achieve not very much, the J-8 took nearly 20 years to enter production, due more to political interference than anything else.

SPECIFICATIONS

CREW:	1
POWERPLANT:	two 65.9kN (14,815lb) thrust Wopen 13A-II afterburning turbojets
MAX SPEED:	2230km/h (1386mph)
SPAN:	9.34m (30ft 8in)
LENGTH:	20.50m (67ft 3in)
HEIGHT:	5.06m (16ft 6in)
WEIGHT:	loaded approx 12,700kg (28,000lb)

Left: The result of 20 years development was little more than an enlarged twin-engined MiG-21, a type which was hot stuff when it first flew in 1955.

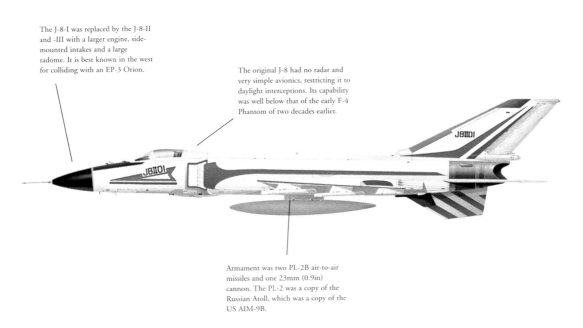

The J-8-I was replaced by the J-8-II and -III with a larger engine, side-mounted intakes and a large radome. It is best known in the west for colliding with an EP-3 Orion.

The original J-8 had no radar and very simple avionics, restricting it to daylight interceptions. Its capability was well below that of the early F-4 Phantom of two decades earlier.

Armament was two PL-2B air-to-air missiles and one 23mm (0.9in) cannon. The PL-2 was a copy of the Russian Atoll, which was a copy of the US AIM-9B.

SHORT SB.6 SEAMEW *(1953)*

The ungainly Seamew was conceived as a cheap, rugged anti-submarine aircraft able to operate from small carriers used by the UK and some other allied nations. To this end it was built with a fixed landing gear and a strong structure. Despite this, the prototype was badly damaged on its first landing, although it was repaired in time for the Farnborough Air Show.

In handling terms the Seamew was described as having some 'vicious tendencies'. It was capable of aerobatics, but the chief test pilot seemed to be the only one able to wring the full manoeuvrability out of the Seamew – until he stalled the prototype Mk.2 during a display and was killed. Production began for RAF Coastal Command and the Royal Navy, but the RAF order was cancelled in 1956 and the Navy's was a victim of the defence cuts of the following year.

SPECIFICATIONS

CREW:	2
POWERPLANT:	one 1327kW (1780hp) Armstrong Siddeley Mamba turboprop
MAX SPEED:	378km/h (235mph)
SPAN:	16.75m (55ft)
LENGTH:	12.50m (41ft)
HEIGHT:	unknown
WEIGHT:	maximum 6804kg (15,000lb)

Left: Described as a 'camel amongst race-horses', the Seamew differed from contemporary anti-submarine aircraft, which tended to be heavy and fast. In keeping the design as simple and strong as possible, compromises were made to the aerodynamics and the Seamew exhibited some unpleasant characteristics.

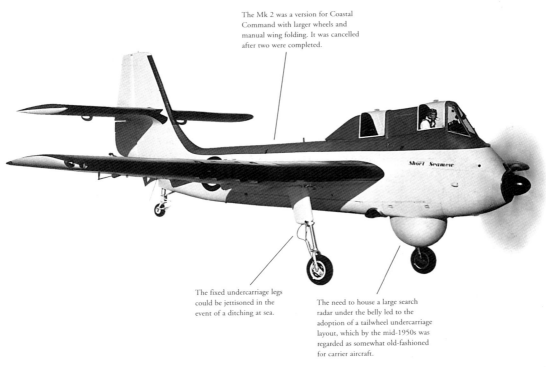

The Mk 2 was a version for Coastal Command with larger wheels and manual wing folding. It was cancelled after two were completed.

Short Seamew

The fixed undercarriage legs could be jettisoned in the event of a ditching at sea.

The need to house a large search radar under the belly led to the adoption of a tailwheel undercarriage layout, which by the mid-1950s was regarded as somewhat old-fashioned for carrier aircraft.

47

SHORT STIRLING (1939)

The Stirling was the first of the RAF's trio of four-engined 'heavies'. It was always hampered by the RAF's 1936 specifications, which restricted the wingspan to under 30.48m (100ft) to fit into the standard hangars of the day. As such the Stirling was unable to reach the optimum operating altitude of 6100m (20,000ft) and was a much easier target for flak and fighters than were the Halifax and Lancaster. The prototype was wrecked when its undercarriage collapsed after its first flight. Many teething troubles and accidents delayed the build-up of squadrons, which soon suffered high losses. The new Stirling III introduced in early 1943 remedied some deficiencies, but within five months, 80 per cent of these had been lost. Late that year the type was withdrawn from the frontline squadrons.

SPECIFICATIONS (Mk III)

CREW:	7
POWERPLANT:	four 1230kW (1650hp) Bristol Hercules XVI radial engines
MAX SPEED:	435km/h (270mph)
SPAN:	30.20m (99ft 1in)
LENGTH:	26.59m (87ft 3in)
HEIGHT:	6.93m (22ft 9in)
WEIGHT:	maximum 31,751kg (70,000lb)

Left: Compared to the Lancaster and Halifax, the Stirling performed poorly at high altitude and suffered the highest loss rates of the RAF's heavy bombers.

The Stirling used a cut-down version of the wing from the Sunderland flying boat, reduced by over 4m (12ft) in span.

The complicated undercarriage legs were very long to increase the wing incidence and reduce the take-off run. The length and design of the legs contributed to many accidents.

The size of the bomb bay restricted the weapons that could be carried to nothing larger than 907kg (2000lb) bombs.

49

SHORT STURGEON AND SB.3 (1946)

Subject to a number of changes in role before it even entered service, the Sturgeon was intended to be a high-performance torpedo-bomber, but the torpedo part was dropped, followed by all offensive capability. A photo-reconnaissance role came and went, but the Sturgeon found its niche as a target tug for naval gunnery. For this role it had a lengthened nose and a winch system. The 25 built had brief careers. The last Sturgeon was modified into the SB.3 anti-submarine aircraft. Any remaining semblance of good looks was ruined by the extremely deep nose, which contained two radar operators. The efflux from the Mamba turboprops seriously destabilized the aircraft at some power settings and destroyed the good handling characteristics. It proved impossible to trim for safe flight on one engine, which was a necessity for long endurance on anti-submarine patrols.

SPECIFICATIONS (SB.3)

CREW:	3
POWERPLANT:	two 1100kW (1475hp) Mamba AS Ma3 turboprops
MAX SPEED:	515km/h (320mph)
SPAN:	18.23m (59ft 11in)
LENGTH:	13.70m (44ft)
HEIGHT:	unknown
WEIGHT:	loaded 10,700kg (23,600lb)

Left: A diagram of the original Sturgeon. Its odd looks were exceeded by the grotesque one-off SB.3 (right), which was unnamed but really did resemble some deep-dwelling fish.

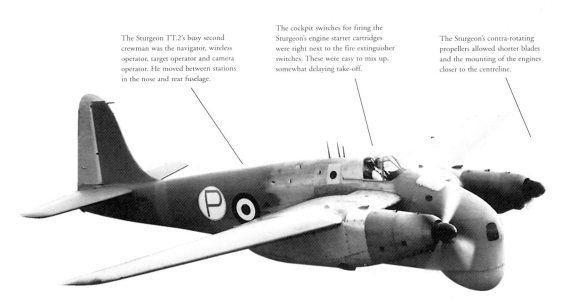

The Sturgeon TT.2's busy second crewman was the navigator, wireless operator, target operator and camera operator. He moved between stations in the nose and rear fuselage.

The cockpit switches for firing the Sturgeon's engine starter cartridges were right next to the fire extinguisher switches. These were easy to mix up, somewhat delaying take-off.

The Sturgeon's contra-rotating propellers allowed shorter blades and the mounting of the engines closer to the centreline.

SOPWITH LRTTr *(1916)*

Sopwith's LRTTr or Long Range Tractor Triplane was one of several designs offered in response to an RFC requirement for an anti-airship fighter. The normal reason for a triplane layout was to give large wing area and thus keep the span down to aid manoeuvrability. For some reason the LRTTr had very long and narrow wings, which would have meant an enormous turning radius, but few details of its performance have survived. It would seem that this clumsy machine would have great difficulty getting within firing range of a Zeppelin. The top gunner in his 'howdah' (as in the seat atop an elephant) would have had a great all-round view, but would only have been able to fire in the front quarter. In any case the LRTTr never saw production or action as new small synchronized-gun fighters soon appeared.

SPECIFICATIONS

CREW:	3
POWERPLANT:	one 187kW (250hp) Rolls-Royce Eagle I piston engine
MAX SPEED:	unknown
SPAN:	16.08m (52ft 9in)
LENGTH:	10.74m (35ft 3in)
HEIGHT:	unknown
WEIGHT:	unknown

Left: With its streamlined gunner's pod and clumsy airframe, the LRTTr was uncharitably known as the 'egg box'. Thankfully, the next design to emerge from the Sopwith factory was the immortal Camel.

The LRTTr was powered by the Rolls-Royce Eagle engine, a fine powerplant also used in the Bristol fighter. The Bristol, however, was more compact with better streamlining and had only two crew.

A very makeshift-looking four-wheel undercarriage kept the nose and tail off the ground. Riding in the 'howdah' for take-off must have been an interesting experience.

Both gunners had a single Lewis gun. The rear hemisphere was covered by a gunner in a more conventional cockpit behind the pilot.

BOGUS CONCEPTS

Here we have aircraft of such variety that it is hard to generalize about the reasons for their failure, but it can be said that they all seemed like good ideas at the time. This category includes a number of radical solutions, some born out of desperation, such as Germany and Japan's manned flying bombs and Japanese fuel-carrying transport that used almost all the fuel en route. Others were solutions looking for a problem such as the Avrocar and the XP-79.

The idea of vertical take-off (VTO) interceptors able to defend point targets against nuclear-armed bombers obsessed military planners in the early Cold War years. Later the emphasis changed to aircraft that could be dispersed away from vulnerable fixed bases. The quest for VTO aircraft produced a number of 'tail-sitters' such as the Pogo, Vertijet and Coléoptère. All of these made transitions from vertical to horizontal flight, where they made pretty mediocre fighters compared with conventional aircraft. Then they had to land while going backwards and downwards, which proved the Achilles heel of all these designs. Other non-starters include anti-Zeppelin triplanes, jet seaplane fighters, an aeroplane that mimicked the birds (or at least attempted to), and a genuine flying tank.

Left: One of the most bizarre-looking aircraft ever to have flown, the SNECMA Coléoptère is pictured being prepared for take-off.

AEROCAR *(1949)*

American inventor Moulton Taylor's dream of a 'roadable aircraft' saw construction of a series of novel, but largely impracticable vehicles over 20 years, none of which reached series production.

Taylor's Aerocar I flew in 1949 but was not certified until 1956. Six were built, followed by a non-roadworthy version called the Aero-Plane and finally the definitive Aerocar III in 1968. The Aerocars were essentially small, lightweight cars with detachable conventional light aircraft wings and an unusual Y-tail with a pusher propeller.

New rules on automobile safety in the 1970s required additional equipment for the car component of the Aerocar, such as bumpers, which increased the weight and expense and reduced performance. Plans to build a sleeker sportscar version were dropped.

SPECIFICATIONS (Aerocar III)

CREW:	1 plus 3 passengers
POWERPLANT:	one 107kW (143hp)
	Avco Lycoming O-320
	piston engine
MAX SPEED:	201km/h (125mph)
SPAN:	10.36m (34ft)
LENGTH:	7.01m (23ft)
HEIGHT:	2.13m (7ft)
WEIGHT:	953kg (2100lb)

Left: The Aerocar was one of several failed attempts to combine motoring and aviating. Neither fish nor fowl, the Aerocars were more novelties than practical cars or touring aircraft and cost more than a conventional light aircraft and a medium-sized car combined.

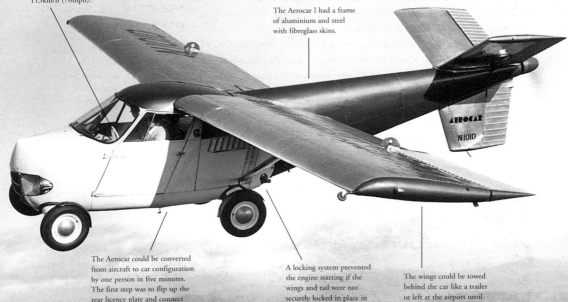

The same steering wheel was used to manoeuvre the Aerocar in flight as on the ground. The engine only gave 30kW (40hp) for road travel and the top road speed was about 113km/h (70mph).

The Aerocar I had a frame of aluminium and steel with fibreglass skins.

The Aerocar could be converted from aircraft to car configuration by one person in five minutes. The first step was to flip up the rear licence plate and connect the propeller shaft.

A locking system prevented the engine starting if the wings and tail were not securely locked in place in aircraft mode.

The wings could be towed behind the car like a trailer or left at the airport until required for flight.

AEROCAR
N101D

AHRENS AR-404 *(1976)*

The AR-404 utility aircraft was the brainchild of a US company who set up a production facility in western Puerto Rico. The company made various claims for the AR-404, including that it could be certified under the same standards as the large jetliners, but in one year rather than four. Suggested uses included fish spotting, Anti-Submarine Warfare, gunship, parachute dropping and training. Through obtaining money from the Puerto Rican government, it was said 1000 locals with no previous aircraft making experience would soon be turning out four per month. A mysterious US government investigation into the company dragged on, preventing the development money and loans going through. The project was abandoned and the principals decamped elsewhere. Only two AR-404s were built. The first prototype was last noted serving as a snack bar.

SPECIFICATIONS

CREW:	2 and 30 passengers
POWERPLANT:	four 313kW (420hp) Allison 250-B17B turboprops
MAX SPEED:	315km/h (195mph)
SPAN:	20.12m (66ft)
LENGTH:	16.08m (52ft 9in)
HEIGHT:	5.79m (19ft)
WEIGHT:	loaded about 7710kg (17,000lb)

Left: A laudable concept to create a cheap and economical utility aircraft for the developing world, the AR-404 was built on shaky financial ground with several parallels to the de Lorean car debacle.

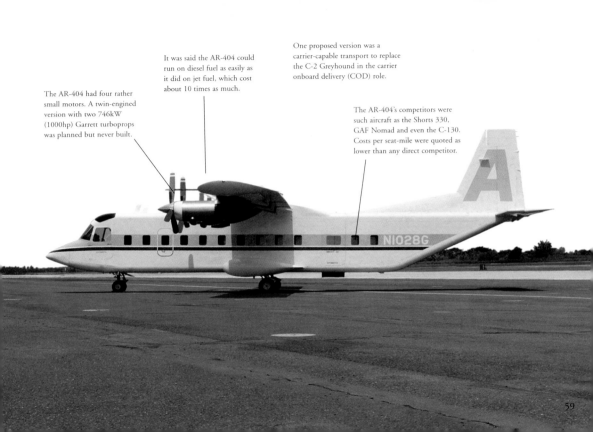

The AR-404 had four rather small motors. A twin-engined version with two 746kW (1000hp) Garrett turboprops was planned but never built.

It was said the AR-404 could run on diesel fuel as easily as it did on jet fuel, which cost about 10 times as much.

One proposed version was a carrier-capable transport to replace the C-2 Greyhound in the carrier onboard delivery (COD) role.

The AR-404's competitors were such aircraft as the Shorts 330, GAF Nomad and even the C-130. Costs per seat-mile were quoted as lower than any direct competitor.

N1028G

ALLIED AVIATION XLRA-1 AND -2 *(1941)*

In April 1941, at the instigation of Captain (later Admiral) Marc Mitscher, the Navy began work on a glider for assaulting enemy beaches carrying squads of Marines.

The basic design worked out by the Bureau of Aeronautics was then handed over to industry for building. The first was built by the Bristol Aeronautical Company as the XLRQ-1, followed by two from the Allied Aviation Corporation as the XLRA-1 and -2. The low-set wing supported the glider in the water, and tow-planes used in tests were amphibians such as the J2F-5 Duck and PBY-5A. Although the XLRA-1/-2 was theoretically ideal for recapturing islands captured by the Japanese in the first months of the Pacific War, actual combat experience showed the strength of beach defences and the vulnerability of even armoured landing craft and amphibious vehicles during opposed invasions. In 1942 orders for 100 XLRA-2s were cancelled as was that for a 22-seat twin-hulled transport glider.

SPECIFICATIONS

CREW:	2 pilots and 10 Marines
POWERPLANT:	none
MAX SPEED:	(towed) 210km/h
	(130mph)
SPAN:	21.95m (72ft)
LENGTH:	12.19m (40ft)
HEIGHT:	3.73m (12ft 3in)
WEIGHT:	unknown

Left: The sight of gliders loaded with Marines swooping into the shallows of Japanese-held islands was not one that came to pass. The naval assault glider was a remarkably ill-thought-out concept that was thankfully shelved before it consumed too much time and resources.

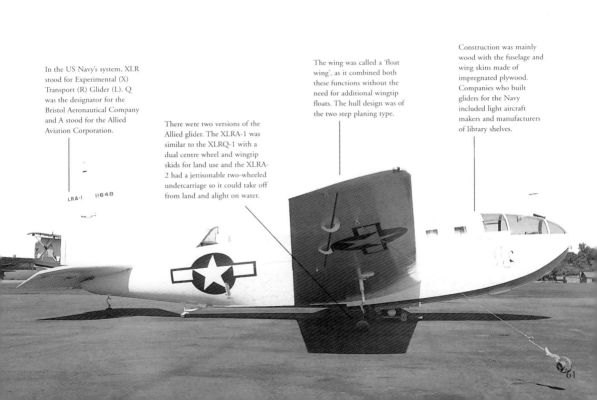

In the US Navy's system, XLR stood for Experimental (X) Transport (R) Glider (L). Q was the designator for the Bristol Aeronautical Company and A stood for the Allied Aviation Corporation.

There were two versions of the Allied glider. The XLRA-1 was similar to the XLRQ-1 with a dual centre wheel and wingtip skids for land use and the XLRA-2 had a jettisonable two-wheeled undercarriage so it could take off from land and alight on water.

The wing was called a 'float wing', as it combined both these functions without the need for additional wingtip floats. The hull design was of the two step planing type.

Construction was mainly wood with the fuselage and wing skins made of impregnated plywood. Companies who built gliders for the Navy included light aircraft makers and manufacturers of library shelves.

LRA-1   11648

ANTONOV KT FLYING TANK (1942)

The extraordinary KT 'Kryl'ya tanka' (Tank's Wings) was a Soviet wartime design intended to supply partisans behind German lines with light armour. The Antonov design bureau quickly developed a set of biplane wings and twin-boomed tail that could be fitted to turn a T-60 tank into a glider.

On its one and only test flight the weight and drag of the KT caused the TB-3 bomber tow-plane's engines to overheat and the glider had to be jettisoned, making a smooth landing in a rough field. The flying surfaces were dropped and the tank drove back to its base, the brave pilot/driver Sergei Anokin reporting enthusiastically about the experience. The lack of a tow-plane with sufficient power was one reason the idea fell out of official favour and was dropped.

SPECIFICATIONS

CREW:	2
POWERPLANT:	as glider, none; as tank, one 63.4kW (85hp) GAZ 202 6-cylinder petrol engine
TOWING SPEED:	160km/h (100mph)
SPAN:	15.00m (49ft 2in)
LENGTH:	11.50m (37ft 9in)
HEIGHT:	unknown
WEIGHT:	8200kg (18,078lb)

Left: The KT was a T-60 light tank fitted with cheap wood and fabric flying surfaces. It was intended to be towed by a heavy bomber and dropped behind enemy lines. Only a single example was converted, making but a single flight. It was thought that the few available heavy towing aircraft would be better used in more conventional frontline roles.

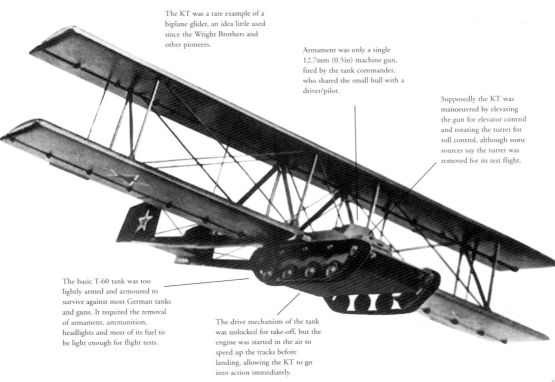

The KT was a rare example of a biplane glider, an idea little used since the Wright Brothers and other pioneers.

Armament was only a single 12.7mm (0.5in) machine gun, fired by the tank commander, who shared the small hull with a driver/pilot.

Supposedly the KT was manoeuvred by elevating the gun for elevator control and rotating the turret for roll control, although some sources say the turret was removed for its test flight.

The basic T-60 tank was too lightly armed and armoured to survive against most German tanks and guns. It required the removal of armament, ammunition, headlights and most of its fuel to be light enough for flight tests.

The drive mechanism of the tank was unlocked for take-off, but the engine was started in the air to speed up the tracks before landing, allowing the KT to go into action immediately.

ARMSTRONG WHITWORTH APE (1926)

To advance the science of aerodynamics, the Royal Aeronautical Establishment (RAE) commissioned an 'infinitely adjustable' aeroplane from Armstrong Whitworth, that by addition and adjustment of various parts would 'provide all the answers' to problems of aircraft design. By varying the length and rake of various struts on the resulting biplane, named the Ape, the wing position, stagger, gap and dihedral could be varied. The fuselage length could be increased by inserting extra bays. Despite all the ingenuity in its construction, the first Ape only had a 134kW (180hp) engine and, unsurprisingly, performance was poor, limiting its utility in exploring the effects of various configurations. The second Ape was later fitted with a more powerful Jupiter engine, but extra gadgets increased the weight and largely nullified the effect of the greater power. It lasted for nine months of 'somewhat protracted' trials before crash-landing near Farnborough in May 1929. A third aircraft was completed but saw little use, the RAE having become somewhat disenchanted with the whole idea.

SPECIFICATIONS

CREW:	2
POWERPLANT:	one 134kW (180hp) Napier Lynx III radial piston engine
MAX SPEED:	145km/h (90mph)
SPAN:	12.19m (40ft)
LENGTH:	8.61m–11.66m (28ft 3in–38ft 3in)
HEIGHT:	3.96m–4.57m (13ft–15ft)
WEIGHT:	1225kg–1474kg (2700lb–3250lb)

Left: The Ape was intended to 'provide all the answers' to questions of aerodynamics, but was hampered by a lack of power and was unable to fully test all the possible permutations of its design.

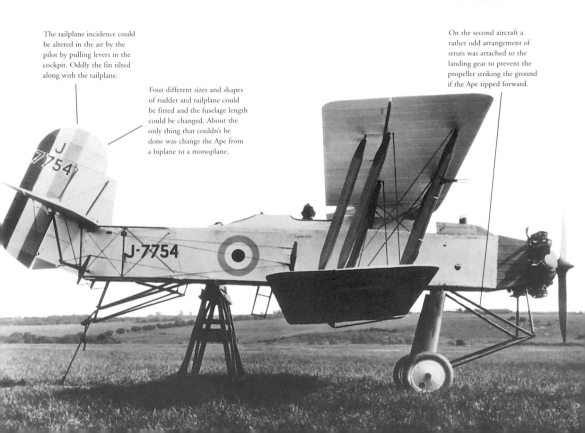

The tailplane incidence could be altered in the air by the pilot by pulling levers in the cockpit. Oddly the fin tilted along with the tailplane.

Four different sizes and shapes of rudder and tailplane could be fitted and the fuselage length could be changed. About the only thing that couldn't be done was change the Ape from a biplane to a monoplane.

On the second aircraft a rather odd arrangement of struts was attached to the landing gear to prevent the propeller striking the ground if the Ape tipped forward.

J-7754

J 7754

ARMSTRONG WHITWORTH F.K.6 (1916)

Designations of some of the Armstrong Whitworth aircraft designed by Dutchman Frederick Koolhoven are confusing to say the least, but it appears that both the company's two three-seat triplanes of 1916 were known as the F.K.6. The first (designated the FK.5 by some sources) had a narrow fuselage, mounted above the lower wing, which had three sets of wheels. Gunners sat in nacelles on either side of the cockpit right beside the propeller. In its original form the company manager refused to allow the F.K.6 to be flown. The second F.K.6 had a larger fuselage, mounted on the wing this time, smaller nacelles, more struts and two pairs of wheels. It was equally inept, but at least achieved limited flight trials. Koolhoven left to form his own company in Holland, which continued to produce unusual designs until the Luftwaffe intervened in 1940.

SPECIFICATIONS

CREW:	3
POWERPLANT:	one 187kW (250hp) Rolls-Royce piston engine
MAX SPEED:	160km/h (100mph)
SPAN:	19.14m (62ft 10in)
LENGTH:	11.29m (37ft 1in)
HEIGHT:	5.18m (17ft)
WEIGHT:	unknown

Left: One of several unsuccessful anti-Zeppelin fighters designed to a 1916 requirement, the first, smaller F.K.6 (or FK.5) was a particularly way-out machine.

The pilot of the original F.K.6 is unlikely to have been able to see much in any direction. The completely revised second example pictured here was only a marginal improvement.

The nacelles were intended to give the gunners a good field of fire but a better solution might have been a single gunner in the rear fuselage. No armament was actually fitted.

The middle wing was much longer than the others, but it is hard to know quite why. The other wings were equal span.

7838

AVRO AVROCAR (1959)

The unique Avrocar began its life in Canada in 1952 as a design for a supersonic fighter-bomber based on the ideas of Avro Canada engineer John Frost. After Canadian government money ran out, the US Army took an interest, but decided they had more use for a 'flying jeep' and helped fund two prototypes as the VZ-9AV, which first made tethered flights in 1959. Powered by three small turbojets, the Avrocar was tested in great secrecy. Although they proved the ability to take-off vertically and operate in ground effect, they proved unstable above about 1m (3ft 3in) altitude, despite an electromechanical stabilization system. NASA wind tunnel tests confirmed the Avrocar's inherent instability. Maximum speed was only 56km/h (35mph).

Despite plans for a civil family-sized 'Avrowagon', an amphibious 'Avropelican', and a large transport version, development was caught in the fall-out from the cancellation of the Avro Arrow, and the Avrocar project was cancelled in December 1961 after the expenditure of $10 million.

SPECIFICATIONS

CREW:	2
POWERPLANT:	three 2.93kN (660lb) thrust Continental J69 turbojets
MAX SPEED:	56km/h (35mph)
DIAMETER:	5.50m (18ft)
HEIGHT:	1.10m (3ft 6in)
WEIGHT:	2563kg (5650lb)

Left: Although the closest flying vehicle to a 'flying saucer' ever developed, the Avrocar is unlikely to have triggered any UFO reports as it barely rose above waist height in all its tests. It was to be the last aircraft developed by the Avro Canada company.

The Avrocar had three turbojets, three intakes and three fuel tanks. Underneath it had three small undercarriage units.

The Avrocar had provision for a pilot and a test observer (who was probably there more for balance reasons) under individual bubble canopies.

The exhausts of the jet engines drove the central fan and provided lift at low speed by being ducted around the circumference. Forward propulsion was achieved by redirecting forward thrust.

US AIR FORCE   US ARMY

69

AVRO TUDOR (1945)

A t the same time as US designers were developing the Super
Constellation and Stratocruiser, both powerful aircraft with worthwhile
passenger loads, Britain was coming up with machines like the Avro Tudor,
essentially a pressurized four-engined Dakota with a commercially worthless
payload. Despite its conservative design and experienced design team, the
early Tudors proved aerodynamically unstable in pitch and yaw and subject
to buffeting at low speeds.

The prototype Tudor 2 crashed when the aileron controls were rigged
backwards, killing designer Roy Chadwick. There were various marks of
different lengths, and by the Tudor 4 Avro had worked out most of the bugs,
but two were lost in the 'Bermuda Triangle' and in 1950 a Tudor 5 crashed
with 80 victims, the worst British civil air disaster up to that time. Most
orders were cancelled and in the end only a handful were built.

SPECIFICATIONS (Tudor 5)

CREW:	3 or 4 crew and 80 passengers
POWERPLANT:	four 1320kW (1770hp) Rolls-Royce Merlin 621 piston engines
MAX SPEED:	475km/h (295mph)
SPAN:	36.58m (120ft)
LENGTH:	32.18m (105ft 7in)
HEIGHT:	7.39m (24ft 3in)
WEIGHT:	loaded 36,287kg (80,000lb)

*Left: Despite a series of improved
versions, the Tudor was never
competitive with the contemporary
US airliners, which British airlines
bought as soon as they could.*

The Tudor I was designed for only 12 passengers, but later models could carry 80. Unfortunately, in total only 11 of the longer, wider Tudor 2, 5 and 11 models were built.

By 1945 most new transport aircraft had tricycle undercarriage and level floors, but the Tudor retained the tailwheel layout of the wartime Avro bombers. Pronounced swinging on take-off was a common problem.

The Merlin engine helped win the war but it was less suitable for a civilian transport aircraft. Contemporary American airliners were using powerful radials, and had transatlantic range, which the Tudors didn't.

G-AGRD

BACHEM BA 349 NATTER (1945)

The desperate concept behind the Bachem Natter (hummingbird) was that young pilots with little or no training would be launched vertically at US bomber formations and blow them apart with a powerful battery of rockets. With no method of landing, the pilot would then bale out, he and the rocket motor descending by parachute for further use (if either could be found again). Several unmanned launches were made and reputedly five manned ones. The first pilot was killed when the canopy came off and struck his head. The SS was more enthusiastic about the idea than the Luftwaffe and wanted 150 of the planned 200 Natters for themselves. Only about 36 were completed and 10 aircraft actually readied for launch. Fortunately for the pilots, American tanks neared the launch site and the aircraft were destroyed.

SPECIFICATIONS

CREW:	1
POWERPLANT:	one 16.67kN (3748lb) thrust Walter 109 rocket
MAX SPEED:	800km/h (497mph)
SPAN:	3.60m (11ft 10in)
LENGTH:	6.10m (20ft)
FIN SPAN:	2.25m (7ft 5in)
WEIGHT:	loaded 2200kg (4850lb)

Left: Of the many crazy aeronautical ideas dreamed up in the last years of the Third Reich, the Natter was the most radical and least practical to reach operational service. Launched from what was little more than an enlarged telephone pole, it could climb at 11,000m (36,415ft) per minute when Allied bombers approached.

In the combat zone the streamlined nosecone would be jettisoned and a battery of 24 unguided rockets exposed. After they were fired, the entire nose would be detached and the pilot flung out by the deceleration from the recovery parachute.

The Natter was constructed mainly of wood, using a furniture hinge for the canopy – which broke off on the first manned flight.

The tail section containing the valuable rocket motor would descend by parachute after use and be recovered for another mission.

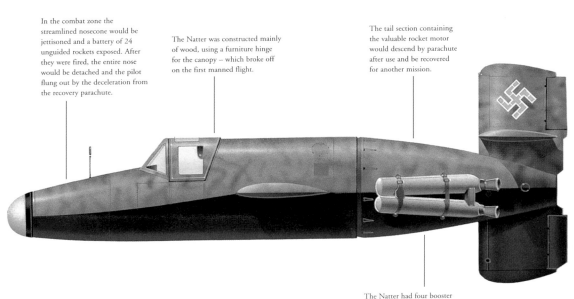

The Natter had four booster rocket motors for its launch and was on autopilot until it reached combat altitude. The sustainer rocket was good for 70 seconds of full thrust, but could be varied in power to give longer endurance.

BELL FM AIRACUDA (1937)

The late 1930s saw a vogue for heavy 'strategic fighters' such as the Messerschmitt BF 110 and the Fokker G.1. These were intended to escort bombers into enemy territory, intercept bombers at long range and carry out ground-attack missions. Wartime experience was to show that these were vulnerable to single-seat fighters and often needed escorting themselves. America's entry in this field was the Bell XFM Airacuda, intended as a 'mobile anti-aircraft platform' against bomber formations.

Mounting the gunners in the forward nacelles gave them a wide field of fire but the engines behind them were impossible to keep cool and frequently overheated on the ground. An emergency bailout would have required feathering both propellers. Despite its sleek looks, there was too much drag and the Airacuda was slower than most bombers and less manoeuvrable than fighters. Its own 272kg (600lb) bomb load was not much use and so it achieved none of its intended roles satisfactorily.

SPECIFICATIONS

CREW:	5
POWERPLANT:	two 813kW (1090hp) Allison V-1710-41 piston engines
MAX SPEED:	431km/h (268mph)
SPAN:	21.34m (70ft)
LENGTH:	14.00m (45ft 11in)
HEIGHT:	5.94m (19ft 6in)
WEIGHT:	maximum 9809kg (21,625lb)

Left: Bell's first aircraft, the Airacuda was an interesting response to an ill-thought-out requirement. A few were built, but they only saw limited service in the training role.

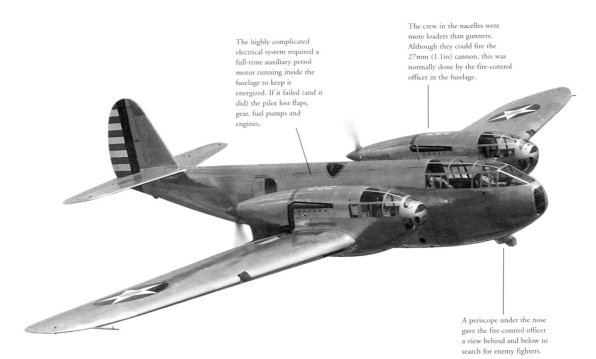

The highly complicated electrical system required a full-time auxiliary petrol motor running inside the fuselage to keep it energized. If it failed (and it did) the pilot lost flaps, gear, fuel pumps and engines.

The crew in the nacelles were more loaders than gunners. Although they could fire the 27mm (1.1in) cannon, this was normally done by the fire-control officer in the fuselage.

A periscope under the nose gave the fire-control officer a view behind and below to search for enemy fighters.

BLACKBURN A.D. SCOUT (SPARROW) (1915)

Harris Booth Air Department of the Admiralty (or A.D.) designed this distinctly odd anti-airship fighter for naval use. Although of conventional wood and fabric construction, unlike what was becoming standard practice, the fuselage nacelle was attached to the top wing rather than the bottom. This gave the pilot/gunner an excellent all-round view but contributed nothing to stability.

The Scout (unofficially called the Sparrow) was intended to carry a Davis two-pounder recoilless gun, but wiser heads prevailed, figuring that, recoilless or not, the structure wasn't up to such a weapon. An ordinary Lewis gun was fitted instead. The ability of a single man to fly the aircraft, load, fire and reload these heavy guns was always doubtful. When RNAS pilots got their hands on the Scout they found it was overweight with extremely poor handling. The Admiralty accepted it, but got rid of it as unsatisfactory within a month.

SPECIFICATIONS

CREW:	1
POWERPLANT:	one 75kW (100hp) 9-cylinder Gnome Monosoupape rotary engine
MAX SPEED:	135km/h (84mph)
SPAN:	10.18m (33ft 5in)
LENGTH:	6.93m (22ft 9in)
HEIGHT:	3.12m (10ft 3in)
WEIGHT:	unknown

Left: Four examples of the A.D. Scout or Sparrow were built, two by Hewlitt & Blondeau and two by Blackburn, who often seem to get the blame for it. Whether the airborne sailor is attempting to leap aboard or falling out is unclear.

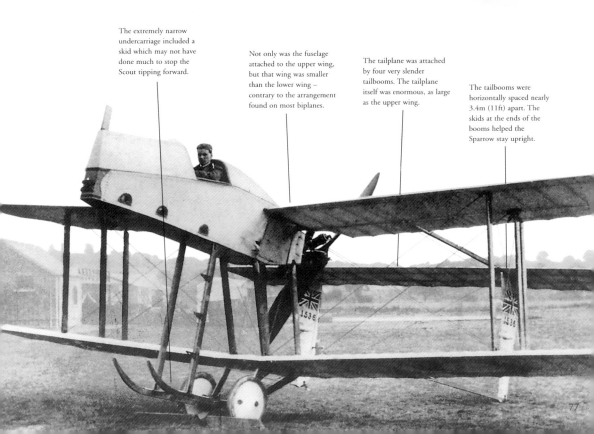

The extremely narrow undercarriage included a skid which may not have done much to stop the Scout tipping forward.

Not only was the fuselage attached to the upper wing, but that wing was smaller than the lower wing – contrary to the arrangement found on most biplanes.

The tailplane was attached by four very slender tailbooms. The tailplane itself was enormous, as large as the upper wing.

The tailbooms were horizontally spaced nearly 3.4m (11ft) apart. The skids at the ends of the booms helped the Sparrow stay upright.

77

BLACKBURN BLACKBURD (1918)

The state of aircraft carriers, or more correctly, aircraft-carrying ships in 1916 was such that a large and heavy aircraft such as a torpedo-bomber might be able to take off given enough headwind, but not land again on the small 'flying-off' decks of the time. Floatplane operations required the ship to stop in potentially dangerous waters. Blackburn's Blackburd (an archaic Scottish spelling) was designed to take off from a ship, jettison its wheels (quickly so they could be recovered) and then its axle so the torpedo could be dropped. At the end of its mission, it was to ditch next to the ship and hopefully be recovered. The Blackburd proved unstable in pitch, being nose heavy with or without a torpedo, and the rudder was ineffective, making deck landings virtually impossible.

SPECIFICATIONS

CREW:	1
POWERPLANT:	one 261kW (350hp) Rolls-Royce Eagle VIII piston engine in nose driving a two-bladed propeller
MAX SPEED:	153km/h (95mph)
SPAN:	15.97m (52ft 5in)
LENGTH:	10.64m (34ft 10in)
HEIGHT:	3.78m (12ft 5in)
WEIGHT:	loaded 2586kg (5700lb)

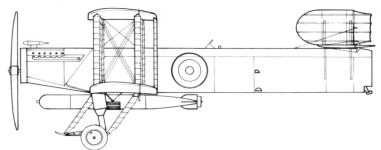

Left: First of a series of Blackburn ship-based attack aircraft, the boxy Blackburd was the poorest of three contenders for the Navy's requirement and was cancelled within a few months of its first flight. The first aircraft crashed at the beginning of its official trials but the sturdy structure did prevent harm to the pilot.

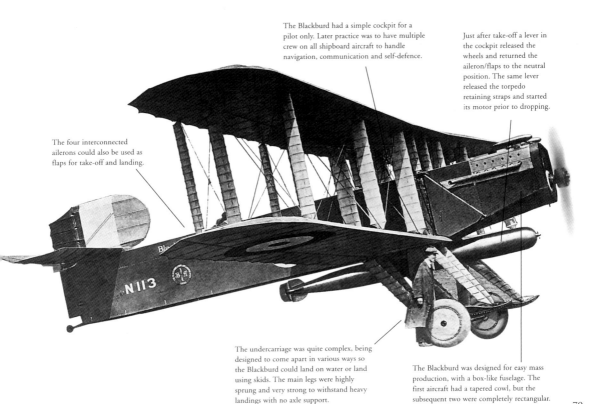

The Blackburd had a simple cockpit for a pilot only. Later practice was to have multiple crew on all shipboard aircraft to handle navigation, communication and self-defence.

Just after take-off a lever in the cockpit released the wheels and returned the aileron/flaps to the neutral position. The same lever released the torpedo retaining straps and started its motor prior to dropping.

The four interconnected ailerons could also be used as flaps for take-off and landing.

The undercarriage was quite complex, being designed to come apart in various ways so the Blackburd could land on water or land using skids. The main legs were highly sprung and very strong to withstand heavy landings with no axle support.

The Blackburd was designed for easy mass production, with a box-like fuselage. The first aircraft had a tapered cowl, but the subsequent two were completely rectangular.

N113

BLACKBURN TB *(1915)*

Technically a fighter, the Blackburn TB was one of the most specialized aircraft ever built – a long-range twin-engined anti-Zeppelin floatplane. This was Blackburn's first twin-engined aircraft (TB stood for Twin Blackburn), but more resembled the collision of two single-engined types. In fact, the rear fuselages and tails came from the BE.2c, then being licence-produced by Blackburn.

Designed for a pair of 112kW (150hp) Smith radial engines, the TB wound up with units giving a third less power. Its war load was only 32kg (70lb) of steel incendiary darts. The TB's attack method was to climb above enemy airships where the observer would fling the darts at them in the hope of causing and igniting a fatal gas leak. The TB had no other armament, but it was unlikely to get within gun range of a Zeppelin, let alone above one.

SPECIFICATIONS

CREW:	2
POWERPLANT:	two 75kW (100hp) Gnome Monosoupape rotary engines
MAX SPEED:	138km/h (86mph)
SPAN:	18.44m (60ft 6in)
LENGTH:	11.13m (36ft 8in)
HEIGHT:	4.11m (13ft 6in)
WEIGHT:	loaded 1588kg (3500lb)

Left: Seven TBs were delivered to the Royal Naval Air Service. They did not give much cause for alarm to Germany's Zeppelin crews, before being broken up in 1917.

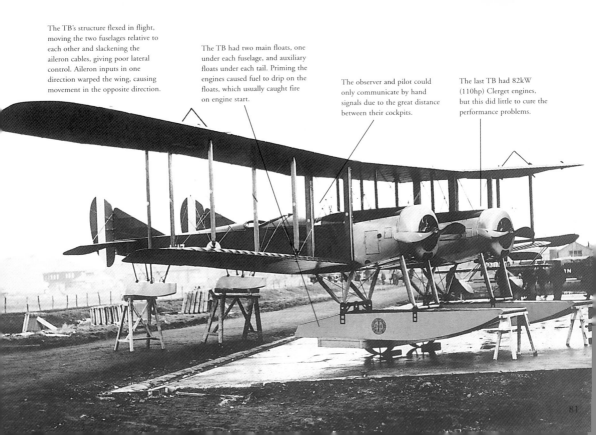

The TB's structure flexed in flight, moving the two fuselages relative to each other and slackening the aileron cables, giving poor lateral control. Aileron inputs in one direction warped the wing, causing movement in the opposite direction.

The TB had two main floats, one under each fuselage, and auxiliary floats under each tail. Priming the engines caused fuel to drip on the floats, which usually caught fire on engine start.

The observer and pilot could only communicate by hand signals due to the great distance between their cockpits.

The last TB had 82kW (110hp) Clerget engines, but this did little to cure the performance problems.

BLOHM UND VOSS BV 40 *(1944)*

By 1943 the enormous swarms of US bombers raiding German cities and factories spurred the Reich Air Ministry (RLM) to seek interesting technical solutions from industry: jet fighters, rocket fighters, surface-to-air missiles and a glider fighter. The theory behind the Blohm und Voss BV 40 was that a tiny glider, armed with powerful cannon, could swoop through a formation of bombers and knock one or two down almost before it was detected. After its firing pass it was proposed that the BV 40 make a second pass towing a bomb on a cable, but this was rejected in favour of a second 30mm (1.18in) cannon. Despite losses of several prototypes, the flight test programme proved the basic functionality of the BV 40, but not the feasibility of the concept, and the idea was abandoned in late 1944.

SPECIFICATIONS

CREW:	1
POWERPLANT:	none
MAX SPEED:	900km/h (560mph) in dive
SPAN:	7.90m (25ft 11in)
LENGTH:	5.70m (18ft 9in)
HEIGHT:	1.66m (5ft 5in)
WEIGHT:	950kg (2094lb)

Left: The BV 40 was another crazy late-war Luftwaffe idea to put partly trained pilots into an aircraft made of non-strategic materials and take on the Eighth Air Force. It required a conventional fighter and its precious fuel to get it above the bombers, and it soon became clear that the glider fighter offered no advantages.

As well as minimizing the target size, the small cross-section theoretically enabled the BV 40 to dive from a height onto the bombers at speeds over 805km/h (500mph).

To minimize the frontal area the pilot lay prone in the cockpit with his head resting on a padded support.

To protect the pilot against return fire from massed heavy bombers, the BV 40's cockpit was heavily armoured on all sides. The windscreen glass was 120mm (5in) thick.

Armament was a pair of heavy Mk 108 30mm (1.18in) cannon as used in the Me 262, mounted in the wing roots and loaded with 35 rounds each.

The BV 40 took off on a wheeled dolly, which was then jettisoned. If it survived its mission it landed on a retractable skid.

BOEING 2707 *(1960s)*

The Boeing 2707 stemmed from President Kennedy's June 1963 call for a supersonic transport (SST) to compete with the Anglo-French Concorde. Unlike Concorde and the Soviet Tu-144, the US SST was to be made largely of titanium, making it capable of Mach 3. In 1966 Boeing's variable-geometry (swing-wing) Model 2707 was chosen over proposals from Lockheed and North American. Boeing built an impressive full-scale mock-up and estimated future sales of 700–1000 SSTs. The technical challenges of a Mach 3 SST were greater than faced by its slower, smaller rivals.

The VG idea was abandoned in 1968 and a smaller fixed-wing version was planned, with test flights planned for 1970 and commercial service in 1974. Two prototypes were begun, but in 1971 the SST programme was cancelled. Increasing oil prices and environmental concerns were the excuses.

SPECIFICATIONS (2707-200)

CREW:	3 and 277 passengers
POWERPLANT:	four 281kN (63,200lb) thrust General Electric GE4/J5P afterburning turbojets
CRUISING SPEED:	Mach 2.7; 2900 km/h (1800mph)
SPAN:	spread, 54.97m (180ft 4in)
LENGTH:	93.27m (306ft)
HEIGHT:	14.10m (46ft 3in)
WEIGHT:	maximum 306,175kg (675,000lb)

Left: Despite great effort and enormous cost, the USA failed to complete its own supersonic airliner. When the Mach 3 project proved an unattainable goal, many US officials did their best to prevent Concorde achieving its full potential.

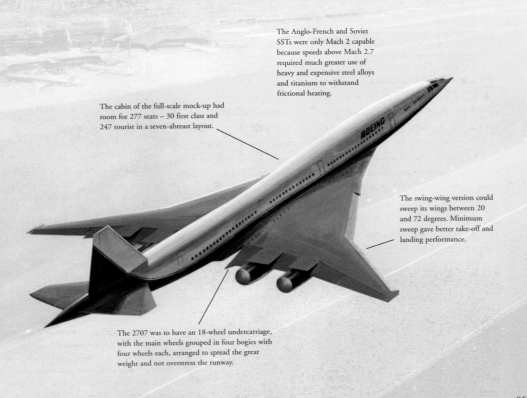

The Anglo-French and Soviet SSTs were only Mach 2 capable because speeds above Mach 2.7 required much greater use of heavy and expensive steel alloys and titanium to withstand frictional heating.

The cabin of the full-scale mock-up had room for 277 seats – 30 first class and 247 tourist in a seven-abreast layout.

The swing-wing version could sweep its wings between 20 and 72 degrees. Minimum sweep gave better take-off and landing performance.

The 2707 was to have an 18-wheel undercarriage, with the main wheels grouped in four bogies with four wheels each, arranged to spread the great weight and not overstress the runway.

BOEING SONIC CRUISER (2001–2002)

Boeing decided not to develop a direct competitor to the 550-seat Airbus A380, but instead drew up plans for a fast (but not supersonic) replacement for the 767, optimized for routes between city pairs, rather than operating within a 'hub-and-spoke' system.

Revealed in March 2001, the Sonic Cruiser's design was a radical departure from traditional airliner configuration. One commentator said that it looked like a 'Beech Starship that was rear-ended by a Lockheed SR-71'. Having had no serious interest from any airline, Boeing abandoned the project in December 2002, blaming a weak market and the effects of the 11 September 2001 attacks. Some of the proposed technologies will find their way into the new, far more conventional 7E7 Dreamliner. Boeing has restarted studies into an A380 competitor.

SPECIFICATIONS

CREW:	2 and 200–250 passengers
POWERPLANT:	two turbofans of up to 511kN (115,000lb) thrust, based on the Pratt & Whitney PW4000, Rolls-Royce Trent, or General Electric GE90
MAX SPEED:	Mach 0.98
SPAN:	50.00m (164ft)
LENGTH:	60.00m (196ft 10in)
HEIGHT:	unknown
WEIGHT:	maximum 200,000kg (440,925lb)

Left: The Sonic Cruiser offered a fast, long-range, efficient new airliner for the 21st century. Unfortunately, it was probably too unconventional for a conservative industry in the post 9/11 era, and came and went within 18 months.

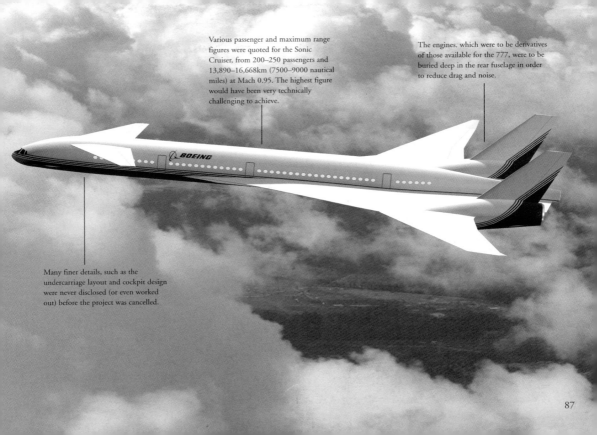

Various passenger and maximum range figures were quoted for the Sonic Cruiser, from 200–250 passengers and 13,890–16,668km (7500–9000 nautical miles) at Mach 0.95. The highest figure would have been very technically challenging to achieve.

The engines, which were to be derivatives of those available for the 777, were to be buried deep in the rear fuselage in order to reduce drag and noise.

Many finer details, such as the undercarriage layout and cockpit design were never disclosed (or even worked out) before the project was cancelled.

BOEING XB-15 *(1937)*

Having messed around with various twin-engined bombers, the USAAF sought true strategic capability in 1933, issuing the requirement that led to the giant XB-15, by far the largest American aircraft built to date. The all-metal XB-15 had features such as auxiliary power units, a flight engineer's position and heavy defensive armament. Unfortunately, the state of airframe development had outstripped that of engine technology and the proposed 1492kW (2000hp) engines were not available until two years after the XB-15 flew. The XB-15 was very underpowered and its performance was inadequate, particularly in comparison to the new fighters then entering service. The first B-17s had flown while the XB-15 was under construction and the XB-15 became the XC-105 transport aircraft, seeing out the war shifting freight around the Caribbean.

SPECIFICATIONS

CREW:	10
POWERPLANT:	four 746kW (1000hp) Pratt & Whitney R-1830-11 radial piston engines
MAX SPEED:	317km/h (197mph)
SPAN:	45.42m (149ft)
LENGTH:	26.70m (87ft 7in)
HEIGHT:	5.56m (18ft 1in)
WEIGHT:	maximum 32,069kg (70,700lb)

Left: Like the Barling Bomber, the XB-15 was a lonely giant. Having become a freighter and never dropping a bomb in anger, it was broken up in Panama at the end of the war.

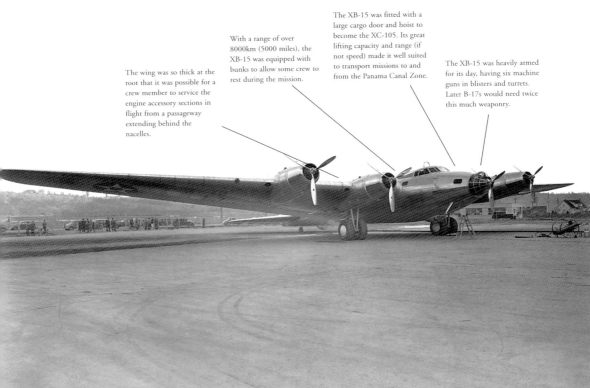

The wing was so thick at the root that it was possible for a crew member to service the engine accessory sections in flight from a passageway extending behind the nacelles.

With a range of over 8000km (5000 miles), the XB-15 was equipped with bunks to allow some crew to rest during the mission.

The XB-15 was fitted with a large cargo door and hoist to become the XC-105. Its great lifting capacity and range (if not speed) made it well suited to transport missions to and from the Panama Canal Zone.

The XB-15 was heavily armed for its day, having six machine guns in blisters and turrets. Later B-17s would need twice this much weaponry.

BONNEY GULL (1928)

Despite 25 years of evidence to the contrary, American pilot and inventor Leonard Warden Bonney believed the secret to manned flight was to emulate the birds as closely as possible. To this end he kept and studied seagulls and devised an aircraft on avian principles. The Bonney Gull emerged in late 1927 and was unlike anything before or since. The wings, which really can be described as gull-like, did everything except actually flap, incorporating variable incidence, variable dihedral, and variable sweep of the outer sections. After four years' work and considerable testing in wind tunnels and on the ground, and despite the protest of friends and observers, Bonney took off in the Gull on 4 May 1928. The Gull wobbled, fishtailed and plunged into the ground, killing Bonney and ending his dream of flying like the birds.

SPECIFICATIONS

CREW:	1
POWERPLANT:	one 134kW (180hp) Kirkham radial piston engine
MAX SPEED:	unknown
SPAN:	12.27m (40ft 3in)
LENGTH:	6.58m (21ft 7in)
HEIGHT:	unknown
WEIGHT:	approx 907kg (2000lb)

Left: The bird-like Gull went against the experience of aviators since the Wright Brothers and returned to earlier ideas. Unfortunately, the Wrights were right and its inventor paid the price.

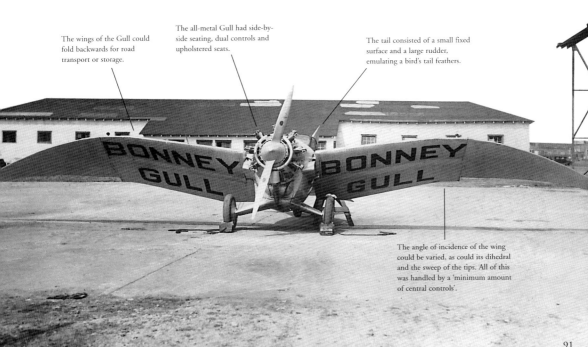

The wings of the Gull could fold backwards for road transport or storage.

The all-metal Gull had side-by-side seating, dual controls and upholstered seats.

The tail consisted of a small fixed surface and a large rudder, emulating a bird's tail feathers.

The angle of incidence of the wing could be varied, as could its dihedral and the sweep of the tips. All of this was handled by a 'minimum amount of central controls'.

BRISTOL BRAEMAR, PULLMAN AND TRAMP (1917–1919)

An unsuccessful contender for a 1917 large bomber requirement, the Bristol Braemar triplane formed the basis of the Pullman, an equally unwanted airliner with a large cabin and enclosed cockpit. The Pullman's crew distrusted this feature and took to carrying axes with which to hack their way out in an emergency.

The Royal Mail Steam Packet Company showed interest in a version called the Tramp to be powered (naturally) by steam engines. By 1919 this was pretty eccentric and a considerable challenge. Two Tramps were built, each with four piston engines in an internal engine room while a light and powerful steam powerplant was developed. This proved impossible, as did making the system that transmitted power from engine room to propellers work reliably, and thus neither of the Tramps ever flew.

SPECIFICATIONS (Pullman)

CREW:	3 and 14 passengers
POWERPLANT:	four 298kW (400hp) Liberty 12 inline piston engines
MAX SPEED:	217km/h (135mph)
SPAN:	24.89m (81ft 8in)
LENGTH:	15.85m (52ft)
HEIGHT:	6.06m (20ft)
WEIGHT:	loaded 8051kg (17,750lb)

Left: Built as a bomber, and considered for the torpedo-bomber role, the Braemar tried to become an airliner, and then a 'spares carrier' for the Royal Mail. In none of these roles did the big Bristol triplanes achieve anything.

The Pullman's engines were installed in the fuselage and ran the propellers by cables and pulleys. This proved its undoing as the gear system was unworkable.

The two Braemars had an open cockpit and gun position in the nose, but the Pullman had a cabin with wraparound windscreens. The RAF test pilots who flew it much preferred the original layout.

The interior of the Pullman was fitted out like a first-class railway coach, but it never carried a paying passenger.

BRISTOL BUCKINGHAM AND BUCKMASTER (1943)

Rendered obsolete by the Mosquito even before it had flown, the Buckingham was delayed until the requirement was finalized, and then by problems with development of the Centaurus engine. Having already been rejected outright by the RAF in Italy, more engine troubles further delayed production until the Buckingham was too late to serve in the Far East either. The Buckinghams were never used as bombers, but the few to enter service were used as high-speed transports. Over 400 were ordered but only 119 production examples were delivered by the war's end. With many Buckinghams unfinished on the production line, about 65 were converted to the unarmed Buckmaster which was also used as a transport and later as a conversion trainer for the Bristol Brigand, which, despite appearances, was also derived from the Buckingham.

SPECIFICATIONS (Mk 1)

CREW:	4
POWERPLANT:	two 1678kW (2250hp) Bristol Centaurus VII or XI radial piston engines
MAX SPEED:	531km/h (330mph)
SPAN:	21.89m (71ft 10in)
LENGTH:	14.27m (46ft 10in)
HEIGHT:	5.33m (17ft 6in)
WEIGHT:	maximum 17,259kg (38,050lb)

Left: Subject to changing RAF requirements during development, only 54 Buckinghams were ever delivered as bombers, the rest as high-speed couriers for four passengers. Many were completed as the equally obscure Buckmaster transport, pictured here.

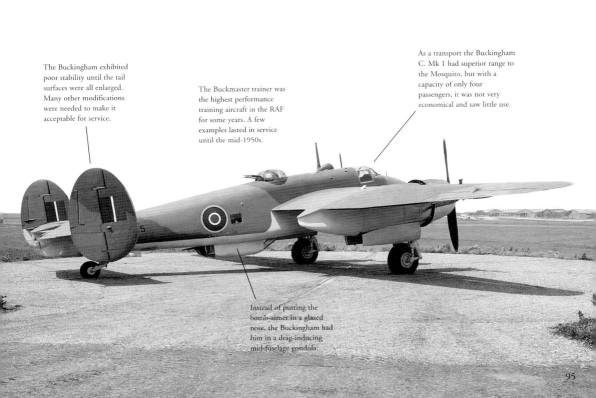

The Buckingham exhibited poor stability until the tail surfaces were all enlarged. Many other modifications were needed to make it acceptable for service.

The Buckmaster trainer was the highest performance training aircraft in the RAF for some years. A few examples lasted in service until the mid-1950s.

As a transport the Buckingham C. Mk 1 had superior range to the Mosquito, but with a capacity of only four passengers, it was not very economical and saw little use.

Instead of putting the bomb-aimer in a glazed nose, the Buckingham had him in a drag-inducing mid-fuselage gondola.

BRITISH AEROSPACE NIMROD AEW.3 *(1980s)*

To replace the 1940s-vintage Avro Shackleton in the airborne early warning (AEW) role, the Royal Air Force began development of a version of the Nimrod maritime patrol aircraft, equipped with GEC Marconi radar in large radomes at the nose and tail. The project quickly fell behind schedule. The second prototype was well underway by the time deficiencies in the first were discovered. The managers of two software departments wouldn't talk with each other, and neither would the two radars. The costs spiralled. After expenditure estimated at around £1.5 billion, the UK government decided to stop throwing good money after bad and cancelled the project in 1986. The Shackleton carried on until 1991 when it was replaced by the US Boeing E-3 Sentry.

SPECIFICATIONS

CREW:	12
POWERPLANT:	four 55.1kN (12,140lb) thrust Rolls-Royce Spey 250 turbofans
MAX SPEED:	(MR.2) 926km/h (525mph)
SPAN:	35.00m (114ft 8in)
LENGTH:	38.60m (126ft 7in)
HEIGHT:	9.08m (29ft 10in)
WEIGHT:	maximum (MR.2) 89,098kg (19,2015lb)

Left: In the 1980s 12 Nimrods were to be converted into AEW.3 radar platforms. Cost rises and technical problems saw the number reduced to six and then zero. The current Nimrod MRA.4 programme has undergone similar tribulations but has (so far) escaped cancellation.

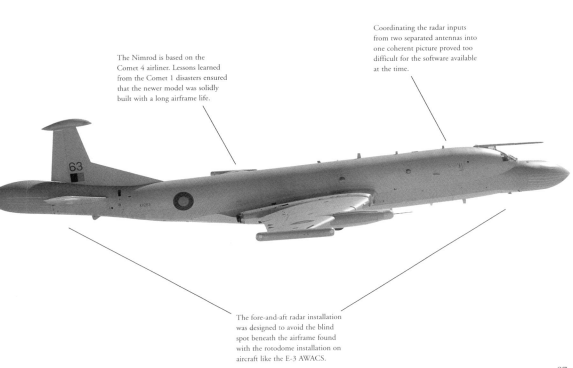

The Nimrod is based on the Comet 4 airliner. Lessons learned from the Comet 1 disasters ensured that the newer model was solidly built with a long airframe life.

Coordinating the radar inputs from two separated antennas into one coherent picture proved too difficult for the software available at the time.

The fore-and-aft radar installation was designed to avoid the blind spot beneath the airframe found with the rotodome installation on aircraft like the E-3 AWACS.

CAPRONI CA.60 NOVIPLANO (1921)

Count Gianni Caproni, builder of some fine aircraft, chose for some reason to build a giant flying boat with no fewer than nine wings and eight engines. With this, or an even bigger version, he hoped to fly over 100 passengers across the Atlantic. Amidst all the struts and wings, the absence of any tail surfaces could easily be overlooked. Reportedly making a short hop without incident, the official first flight was less successful. Rising to about 18m (60ft) above Lake Maggiore, the Ca.60 suddenly nosed down and dived into the water. Some said that testing had shown the need for a lot of lead ballast and that this had shifted in flight. Test pilot Semprini crawled out of the wreck unscathed. Later a mysterious fire destroyed the remains and ended the Count's transatlantic dream.

SPECIFICATIONS

CREW:	8
POWERPLANT:	eight 297kW (400hp) Liberty piston engines
CRUISING SPEED:	estimated 112km/h (70mph)
SPAN:	30m (98ft 5in)
LENGTH:	23.47m (77ft)
HEIGHT:	9.24m (30ft)
WEIGHT:	24,993kg (55,100lb)

Left: Noviplano meant 'nine wings', but the Ca.60 was sometimes called the 'Flying Houseboat' and other uncomplimentary things. One commentator likened it to a left-over from the Spanish Armada.

The Ca-60 had twice the wing area of a B-52 bomber. The equal size wings would have nearly equal loading, making it longitudinally unstable. Supposedly differential use of front and rear ailerons would have controlled pitch.

The eight Liberty engines were arranged with three pulling and pushing on the front wing and three pushing and one pulling at the back. The centre engines had four-bladed propellers.

The pilot had an open cockpit, but the passengers in the cabin had more window glazing than any airliner before or since.

CONVAIR NB-36 *(1955)*

Sometimes known as the Crusader, the NB-36 was intended to prove the feasibility of carrying a nuclear reactor in flight, towards an eventual goal of a nuclear-powered aircraft with unlimited endurance. The NB-36H was built using components from a B-36 destroyed in a tornado with a new nose compartment heavily lined with lead and thick yellow tinted glass to protect the crew from radiation. The consequences of an NB-36H crash were so frightening that several support planes, including one filled with a team of paratroopers, followed the aircraft on every flight. Should the NB-36H crash or have to jettison its reactor, they would jump and secure the site and help with clean-up. A hotline to the president's office was set up in case of disaster. It was nearly used on one flight when a smoke marker went off in the reactor compartment.

SPECIFICATIONS

CREW:	5
POWERPLANT:	six 2835kW (3800hp) Pratt & Whitney R-4360-53 radials and four 23.1kN (5200lb) thrust General Electric J47-GE-19 turbojets
MAX SPEED:	676km/h (420mph)
SPAN:	70.10m (230ft)
LENGTH:	49.38m (162ft 1in)
HEIGHT:	14.23m (46ft 8in)
WEIGHT:	162,305kg (357,500lb)

Left: The USA's Nuclear Powered Aircraft (NPA) programme lasted 15 years and cost a billion dollars, but achieved little more than getting a small reactor airborne. No one really came up with a convincing case for a bomber that could stay aloft indefinitely, well beyond the endurance of any crew. The development of all-jet bombers and aerial refuelling obviated the need for a nuclear-powered aircraft.

The five-man crew, which included a pilot, copilot, flight engineer and two nuclear engineers, were located in the forward section of the aircraft, while the atomic reactor was located in the rear section.

The crew were so isolated from the engines and the outside world because of the thick shielding that they could barely hear the very noisy engines and likened the experience to flying a submarine.

Contrary to belief at the time, the USSR never flew an atomic-powered aircraft. They did test a reactor in a Tu-95 'Bear' but didn't bother with heavy shielding. Most of the crew died within a few years of the tests.

The engines of a normal B-36 were inspected in flight by the aft crew members. On the NB-36H this was done by a television camera system, as was observation of the reactor itself.

The reactor did not power the aircraft or any of its systems. It was only operated when the XB-36 was over a test range in New Mexico. In all the 'Crusader' only made 47 flights, all of them in daylight and beginning and ending at Carswell AFB, Texas.

CONVAIR R3Y TRADEWIND (1950)

In the 1950s the Tradewind was part of the US Navy's grand plans for fleets of seaplane fighters, bombers and transports. Originally designed as the XP5Y-1 patrol plane, the Tradewind was completely revised as the unarmed R3Y transport soon after its first flight when the Navy brass changed their minds as to what they wanted.

The Tradewind was intended to carry 103 troops or 92 casualty litters. Many publicity photos show apparent battalions of Marines disgorged from the nose doors storming across beaches. In reality the unwieldy flying boat would have been very vulnerable in any opposed landing.

Only one squadron operated the R3Y, but the extremely complex T40 turboprop engines gave no end of trouble and the contra-rotating propellers often got out of synchronization and overheated. After one near disaster when a propeller and gearbox flew off, the R3Ys were grounded and scrapped.

SPECIFICATIONS

CREW:	5
POWERPLANT:	four 4362kW (5860hp) Allison T40 turboprops
MAX SPEED:	624km/h (388mph)
SPAN:	43.45m (142ft 7in)
LENGTH:	42.57m (139ft 8in)
HEIGHT:	13.67m (44ft 10in)
WEIGHT:	loaded 63,674kg (140,374lb)

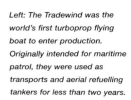

Left: The Tradewind was the world's first turboprop flying boat to enter production. Originally intended for maritime patrol, they were used as transports and aerial refuelling tankers for less than two years.

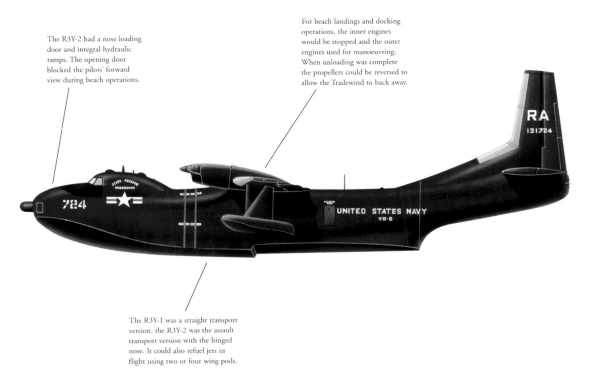

The R3Y-2 had a nose loading door and integral hydraulic ramps. The opening door blocked the pilots' forward view during beach operations.

For beach landings and docking operations, the inner engines would be stopped and the outer engines used for manoeuvring. When unloading was complete the propellers could be reversed to allow the Tradewind to back away.

The R3Y-1 was a straight transport version, the R3Y-2 was the assault transport version with the hinged nose. It could also refuel jets in flight using two or four wing pods.

RA
131724

724

UNITED STATES NAVY
VR-2

CONVAIR F2Y SEA DART (1953)

In the late 1940s the US Navy found they could not exploit the new swept-wing technology, and thus supersonic flight, with aircraft able to use the small carriers of the day. A delta-winged seaplane fighter was Convair's solution and they were awarded a contract in 1951. Delays in the intended Westinghouse J46 engines saw their substitution by the J34, another of Westinghouse's inadequate engines. The J34s were eventually replaced by XJ46s, which each only gave 3.03kN (680lb) more thrust and far less than promised. Like Convair's original F-102, the XF2Y had too much drag to be supersonic in level flight.

Convair suggested a complete redesign but the Navy for some reason went cold on the whole idea. The US Navy decided to re-evaluate the F2Y in 1954 but the first pre-production YF2Y-1 broke up in the air during a public demonstration. Only one of the three other YF2Y-1s was ever flown before the whole thing was abandoned in 1957.

SPECIFICATIONS

CREW:	1
POWERPLANT:	two 15.12kN (3400lb) thrust Westinghouse J34 turbojets
MAX SPEED:	1325km/h (825mph)
SPAN:	9.96m (32ft 8in)
LENGTH:	16.03m (52ft 7in)
HEIGHT:	4.93m (16ft 2in)
WEIGHT:	loaded 7497kg (16,527lb)

Left: The Sea Dart was the only flying boat to go supersonic, if only just. Before the bugs were sorted out, development of the 'supercarrier' allowed true high-performance aircraft to go to sea.

It was intended that a
production version would have
armament of 20mm (0.79in)
cannon and a pack of unguided
rockets.

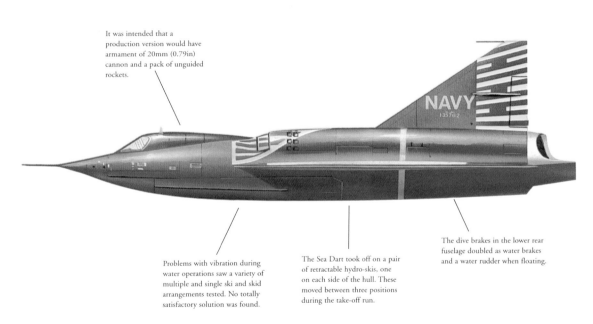

NAVY
135762

Problems with vibration during
water operations saw a variety of
multiple and single ski and skid
arrangements tested. No totally
satisfactory solution was found.

The Sea Dart took off on a pair
of retractable hydro-skis, one
on each side of the hull. These
moved between three positions
during the take-off run.

The dive brakes in the lower rear
fuselage doubled as water brakes
and a water rudder when floating.

CONVAIR XFY-1 POGO (1954)

Along with the Lockheed XFV-1 Salmon, the Convair XFY-1 Pogo was designed as a point defence fighter that could take-off and land vertically, using a powerful turboprop with a contra-rotating propeller. Although the idea had some merit, not enough thought was put into how, once the mission was over, the pilot would bring the aircraft back to the landing pad or ship. Wind tunnel tests showed that a rate of descent greater than 3m (10ft) per second could lead to the Pogo tumbling out of control. During the landing, pilot 'Skeets' Coleman, the only man to fly the XFY-1, had to look over his shoulder, adjust his ejection seat to 45 degrees and carefully judge the rate of descent while travelling backwards. The unreliability of the T-40 engine and lack of an effective zero-zero ejection seat helped kill the turboprop 'tail-sitter' and both the XFY and XFV programmes were cancelled in mid-1955.

SPECIFICATIONS

CREW:	1
POWERPLANT:	one 4362kW (5850hp) Allison XT-40 turboprop
MAX SPEED:	982km/h (610mph)
SPAN:	8.43m (27ft 7in)
LENGTH:	10.66m (35ft)
TAIL SPAN:	6.98m (22ft 11in)
WEIGHT:	maximum 7371kg (16,250lb)

Left: The Pogo pilot's life depended entirely on proper functioning of the XT-40 engine, described as 'not the world's most reliable'. Unlike a helicopter, the XFY-1 could not autorotate to a safe landing.

The spinner was so large because the production version was intended to carry an air-intercept radar, although no mechanism was devised to stop it rotating with the spinner.

To board the Pogo, the pilot had to climb a very tall ladder and lie on his back throughout the startup and take-off process. Special moveable hangars were needed so that groundcrews could work on the engines.

Although the XFY-1 was never armed, a production Pogo would have had four 20mm (0.79in) cannon or a battery of air-to-air rockets.

Castoring wheels were fitted to the ends of the wings and tail surfaces.

NAVY

107

FAIREY ROTODYNE (1957)

The Rotodyne was a compound aircraft with wings, tractor engines and a tip-driven rotor system. Unfortunately, it was use of the tip jets at and near the airport that was the problem. The Rotodyne put out a painful 106 decibels of shrieking noise. Much work was done on silencers, but it was never reduced to the 96 decibels that the authorities demanded. Budgetary problems of the time saw the RAF and British Army withdraw their interest and the Rotodyne became a wholly civil project. Fairey talked up expressions of interest from BEA in the UK, New York Airways and the US Army, but the crucial launch order never came. British government policy to rationalize the industry saw the end of the Rotodyne and Fairey as an airframe maker in 1962.

SPECIFICATIONS

CREW:	3 and 40 passengers
POWERPLANT:	two 2089kW (2800hp) Napier Eland NEL7 turboprops
CRUISING SPEED:	298km/h (185mph)
ROTOR DIAMETER:	27.43m (90ft)
LENGTH:	17.95m (58ft 8in)
HEIGHT:	6.80m (22ft 2in)
WEIGHT:	loaded 14,969kg (33,000lb)

Left: The Rotodyne offered a new fast method of intercity transport but it proved too noisy and too expensive and was an easy victim of budget cuts and politics.

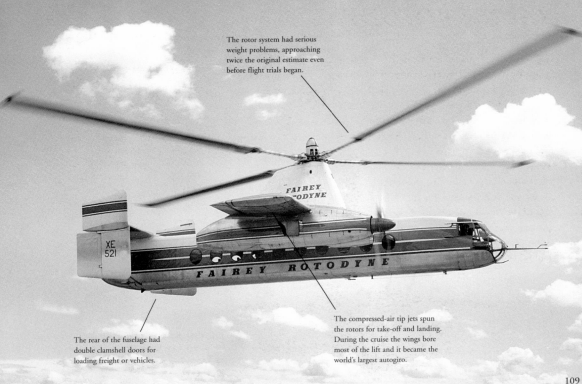

The rotor system had serious weight problems, approaching twice the original estimate even before flight trials began.

The rear of the fuselage had double clamshell doors for loading freight or vehicles.

The compressed-air tip jets spun the rotors for take-off and landing. During the cruise the wings bore most of the lift and it became the world's largest autogiro.

FAIREY ROTODYNE

XE 521

FIESELER FI 103R-IV FLYING BOMB (1944)

SS officer Otto Skorzeny is credited with the idea of a piloted version of the V-1 flying bomb able to make precision attacks, and design began before the first unguided V-1s fell on London in June 1944. To study why many test V-1s crashed soon after launch an earlier piloted version was tested. Two pilots were injured before famed woman test pilot Hanna Reitsch confirmed that the engine noise was vibrating the airframe off course. The operational manned V-1, also called the Reichenberg IV, was not intended as a suicide weapon, unlike the Japanese 'Ohka', although in practice the distinction would have been narrow. The 100 volunteers who signed up to fly the bombs were known unofficially as 'Selbstopfermaenner' or 'Self-sacrifice Men'. Although about 70 Reichenberg IVs were built for use by special unit KG 200, none were actually used operationally and development stopped in October 1944.

SPECIFICATIONS

CREW:	1
POWERPLANT:	one 3.43kN (772lb) thrust Argus As 14 pulse jet
MAX SPEED:	650km/h (404mph)
SPAN:	5.72m (18ft 9in)
LENGTH:	8.00m (26ft 3in)
HEIGHT:	1.42m (4ft 8in)
WEIGHT:	(unmanned V-1) 2150kg (4750lb)

Left: A suicide weapon in all but name, the Reichenberg IV would have taken a very brave or fanatical pilot to use it in action. Fortunately for all concerned, even the Nazis decided it was a bad idea.

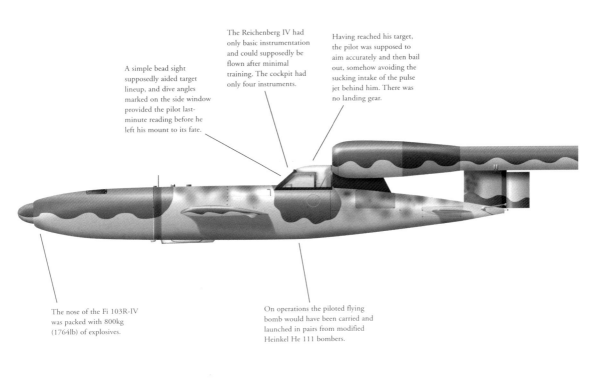

A simple bead sight supposedly aided target lineup, and dive angles marked on the side window provided the pilot last-minute reading before he left his mount to its fate.

The Reichenberg IV had only basic instrumentation and could supposedly be flown after minimal training. The cockpit had only four instruments.

Having reached his target, the pilot was supposed to aim accurately and then bail out, somehow avoiding the sucking intake of the pulse jet behind him. There was no landing gear.

The nose of the Fi 103R-IV was packed with 800kg (1764lb) of explosives.

On operations the piloted flying bomb would have been carried and launched in pairs from modified Heinkel He 111 bombers.

FISHER P-75 EAGLE (1943)

To build the USAAF a fighter of 'exceptional performance' with high speed, long range and a fast climb rate, someone had the bright idea of assembling parts from several different aircraft and getting a car parts maker to build it. The Fisher Body Division of auto maker General Motors combined Curtiss Warhawk, Douglas Dauntless and Vought Corsair parts with a complicated new engine to create the XP-75. By the time the prototypes were flying, the USAAF decided it needed an escort fighter more than an interceptor and ordered 2500 XP-75As, a revised version with a bubble canopy and fewer borrowed parts. These proved unstable in yaw and sluggish in roll, and they spun badly. The mid-mounted engine gave less power than expected and tended to overheat. Thankfully the P-51D proved up to the job and the Eagle was grounded.

SPECIFICATIONS

CREW:	1
POWERPLANT:	one 2151kW (2885hp) Allison V-3420-23 inline piston engine
MAX SPEED:	643km/h (400mph)
SPAN:	15.04m (49ft 4in)
LENGTH:	12.32m (40ft 5in)
HEIGHT:	4.72m (15ft 6in)
WEIGHT:	maximum 8260kg (18,210lb)

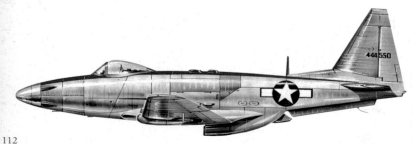

Left: Called the Eagle but more of a turkey, the P-75 was a 'bitzer', created largely from bits of other aircraft. This was no way to design a fighter aircraft, no matter how cheaply it was done.

The engine was a 24-cylinder monstrosity, created by joining two Allison V-1710s on a common shaft.

The engine was mounted behind the cockpit like that on the P-39 and P-63, driving contra-rotating propellers through an extension shaft.

The Eagle's outer wings came from the P-40 Warhawk, the landing gear was from an F4U Corsair and the tail originated with the SBD Dauntless.

It was originally planned to use outer wings from the P-51, but those from the P-40, designed by the same man behind the XP-75, were used instead.

432166

FOCKE-WULF TA-154 MOSKITO (1943)

Inspired by the RAF's 'Wooden Wonder', the de Havilland Mosquito, Kurt Tank of Focke-Wulf created the Ta-154 in response to an urgent requirement for a night-fighter to protect Germany from the RAF's bombers. Like the Mosquito, the Ta-154, inevitably dubbed 'Moskito', was a heavily armed two-seat, twin-engined aircraft made largely of wood. Unfortunately, the RAF reached the factory producing the specialized glue first and the production aircraft were assembled using a cheaper alternative. Three aircraft soon disintegrated in flight and production was stopped while a solution was sought. Hermann Goering, who knew little about the programme, accused Tank of sabotage, and an unrelated crash saw cancellation of the whole programme in August 1944. A plan to use some of the completed aircraft packed with explosives to blow up US bomber formations did not proceed.

SPECIFICATIONS

CREW:	2
POWERPLANT:	two 1119kW (1500hp) Jumo 211R piston engines
MAX SPEED:	650km/h (404mph)
SPAN:	16.00m (52ft 6in)
LENGTH:	12.10m (39ft 9in)
HEIGHT:	3.50m (11ft 6in)
WEIGHT:	8930kg (19,687lb)

Left: Only a handful of examples of the otherwise promising Ta-154 were delivered to the Luftwaffe due to the type's propensity to come unglued in flight.

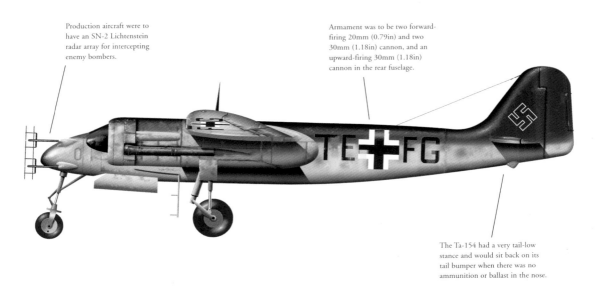

Production aircraft were to
have an SN-2 Lichtenstein
radar array for intercepting
enemy bombers.

Armament was to be two forward-
firing 20mm (0.79in) and two
30mm (1.18in) cannon, and an
upward-firing 30mm (1.18in)
cannon in the rear fuselage.

The Ta-154 had a very tail-low
stance and would sit back on its
tail bumper when there was no
ammunition or ballast in the nose.

TE+FG

FOKKER V8 (1917)

The Fokker V8, which is one of those few aircraft that fall into the category of quintrupriplane, is mainly remarkable in appearing months after the successful V6, prototype for the famous Dr.1 Triplane. The V8 resembled the V6 in some respects, but had an inline engine and three wings at the front and two at the back. In October 1917 it was test flown by Anthony Fokker himself, but by all accounts this was little more than a hop. It was apparent that modifications were needed, which were duly carried out, and two weeks later another short flight was made. This was to be the V8's last and it was scrapped soon afterwards. One almost thinks it was created on a bet, to prove that five wings were no better than three.

SPECIFICATIONS

CREW:	1
POWERPLANT:	one 90kW (120hp) Mercedes DIII engine
MAX SPEED:	unknown
SPAN:	unknown
LENGTH:	unknown
HEIGHT:	unknown
WEIGHT:	unknown

Left: The Fokker V8 was abandoned in favour of the Dr.1, which had many similar features but fewer wings. It became the archetypal German fighter of World War I.

The forward wings were mounted about as far forward as physically possible, and unlike the Dr.1's were not staggered.

The middle wings were affixed to the top and bottom of the fuselage just behind the pilot's cockpit. All the top wings had ailerons.

The tail surfaces were conventional for the time, being essentially the same as those on the Dr.1, having a large tailplane with elevators but a single moveable fin surface.

GENERAL AIRCRAFT FLEET SHADOWER (1940)

Designed for the extremely specific role of following enemy surface ships at night, the G.A.L.38 was an extremely strange-looking creature, looking something like the offspring of a Stirling bomber and a Sunderland flying boat. Of all-wooden construction, the Fleet Shadower (also known as the Night Shadower) had full-span flaps which were 'blown' by airflow from the engines to give the shortest possible take-off and landing distances for aircraft-carrier operations and to maintain contact with enemy warships. The four tiny engines were very quiet, and generally the AS.39 could be described as an early stealth aircraft, following a German battleship at night out of earshot, and hopefully gunshot. The development of effective ASV (Air to Surface Vessel) radar that could be fitted in long-range patrol aircraft removed the need for such a specialized machine.

SPECIFICATIONS

CREW:	3
POWERPLANT:	four 97kW (130hp) Pobjoy Niagara piston engines
MAX SPEED:	185km/h (115mph)
SPAN:	17.02m (55ft 10in)
LENGTH:	11.00m (36ft 1in)
HEIGHT:	3.86m (12ft 8in)
WEIGHT:	4290kg (9458lb)

Left: The Fleet Shadower was one of the most specialized aircraft of all time. In action it would have chugged along all night behind heavily armed warships. At dawn it would have been defenceless.

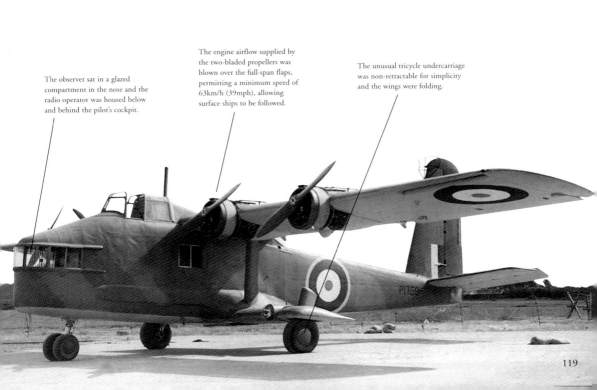

The observer sat in a glazed
compartment in the nose and the
radio operator was housed below
and behind the pilot's cockpit.

The engine airflow supplied by
the two-bladed propellers was
blown over the full-span flaps,
permitting a minimum speed of
63km/h (39mph), allowing
surface ships to be followed.

The unusual tricycle undercarriage
was non-retractable for simplicity
and the wings were folding.

GENERAL DYNAMICS F-111B *(1960s)*

Spiralling costs of combat aircraft and the diverse range of warplanes in US military service encouraged the US Defense Department to seek 'commonality' between the services' equipment. Flagship for this philosophy was to be the F-111, in F-111A bomber form for the Air Force and as the F-111B fleet defence fighter for the Navy. As early as 1964 General Dynamics warned the Navy that the F-111B would not meet its requirements. They were right. The Navy's weight limit was 25,000kg (55,000lb), but early tests indicated a fully equipped F-111B would weigh 35,455kg (78,000lb). A Super Weight Improvement Program (SWIP) was followed without irony by three separate Colossal Weight Improvement Programs (CWIP). The Navy and USAF versions began to diverge. Testing proved that carrier suitability was marginal. Testifying before Congress, an Admiral said 'all the thrust in Christendom couldn't make a fighter out of that airplane'.

SPECIFICATIONS

CREW:	2
POWERPLANT:	two 82.3kN (18,500lb) Pratt & Whitney TF30-P-1 afterburning turbofans
MAX SPEED:	2334km/h (1450mph)
SPAN:	21.34m (70ft) extended
LENGTH:	20.97m (68ft 10in)
HEIGHT:	5.10m (16ft 8in)
WEIGHT:	maximum 39,264kg (86,563lb)

Left: The F-111B served to prove that the needs of the US Air Force and Navy were quite different. The F-111B was cancelled in 1968 after nearly $400 million had been wasted.

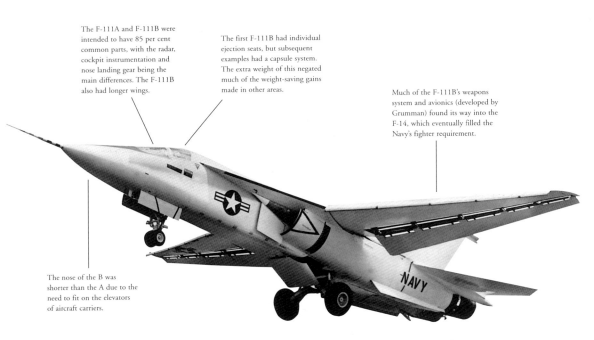

The F-111A and F-111B were intended to have 85 per cent common parts, with the radar, cockpit instrumentation and nose landing gear being the main differences. The F-111B also had longer wings.

The first F-111B had individual ejection seats, but subsequent examples had a capsule system. The extra weight of this negated much of the weight-saving gains made in other areas.

Much of the F-111B's weapons system and avionics (developed by Grumman) found its way into the F-14, which eventually filled the Navy's fighter requirement.

The nose of the B was shorter than the A due to the need to fit on the elevators of aircraft carriers.

GLOSTER METEOR (PRONE PILOT) (1954)

The increasing performance of combat aircraft in the postwar years saw aircrews subjected to greater and greater acceleration or g forces during manoeuvres. Reducing the distance that blood has to pump from the heart to the brain increases tolerance to g. Lying prone would theoretically give the pilot an edge in a dogfight. To test this concept for a proposed British rocket interceptor, a Meteor F.8 fighter was modified with an additional cockpit in a forward fuselage extended by 2.39m (7ft 10in). A safety pilot remained in the normal cockpit. Tests showed the prone pilot could indeed endure slightly more g, but suffered from vertigo, couldn't see very much – particularly behind him – and became tired quickly. After 55 hours of flight testing the idea was abandoned.

SPECIFICATIONS

CREW:	2
POWERPLANT:	two 16kN (3600lb) thrust Rolls-Royce Derwent 8 turbojets
MAX SPEED:	(F.8) 962km/h (598mph)
SPAN:	11.32m (37ft 2in)
LENGTH:	15.98m (52ft 3in)
HEIGHT:	4.24m (13ft 11in)
WEIGHT:	(F.8) loaded 7122kg (15,700lb)

Left: Prone flying promised better combat performance and a slimmer fuselage, but introduced its own difficulties. It proved uncomfortable. The problem of quick escape was never quite solved.

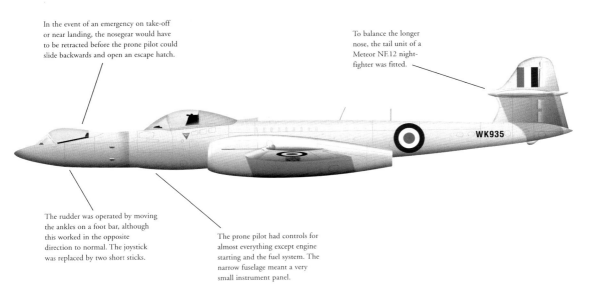

In the event of an emergency on take-off or near landing, the nosegear would have to be retracted before the prone pilot could slide backwards and open an escape hatch.

To balance the longer nose, the tail unit of a Meteor NF.12 night-fighter was fitted.

The rudder was operated by moving the ankles on a foot bar, although this worked in the opposite direction to normal. The joystick was replaced by two short sticks.

The prone pilot had controls for almost everything except engine starting and the fuel system. The narrow fuselage meant a very small instrument panel.

WK935

GENERAL DYNAMICS/MCDONNELL DOUGLAS A-12 AVENGER II (CANCELLED 1991)

General Dynamics and McDonnell Douglas appropriated the name of an earlier Grumman product for their proposed stealth replacement for the A-6 Intruder all-weather attack bomber. Sadly, the Avenger II was not destined to be a classic like the wartime TBF. Intended to use more sophisticated stealth techniques than the USAF's F-117A Nighthawk, the A-12 was a trapezoidal shape with smooth, rather than faceted, surfaces for scattering radar beams. It would have carried more weapons than the F-117 and had an air-to-air capability. Developed largely in secrecy and without proper oversight, the cost rose to a reported $100 million per aircraft. The Avenger II was cancelled by Defense Secretary Dick Cheney in January 1991, just before the Gulf War and a few months before the prototype's expected first flight. Four senior naval officers were forced into retirement over the fiasco. The Navy eventually wound up with the Super Hornet, in many ways a less capable aircraft than the Intruder, which was retired in 1996 without an immediate replacement. The Navy sued the contractors and the contractors sued back for more. The issue has been in and out of the courts ever since.

Few images of the A-12 other than artists' impressions and mock-up photos ever emerged, and more than $2 billion was spent for little tangible result.

SPECIFICATIONS

CREW:	2
POWERPLANT:	two 57.8kN (13,000lb) thrust General Electric F412-400 turbofan engines
MAX SPEED:	933km/h (580mph)
SPAN:	21.41m (70ft 3in)
LENGTH:	11.35m (37ft 3in)
HEIGHT:	3.44m (11ft 3.75in)
WEIGHT:	unknown

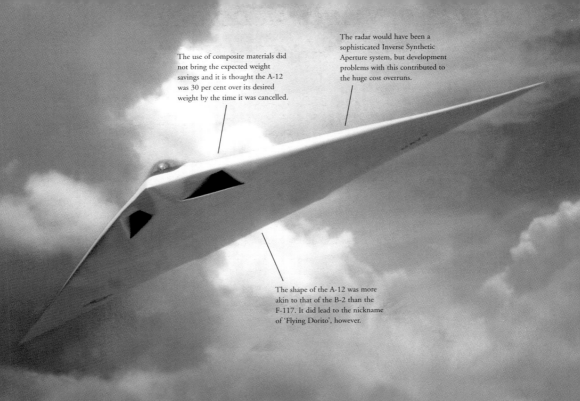

The use of composite materials did not bring the expected weight savings and it is thought the A-12 was 30 per cent over its desired weight by the time it was cancelled.

The radar would have been a sophisticated Inverse Synthetic Aperture system, but development problems with this contributed to the huge cost overruns.

The shape of the A-12 was more akin to that of the B-2 than the F-117. It did lead to the nickname of 'Flying Dorito', however.

GOODYEAR INFLATOPLANE *(1956)*

As well as their famous blimps, the Goodyear Company built military aircraft under licence, such as versions of the Vought Corsair. Of course, what they really wanted to do was build rubber aeroplanes and they got their chance in the 1950s. The US Army was particularly open to new ideas and sponsored development of the Inflatoplane (sometimes called the Inflatibird). Goodyear claimed it was 'suitable for all types of Army field operations, particularly reconnaissance'. It could be packed into a 1.25 cubic metre (44 cubic foot) container and transported by truck, jeep trailer or aircraft. One proposed use was to drop the container behind enemy lines so downed pilots could rescue themselves. Testing of a single- and two-seat version carried on into the 1970s, but no orders were ever forthcoming.

SPECIFICATIONS
(two-seat Inflatoplane)

CREW:	2
POWERPLANT:	one 45kW (60hp) McCulloch 4318 piston engine
CRUISING SPEED:	113km/h (70mph)
SPAN:	8.53m (28ft)
LENGTH:	5.82m (19ft 2in)
HEIGHT:	1.22m (4ft)
WEIGHT:	loaded 336kg (740lb)

Left: The Inflatoplane was one of the more unusual of the many attempts to bring aviation to the troops in the field. Years of tests failed to find a valid military use for an aircraft that could be brought down with a well-aimed bow and arrow.

The Inflatoplane was pressurized at 544mbar (8psi), less than a car tyre, and could be inflated in less than 10 minutes. Endurance was over five hours on the two-seater.

The original single-seat model had a 30kW (40hp) Nelson engine and the two-seater had a 45kW (60hp) McCulloch. In both cases the engine was started by hand-swinging the propeller.

The Inflatoplane's undercarriage allowed the packed-up aeroplane to be moved around like a wheelbarrow.

HAFNER ROTABUGGY FLYING JEEP (1943)

Designed by Austrian Raoul Hafner of the British Airborne Forces Experimental Establishment, the Rotabuggy was essentially a jeep converted into an autogiro as a way of giving airborne forces some ground transport. Initial flight trials, with the Rotabuggy towed behind a Whitley bomber, proved exhausting to the pilot who had to hang on to the control column which thrashed continuously around the cockpit. On flights where the tow cable remained attached there were some scary moments as the Rotabuggy, on the edge of a stall, touched down after the tow plane left and the driver took over. Development of vehicle-carrying gliders provided a safer and more efficient way of getting jeeps with more equipment (such as towed light guns) to the battlefield and the Rotabuggy never saw service. Another of Hafner's ideas was the Rotatank, a modified Valentine tank, which fortunately never left the drawing board.

SPECIFICATIONS

CREW:	2
POWERPLANT:	none
MAX SPEED:	241km/h (150mph) in flight
ROTOR DIAMETER:	12.40m (40ft 8in)
HEIGHT:	unknown
WEIGHT:	1411kg (3110lb)

Left: One of several failed concepts for equipping airborne forces, the effort and risk in getting the Rotabuggy into battle would probably have outweighed its utility.

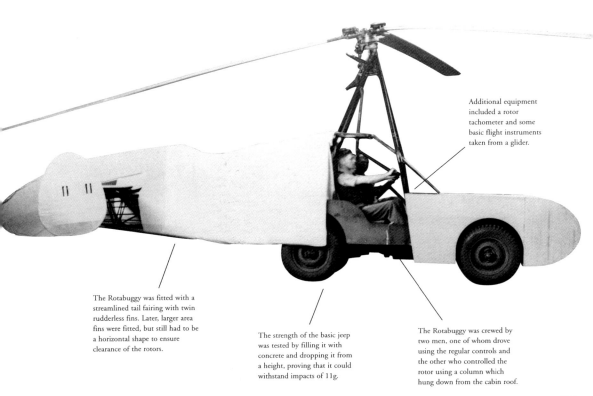

Additional equipment included a rotor tachometer and some basic flight instruments taken from a glider.

The Rotabuggy was fitted with a streamlined tail fairing with twin rudderless fins. Later, larger area fins were fitted, but still had to be a horizontal shape to ensure clearance of the rotors.

The strength of the basic jeep was tested by filling it with concrete and dropping it from a height, proving that it could withstand impacts of 11g.

The Rotabuggy was crewed by two men, one of whom drove using the regular controls and the other who controlled the rotor using a column which hung down from the cabin roof.

HILLER VZ-1 PAWNEE (1955)

US scientist Charles Zimmerman determined that a helicopter rotor could work just as well if put below a vehicle as above it. After a scary-looking device with uncovered blades called the De Lackner Aerocycle was flown, the Hiller Company built the VZ-1 Pawnee.

The Pawnee worked on the basis of so-called 'kinesthetic control'. In other words, the vehicle's direction and speed was controlled by the pilot shifting his body. It was thought that any soldier could learn this instinctive form of control.

Second and third versions, each with a larger, deeper rotor duct were built. The third was so large that kinesthetic control was ineffective and it had a seat and conventional helicopter controls. These designs flew well enough, but the army judged them to be too small, slow and of limited usefulness and practicality for combat service.

SPECIFICATIONS
(First model VZ-1)

CREW:	1
POWERPLANT:	two 30kW (40hp) Nelson H-56 two-stroke piston engines
MAX SPEED:	26km/h (16mph)
PLATFORM DIAMETER:	2.50m (8ft 4in)
HEIGHT:	2.10m (7ft)
WEIGHT:	empty 167.8kg (370lb)

Left: The Pawnee proved the basic feasibility of a ducted flying platform, although a useful purpose was never found for it. The idea that a soldier could snipe at the enemy in this manner for any length of time was a fantasy.

130

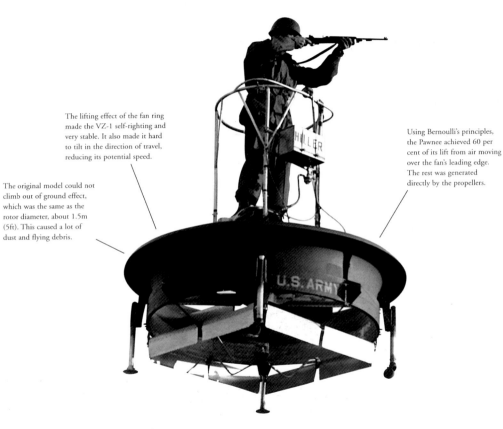

The lifting effect of the fan ring made the VZ-1 self-righting and very stable. It also made it hard to tilt in the direction of travel, reducing its potential speed.

The original model could not climb out of ground effect, which was the same as the rotor diameter, about 1.5m (5ft). This caused a lot of dust and flying debris.

Using Bernoulli's principles, the Pawnee achieved 60 per cent of its lift from air moving over the fan's leading edge. The rest was generated directly by the propellers.

131

HUGHES H-4 HERCULES 'SPRUCE GOOSE' *(1947)*

In 1942 famed shipbuilder Henry Kaiser and eccentric millionaire Howard Hughes conceived of a 'flying liberty ship' to carry freight over the Atlantic above the U-boat threat and got $18 million in government funding for a prototype.

Kaiser believed the HK-1 (for Hughes-Kaiser) could be built in 10 months, but a year later when it was still in the design stage he withdrew from the project. In the end, the giant aircraft, now renamed the H-4 and known unofficially as the 'Spruce Goose' (although it was made mainly of birch) was not completed until mid-1946.

Howard Hughes took the H-4 on its one and only flight in October 1947. The 'Spruce Goose' flew in a straight line for about one minute, covering a little over a mile at a height of about 20m (70ft). He put it down on the water and then locked it away in a climate-controlled hangar where it was discovered in 1980, four years after his death.

SPECIFICATIONS

CREW:	unknown
POWERPLANT:	eight 2236kW (3000hp) Pratt & Whitney R-4360 radial engines
MAX SPEED:	estimated 378km/h (235mph)
SPAN:	97.50m (319ft 11in)
LENGTH:	66.60m (218ft 8in)
HEIGHT:	24.10m (79ft 4in)
WEIGHT:	136,078kg (300,000lb)

Left: By far the largest aircraft built up to the late 1980s, the 'Spruce Goose' was a giant white elephant. Despite vast effort and expense all it achieved was taking its inventor on a short hop across Long Beach harbour.

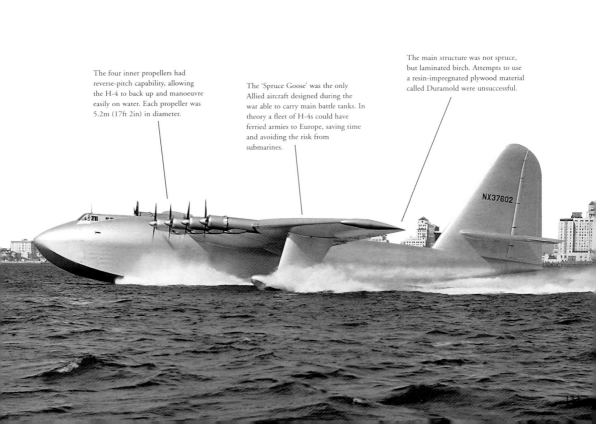

The four inner propellers had reverse-pitch capability, allowing the H-4 to back up and manoeuvre easily on water. Each propeller was 5.2m (17ft 2in) in diameter.

The 'Spruce Goose' was the only Allied aircraft designed during the war able to carry main battle tanks. In theory a fleet of H-4s could have ferried armies to Europe, saving time and avoiding the risk from submarines.

The main structure was not spruce, but laminated birch. Attempts to use a resin-impregnated plywood material called Duramold were unsuccessful.

NX37602

HUGHES XH-17 FLYING CRANE *(1952)*

The XH-17 began as a ground test stand for a huge tip-jet-powered rotor system. In 1949, Hughes Aircraft got a contract to turn it into a flying machine. The giant rotors promised a huge lifting capacity, so they were attached to stilt-like legs and a box-like fuselage. Cargo such as radar vans could be driven underneath and lifted away. It was proposed that tanks could be carried this way, but as an operational aircraft the XH-17 was just too bulky and cumbersome to be practical and had a range of only 64km (40 miles), well below the US Army's requirement. The rotor blades were subject to vibration stresses and the XH-17 was frequently grounded. After three years of sporadic testing, the whole programme came to an end when the one set of rotors reached the end of its design life.

SPECIFICATIONS

CREW:	2
POWERPLANT:	two General Electric J35 turbojets
CRUISING SPEED:	97km/h (60mph)
ROTOR DIAMETER:	39.62m (130ft)
HEIGHT:	unknown
WEIGHT:	loaded 23,587kg (52,000lb)

Left: With a loaded weight twice as heavy as any conventional rotorcraft, the XH-17 was an impressive, if impractical, machine. As if the height and wide stance of the machine weren't impressive enough, the 40-m (130-ft) rotors were the largest ever built.

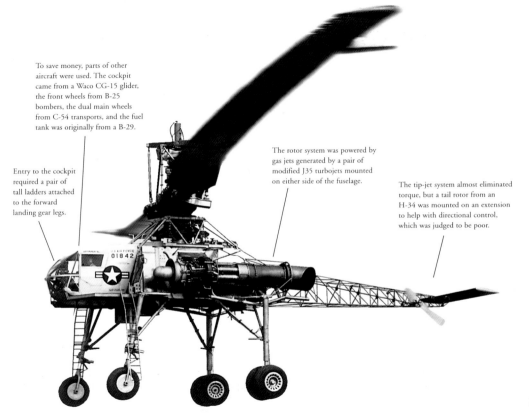

To save money, parts of other aircraft were used. The cockpit came from a Waco CG-15 glider, the front wheels from B-25 bombers, the dual main wheels from C-54 transports, and the fuel tank was originally from a B-29.

Entry to the cockpit required a pair of tall ladders attached to the forward landing gear legs.

The rotor system was powered by gas jets generated by a pair of modified J35 turbojets mounted on either side of the fuselage.

The tip-jet system almost eliminated torque, but a tail rotor from an H-34 was mounted on an extension to help with directional control, which was judged to be poor.

01842

135

KOKUSAI KI-105 OHTORI *(1945)*

T he Ki-105 Ohtori, ('Phoenix') was a desperate project fomented in the last months of the Pacific War. With Allied attacks on ports and shipping, Japan's sources of oil to fuel its defensive fighters were drying up. To meet the demand for aviation fuel, the experimental Kokusai Ku-7 transport glider was developed into a powered version for use in transporting fuel from the oilfields still held in Sumatra to Japan. This required a very long range of 2500km (1553 miles), and to achieve this the Ki-105's engines drew on the transported fuel, and used 80 per cent of it to reach Japan (plus what it used to reach Sumatra unloaded). Japan developed a process to make gasoline from pine tree oil, which saw whole forests destroyed to fill the tanks of a few fighter aircraft. In light of such desperation, the development of the Ki-105 as a gas-guzzling flying fuel truck seems almost sensible.

SPECIFICATIONS

CREW:	2
POWERPLANT:	two 701kW (940hp) Mitsubishi Ha-26-II radial piston engines
CRUISING SPEED:	220km/h (137mph)
SPAN:	35.00m (114ft 10in)
LENGTH:	19.92m (65ft 4in)
HEIGHT:	5.56m (18ft 3in)
WEIGHT:	maximum 12,500kg (27,558lb)

Left: The Ki-105 was developed from the Ku-7 Manazuru (Crane) transport glider of 1944, shown here, which could carry 32 troops or a tank, but arrived too late for any war use. The powered Ki-105 did not appear until April 1945 and despite testing of nine prototypes, the planned production of up to 300 Ohtoris did not take place before the war's end.

Details are scarce on some aspects of the Ki-105, and it is unclear how the fuel was to be carried and transferred to the aircraft's own tanks in flight.

The large and slow Ohtori, filled with gasoline, would have been an easy target for Allied fighters en route from Sumatra to Japan.

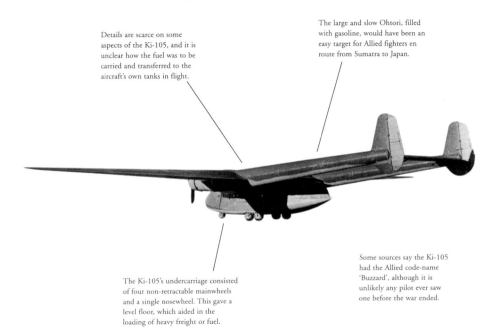

The Ki-105's undercarriage consisted of four non-retractable mainwheels and a single nosewheel. This gave a level floor, which aided in the loading of heavy freight or fuel.

Some sources say the Ki-105 had the Allied code-name 'Buzzard', although it is unlikely any pilot ever saw one before the war ended.

The story of the LearFan is a complex one. Designed by Bill Lear as a cheaper alternative to business jets, with nearly the same performance but a pusher propeller, the LearFan became the first business aircraft with a composite (carbon fibre) structure, as opposed to conventional metal construction. Unfortunately in the late 1970s this was all a bit radical for the Federal Aviation Administration, who repeatedly refused certification of the LearFan. Bill Lear died in 1978 and his widow carried on the programme, seeing the first of three prototypes fly in 1981. Problems with the gearbox, which managed the two PT-6 turboprops on a common shaft, and structural problems with the new composite materials caused costs to escalate, and despite orders and options at one time for over 130 aircraft, the company went bankrupt in 1984 with debts approaching 500 million dollars.

SPECIFICATIONS

CREW:	2 and 8 passengers
POWERPLANT:	two 485kW (650hp) Pratt & Whitney PT6B-35F turboshafts
MAX SPEED:	684km/h (425mph)
SPAN:	11.99m (39ft 4in)
LENGTH:	12.50m (40ft 7in)
HEIGHT:	3.70m (12ft 2in)
WEIGHT:	max take-off 3334kg (7350lb)

Left: The LearFan had its share of technical troubles, but suffered from official disdain and a lack of capital. A factory in Northern Ireland never built a production aircraft but an Iraqi front company tried to buy it for military purposes.

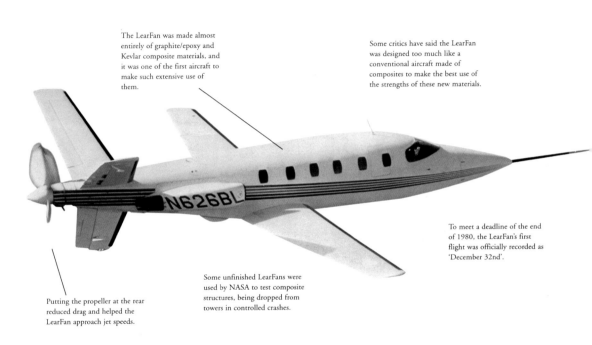

The LearFan was made almost entirely of graphite/epoxy and Kevlar composite materials, and it was one of the first aircraft to make such extensive use of them.

Some critics have said the LearFan was designed too much like a conventional aircraft made of composites to make the best use of the strengths of these new materials.

To meet a deadline of the end of 1980, the LearFan's first flight was officially recorded as 'December 32nd'.

Putting the propeller at the rear reduced drag and helped the LearFan approach jet speeds.

Some unfinished LearFans were used by NASA to test composite structures, being dropped from towers in controlled crashes.

MARTIN P6M SEAMASTER (1955)

In the late 1940s the US Navy realized that the limitations of its current attack aircraft and seaplanes meant that the US Air Force was likely to take over the strategic (nuclear) role in the future. The concept of a 'Seaplane Striking Force' was developed. Along with the R3Y transports and F2Y fighters would be the P6M jet flying-boat atom bomber. Convair's SeaMaster design was chosen in 1951. The prototype flew in July 1955 and was lost in mysterious circumstances in December. It was not until 1959 that production deliveries commenced and rising costs saw planned numbers fall from 24 to 18 to 8. The P6M took so long to come to fruition that other developments such as the nuclear-powered aircraft carrier and the Polaris missile submarine had superseded it. Citing 'unforeseen technical difficulties' the Navy cancelled the SeaMaster just as it was entering service. Martin gave up aircraft production and decided to concentrate on missiles and electronics instead.

SPECIFICATIONS (XP6M-1)

CREW:	4
POWERPLANT:	four 57.8kN (13,000lb) thrust Allison J71-A-4 afterburning turbojets
MAX SPEED:	965km/h (600mph)
SPAN:	31.27m (102ft 7in)
LENGTH:	40.54m (133ft 1in)
HEIGHT:	9.75m (32ft 1in)
WEIGHT:	loaded 72,640kg (160,000lb)

Left: Designed during a period of rapid technological change, the P6M was obsolete by the time it was ready for service. A total of 16 were built, 8 of them test models. The fastest large flying boat ever built, the SeaMaster became the last major aircraft designed under the Martin name.

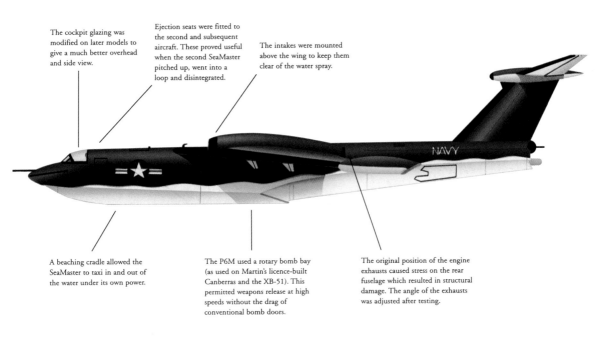

The cockpit glazing was modified on later models to give a much better overhead and side view.

Ejection seats were fitted to the second and subsequent aircraft. These proved useful when the second SeaMaster pitched up, went into a loop and disintegrated.

The intakes were mounted above the wing to keep them clear of the water spray.

A beaching cradle allowed the SeaMaster to taxi in and out of the water under its own power.

The P6M used a rotary bomb bay (as used on Martin's licence-built Canberras and the XB-51). This permitted weapons release at high speeds without the drag of conventional bomb doors.

The original position of the engine exhausts caused stress on the rear fuselage which resulted in structural damage. The angle of the exhausts was adjusted after testing.

NAVY

MCDONNELL XF-85 GOBLIN (1948)

The XF-85 Goblin was intended to let heavy bombers bring along their own fighter escort along the lines of various 'parasite fighter' experiments conducted with US airships and Soviet bombers in the 1930s. The Goblin itself was designed entirely around the constraints of the bomb bay of the B-36 and thus lacked the performance of a conventional fighter. After fighting off the enemy (with its four machine guns) the Goblin was to return to the bomber and hook on to its trapeze. In its test programme, using a B-29, turbulence under the bomber made this very difficult and it was only achieved three times. On another flight the hook broke the canopy and knocked off the pilot's helmet. Experiments were abandoned, but later on modified F-84s were flown under B-36s.

SPECIFICATIONS

CREW:	1
POWERPLANT:	one 13.4kN (3000lb) thrust Westinghouse XJ34 turbojet
MAX SPEED:	1066km/h (664mph)
SPAN:	6.43m (21ft 1in)
LENGTH:	4.30m (14ft 1in)
HEIGHT:	2.51m (8ft 3in)
WEIGHT:	2063kg (4550lb)

Left: The XF-85 was only tested from a modified B-29 and never flew under a B-36. Its performance and armament would have been inadequate to deal with the MiG fighters it would have encountered in action.

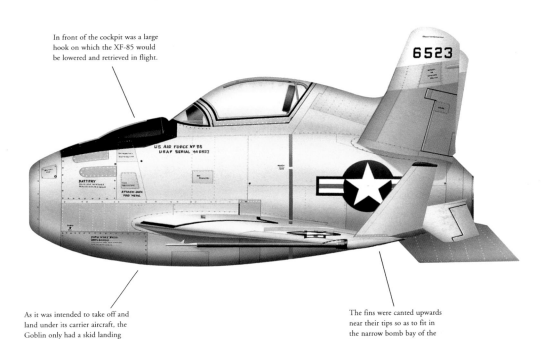

In front of the cockpit was a large hook on which the XF-85 would be lowered and retrieved in flight.

6523

US AIR FORCE XF 85
USAF SERIAL 44 6523

BATTERY

ATTACH JACK
PAD HERE.

As it was intended to take off and land under its carrier aircraft, the Goblin only had a skid landing gear and needed a surface such as a dry lake to land on.

The fins were canted upwards near their tips so as to fit in the narrow bomb bay of the B-29. The wings folded for stowage in the bomber.

143

MITSUBISHI F-2 (1995)

The Japanese Air Self-Defence Force (JASDF) began the search for a replacement for the Mitsubishi F-1 in the maritime attack (or 'anti-landing craft') role in 1982. The F/A-18 was rejected as too expensive and the Tornado lost out because Japan was wary of dealing with multiple foreign nations. After exploring an all-indigenous design and rejecting it for cost and timescale reasons, in 1987 the JASDF announced a development of the F-16C/D designated the FS-X, later the F-2. Reinventing the F-16 and duplicating production facilities eliminated any cost savings. The new composite wing developed cracks with a full load, contributing to delays. A requirement for up to 200 F-2s was reduced to 130, but development problems and slow funding saw production drop below the economical minimum of eight per year, and in 2004 it was decided to halt deliveries at about 85 aircraft.

SPECIFICATIONS (F-2A)

CREW:	1
POWERPLANT:	one 131.7kN (29,600lb) thrust General Electric F110-GE-129 afterburning turbofan
MAX SPEED:	2174km/h (1315mph)
SPAN:	11.13m (36ft 6in)
LENGTH:	15.52m (50ft 11in)
HEIGHT:	4.96m (16ft 3in)
WEIGHT:	maximum 22,100kg (48,722lb)

Left: Under US pressure, Japan developed a version of the F-16 that cost several times as much. For the expenditure of an estimated US $100 million per aircraft, Japan got a less capable aircraft than the F-16C Block 52, much later and in fewer numbers than desired.

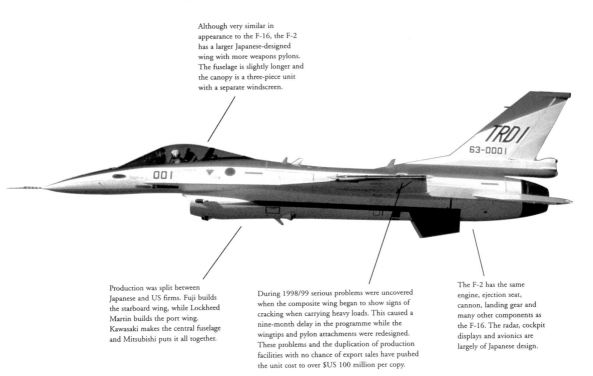

Although very similar in appearance to the F-16, the F-2 has a larger Japanese-designed wing with more weapons pylons. The fuselage is slightly longer and the canopy is a three-piece unit with a separate windscreen.

Production was split between Japanese and US firms. Fuji builds the starboard wing, while Lockheed Martin builds the port wing. Kawasaki makes the central fuselage and Mitsubishi puts it all together.

During 1998/99 serious problems were uncovered when the composite wing began to show signs of cracking when carrying heavy loads. This caused a nine-month delay in the programme while the wingtips and pylon attachments were redesigned. These problems and the duplication of production facilities with no chance of export sales have pushed the unit cost to over $US 100 million per copy.

The F-2 has the same engine, ejection seat, cannon, landing gear and many other components as the F-16. The radar, cockpit displays and avionics are largely of Japanese design.

MYASISHCHEV M-50 'BOUNDER' (1959)

The M-50 'Bounder' was yet another failed attempt by the Myasishchev design bureau to supply the USSR's strategic forces with its main bomber, but did at least reach the hardware stage.

Delays with the intended Zubets engines saw substitution of lower-powered Soloviev D-15s instead, and the 'supersonic' M-50 only achieved Mach 0.99 in this form. The Soviets, however, convinced the West that on the basis of its flight tests: 'a strategic bomber with nuclear engines and unlimited range has been designed'.

The most often seen quote about the M-50 is that it was 'an outstanding failure which revealed an embarrassing lack of understanding of the problems of high-speed flight'. In 1960, following the lead of the UK defence secretary, Nikita Khrushchev declared that missiles and space vehicles would replace the work of manned combat aircraft. Work on new aircraft was halted and the Myasishchev design bureau was broken up.

SPECIFICATIONS

CREW:	2
POWERPLANT:	four 137.3kN (30,865lb) thrust ND-7 turbojets
MAX SPEED:	1950km/h (1211mph)
SPAN:	37.00m (121ft 3in)
LENGTH:	57.00m (187ft)
HEIGHT:	12.00m (39ft 3in)
WEIGHT:	maximum 200,000kg (440,800lb)

Left: Although superficially a high-performance aircraft, the design of the M-50 lacked many of the subtleties needed for supersonic cruising flight. It appeared at a time when ballistic missiles and airborne stand-off weapons were emerging and fell victim to the belief that the day of the bomber was over.

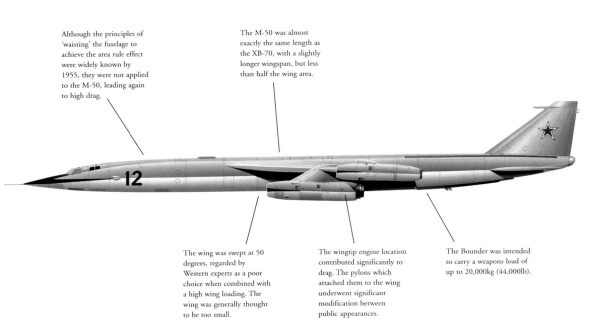

Although the principles of 'waisting' the fuselage to achieve the area rule effect were widely known by 1955, they were not applied to the M-50, leading again to high drag.

The M-50 was almost exactly the same length as the XB-70, with a slightly longer wingspan, but less than half the wing area.

The wing was swept at 50 degrees, regarded by Western experts as a poor choice when combined with a high wing loading. The wing was generally thought to be too small.

The wingtip engine location contributed significantly to drag. The pylons which attached them to the wing underwent significant modification between public appearances.

The Bounder was intended to carry a weapons load of up to 20,000kg (44,000lb).

12

NORTH AMERICAN XB-70A VALKYRIE (1964)

The XB-70 project was begun in 1958 as a highly ambitious attempt to build a Mach 3 strategic bomber. The programme stopped and started, mainly for political reasons and was eventually reduced to two prototypes for use as research aircraft. The first prototype needed rebuilding when corrosion was discovered and the second was delayed by a fuel leak. The first flight did not occur until September 1964. The XB-70s achieved Mach 3 and other milestones, but on 8 June 1966 a photo session went horribly wrong and an F-104 Starfighter collided with the No. 2 XB-70. One of the XB-70 crew and the F-104 pilot were killed. After that the remaining aircraft flew on for a couple more years before going to the USAF Museum. It was estimated that development of two prototypes cost $1.5 billion or about ten times their weight in gold.

SPECIFICATIONS

CREW:	4
POWERPLANT:	six 800.71kN (180,000lb) thrust General Electric YJ93-GE-3 afterburning turbojets
MAX SPEED:	Mach 3.0
SPAN:	32.05m (105ft)
LENGTH:	56.69m (185.83ft) without pitot tube
HEIGHT:	9.38m (30.75ft)
WEIGHT:	maximum 246,365kg (542,000lb)

Left: The Valkyrie was the fastest bomber ever built but came along when ICBMs had reached maturity, and fell victim to its massive technical complexity and great cost.

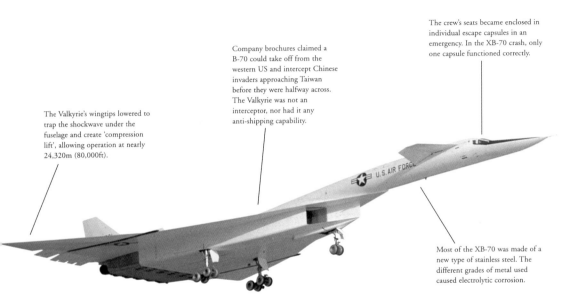

The Valkyrie's wingtips lowered to trap the shockwave under the fuselage and create 'compression lift', allowing operation at nearly 24,320m (80,000ft).

Company brochures claimed a B-70 could take off from the western US and intercept Chinese invaders approaching Taiwan before they were halfway across. The Valkyrie was not an interceptor, nor had it any anti-shipping capability.

The crew's seats became enclosed in individual escape capsules in an emergency. In the XB-70 crash, only one capsule functioned correctly.

U.S. AIR FORCE

Most of the XB-70 was made of a new type of stainless steel. The different grades of metal used caused electrolytic corrosion.

NORTHROP XP-79B *(1945)*

Begun as an extremely ambitious project for a rocket-powered gun-armed interceptor, the XP-79B emerged as a jet, intended to ram enemy bombers and survive due to its strong magnesium structure. This idea, worthy of the Nazis or the Japanese with their backs against the wall, was conceived in the US just as the tide was turning for Allied forces and any need for such desperate measures was waning. The aircraft was not flown until the war was over, and then only once. After a near collision with a fire truck on take-off, the XP-79 flew well enough for a few minutes until it entered a spin from 2440m (8,000ft) and crashed at high speed, killing test pilot Harry Crosby. Plans to continue with the rocket-powered versions of the XP-79 ended there, although Northrop's slightly less radical development vehicle, the MX-334 became the first American rocket aircraft.

SPECIFICATIONS

CREW:	1
POWERPLANT:	two 5.1kN (1150lb) thrust Westinghouse 19B (J30) turbojets
MAX SPEED:	unknown
SPAN:	11.58m (38ft)
LENGTH:	4.27m (14ft)
HEIGHT:	2.29m (7ft 6in)
WEIGHT:	empty 2649kg (5840lb)

Left: One of the first American jet aircraft, the XP-79B had one of the shortest and most spectacular flying careers ever. By the time it was built, the need for a high-speed ramming interceptor was nil.

The XP-79B's pilot lay in a prone position, theoretically giving tolerance of up to 20g. Although the intention was to strike enemy aircraft using the leading edges of the wings, finding volunteers to dive on enemy bombers headfirst in a plastic bubble may have proved difficult.

The XP-79B's structure was largely magnesium, assembled using Northrop's patented Heliarc welding process.

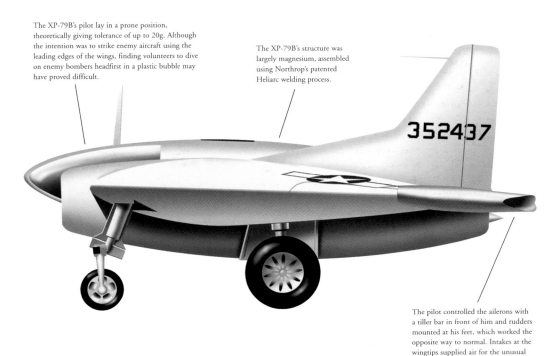

352437

The pilot controlled the ailerons with a tiller bar in front of him and rudders mounted at his feet, which worked the opposite way to normal. Intakes at the wingtips supplied air for the unusual bellows-boosted ailerons.

PEMBERTON-BILLING (SUPERMARINE) NIGHTHAWK (1917)

Outspoken aircraft maker and sometime Member of Parliament Noel Pemberton-Billing built a number of unsuccessful fighters for the Admiralty. The quadruplane (four-winged) P.B.29E anti-Zeppelin fighter crashed fairly quickly, but its design formed the basis of the larger P.B.31E Nighthawk. The concept of the Nighthawk was that it would use its extreme endurance (up to 18 hours) to lie in wait all night for any airships, pick them up with its searchlight and then despatch them with its one-and-a-half-pounder recoilless Davis gun and two machine guns. The Davis gunner was perched atop the stack of wings, struts and wires where he would have been afforded an excellent view of the lumbering Zeppelins retreating into the distance – if the Nighthawk had ever entered service.

SPECIFICATIONS

CREW:	3
POWERPLANT:	two 76kW (100hp) Anzani radial engines
MAX SPEED:	121km/h (75mph)
SPAN:	18.29m (60ft)
LENGTH:	11.24m (36ft 11in)
HEIGHT:	5.40m (37ft 9in)
WEIGHT:	loaded 2788kg (6146lb)

Left: The ungainly Nighthawk was one of many wacky attempts to defeat the 'Zepp Menace' facing Britain. Although the idea of a long-endurance standing patrol was a good one, the Nighthawk lacked the performance to engage the well-armed Zeppelins.

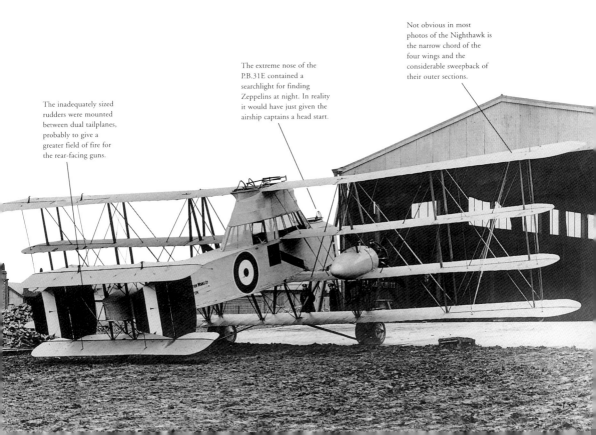

The inadequately sized rudders were mounted between dual tailplanes, probably to give a greater field of fire for the rear-facing guns.

The extreme nose of the P.B.31E contained a searchlight for finding Zeppelins at night. In reality it would have just given the airship captains a head start.

Not obvious in most photos of the Nighthawk is the narrow chord of the four wings and the considerable sweepback of their outer sections.

PZL-MIELEC M-15 BELPHEGOR (1973)

In order to replace the 1940s-era Antonov An-2 in the crop-spraying role, Poland's PZL-Mielec came up with one of the weirdest aircraft ever – the Belphegor, probably the world's only production jet biplane. Flown in 1973, it was not certified until 1979. A requirement for up to 3000 was foreseen, but according to one commentator 'low accuracy, numerous design flaws and high fuel consumption' effectively killed the project. Production ended in 1981, with only 175 aircraft completed. In the USSR agricultural spraying was entirely state-sponsored and without profit. In the West agricultural aircraft were generally designed for high intensity operations with low costs, great efficiency and high ecological standards. None of these applied to the Belphegor. There is speculation that a secondary role would have been to lay a blanket of chemical weapons over the frontline during any Warsaw Pact invasion of Europe.

SPECIFICATIONS

CREW:	1–2
POWERPLANT:	one 14.7kN (3306lb) thrust AI-25 turbofan
MAX SPEED:	180km/h (97mph)
SPAN:	22.40m (73ft 6in)
LENGTH:	12.72m (41ft 9in)
HEIGHT:	5.20m (17ft)
WEIGHT:	gross 5650kg (12,456lb)

Left: The M-15 was in some ways a 'jet An-2', although lacking that piston-engined biplane's versatility. Despite some advantages, it never caught on and the An-2 remained in production in Poland and elsewhere.

The upper wing was equipped with a variety of high-lift devices, while the lower wing had nozzles for the dispensing of granular or liquid chemicals.

The chemical hoppers were contained within the large interplane struts. Along with the fixed undercarriage these created a lot of drag and increased the fuel consumption.

The cabin normally housed a mechanic or two, but could carry up to 21 passengers for ferry purposes. These could have been agricultural workers or perhaps Special Forces troops.

ROCKWELL XFV-12A *(1976)*

I n 1972 the US Navy began a programme for a follow-on to the AV-8A
Harrier for use on the proposed small aircraft carriers called Sea Control
Ships. Rockwell responded with the XFV-12A, which was partly comprised
of components from other aircraft, mainly the A-4 Skyhawk and F-4
Phantom. The engine may have been left over from F-14B Tomcat testing.
The thrust from this was ejected through a type of venetian blind
arrangement in the wings and canards to provide vertical lift. Lab tests
proved that only about 25 per cent of engine thrust was available for vertical
lift, instead of 55 per cent, enough to lift only 75 per cent of the aircraft.
Increasing costs saw only one prototype completed, and it seems it never
flew. Rockwell preferred to ignore this inglorious chapter in its history.

SPECIFICATIONS

CREW:	1
POWERPLANT:	one 133.4kN (30,000lb) thrust Pratt & Whitney F401-PW-400 turbofan
MAX SPEED:	(estimated) Mach 2.4 (2560km/h; 1380kt)
SPAN:	8.69m (28ft 6in)
LENGTH:	13.35m (43ft 10in)
HEIGHT:	3.15m (10ft 4in)
WEIGHT:	11,000kg (24,250lb)

*Left: The US Navy preferred the risky lift
system of the XFV-12 to further development
of the Harrier, but backed the wrong horse.
Eventually it was cancelled, as was the class
of ship for which it was intended.*

The whole XFV-12 programme was conducted on the cheap. The main landing gear, canopy and other cockpit parts came from an A-4 Skyhawk. The main wing box and parts of the inlets were from an F-4 Phantom.

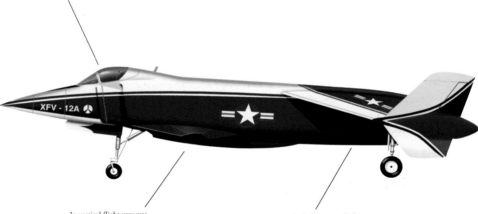

In vertical flight yaw was controlled by vectoring the ejector units. Roll control came from varying the amount of thrust supplied to each.

The XFV-12 had what was called a 'thrust augmentor wing'. Engine gases were to be channelled along ducts in the canard and wing surfaces for vertical flight.

RYAN X-13 VERTIJET *(1955)*

In the early 1950s, some senior officers thought that all US Navy carrier aircraft would be Vertical Take Off (VTO) machines within 10 years. They were wrong, but it took such machines as the X-13 Vertijet to prove it. The delta-winged X-13 used a unique landing method, involving a special trailer, a hook and a striped pole. To land the pilot had to approach the trailer's vertical base board without being able to see it. A pole marked with gradations protruded from the board and the pilot had to use this to judge his 'altitude' from the landing wire. In one demonstration at the Pentagon, the X-13 flew from its trailer, crossed the Potomac River, destroyed a rose garden with its thrust and landed in a net. Although this impressed the top brass, further funding was not forthcoming and the project petered out.

SPECIFICATIONS

CREW:	1
POWERPLANT:	one 44.5kN (10,000lb) thrust Rolls-Royce Avon RA.28-49 turbojet
MAX SPEED:	777km/h (483mph)
SPAN:	6.40m (21ft)
LENGTH:	7.13m (23ft 5in)
HEIGHT:	(on wheels) 4.60m (15ft 2in)
WEIGHT:	loaded 3317kg (7313lb)

Left: The only successful US jet 'tail-sitter', the Vertijet suffered from the same limitations as the Pogo and similar machines. The small payload and short range failed to excite enthusiasm for a production version.

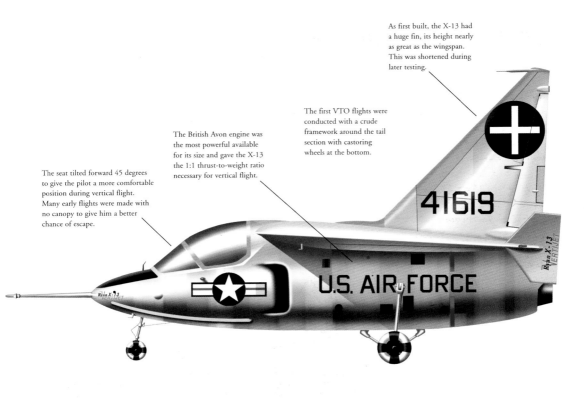

As first built, the X-13 had a huge fin, its height nearly as great as the wingspan. This was shortened during later testing.

The first VTO flights were conducted with a crude framework around the tail section with castoring wheels at the bottom.

The British Avon engine was the most powerful available for its size and gave the X-13 the 1:1 thrust-to-weight ratio necessary for vertical flight.

The seat tilted forward 45 degrees to give the pilot a more comfortable position during vertical flight. Many early flights were made with no canopy to give him a better chance of escape.

41619

U.S. AIR FORCE

SAUNDERS ROE S.R./A.1 (1947)

The result of a 1944 requirement, the S.R./A.1 was the world's first jet-fighter flying boat. Its concept was influenced by the outwardly successful Japanese seaplane fighters, which were able to operate from islands which didn't have airfields. In the Pacific the Americans simply built airfields. The S.R./A.1 did not fly until 1947, by which time the war was long gone, as was the requirement for a flying-boat fighter. One of the three S.R./A.1s crashed while practising aerobatics and another flipped over and sank after hitting a piece of wood in the water. Some more testing was carried out with the remaining example in 1950 when the Korean War broke out, but by then the S.R./A.1 was outperformed by its potential adversaries and became a museum piece.

SPECIFICATIONS

CREW:	1
POWERPLANT:	two 14.5kN (3250lb) thrust Metropolitan-Vickers MVB-1 Beryl turbojets
MAX SPEED:	824km/h (512mph)
SPAN:	14.02m (46ft)
LENGTH:	15.24m (50ft)
HEIGHT:	5.10m (16ft 9in)
WEIGHT:	8872kg (19,560lb)

TG263

Left: Obsolete by the time it flew, the S.R./A.1 was like the Japanese 'Rufe' and other floatplane fighters in that its performance was inferior to contemporary landplanes.

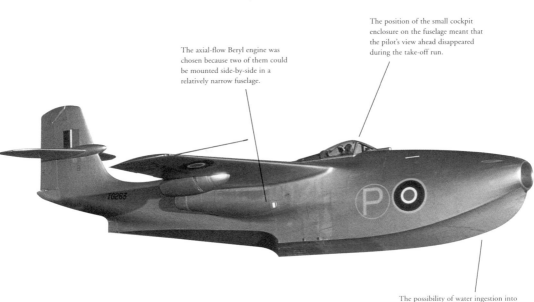

The axial-flow Beryl engine was chosen because two of them could be mounted side-by-side in a relatively narrow fuselage.

The position of the small cockpit enclosure on the fuselage meant that the pilot's view ahead disappeared during the take-off run.

The possibility of water ingestion into the nose-mounted intake was the reason for its high position in the nose.

SNECMA COLÉOPTÈRE (1959)

One of the most extraordinary of the 1950s and 60s vertical take-off (VTO) projects was the French Coléoptère ('annular wing'). The wing design was unique enough, but combining it with a tail-sitting format was a huge technological leap. More or less normal control surfaces directed the aircraft in horizontal flight and thrust vectoring was used to make manoeuvres while vertical.

The difficulty with tail-sitting aircraft is landing them, with the pilot looking downwards over his shoulder. Transitioning to and from the horizontal to the vertical is also fraught with danger. So it was on only the Coléoptère's ninth flight, when it failed to hover and began to plummet instead, oscillating about all three axes for good measure. The pilot ejected and the Coléoptère shot off at about 50 degrees before crashing, bringing an end to the programme.

Left: The Coléoptère proved the feasibility of an annular wing, although it had little opportunity to test it in horizontal flight before crashing during a vertical landing.

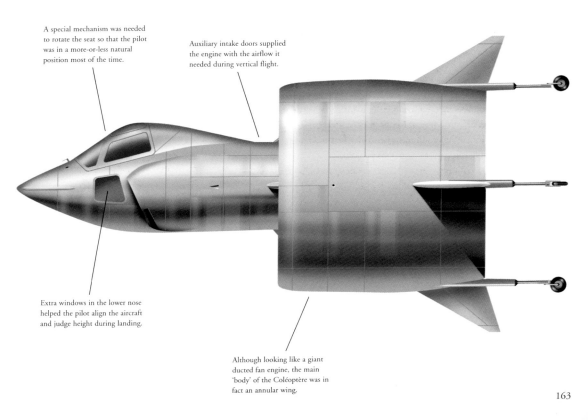

A special mechanism was needed to rotate the seat so that the pilot was in a more-or-less natural position most of the time.

Auxiliary intake doors supplied the engine with the airflow it needed during vertical flight.

Extra windows in the lower nose helped the pilot align the aircraft and judge height during landing.

Although looking like a giant ducted fan engine, the main 'body' of the Coléoptère was in fact an annular wing.

163

TUPOLEV ANT-20 MAXIM GORKII *(1934)*

Built entirely for propaganda purposes at the behest of the Union of Soviet Writers and Editors to celebrate the career of the writer Maxim Gorkii (or Gorky), and paid for by public subscription, the giant ANT-20 toured the otherwise inaccessible areas of the USSR, bringing the communist message to the masses. To this end, the ANT-20 contained a small printing plant, a photographic studio, a cinema and a radio station. Of course, to show the wider world the superiority of Soviet aeronautics, the Maxim Gorkii had to be the largest aircraft in the world. Only a few subsequent aircraft (such as the B-36 and the An-124) have had greater wingspans. The six engines originally fitted were not enough and an extra pair were added on a pod above the fuselage. The Maxim Gorkii was lost when a Polikarpov I-5 fighter plane attempted a barrel roll around it. The fighter pilot, all 49 occupants of the ANT-20 and three people on the ground perished.

SPECIFICATIONS

CREW:	8–10 and 72 passengers
POWERPLANT:	eight 671kW (900hp)
	Mikulin AM-34FRN
	piston engines
CRUISING SPEED:	220km/h (137mph)
SPAN:	63.00m (206ft 8in)
LENGTH:	32.46m (106ft 6in)
HEIGHT:	11.25m (36ft 11in)
WEIGHT:	41,731kg (92,595lb)

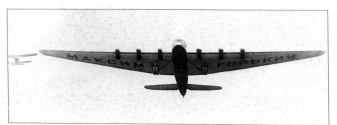

Left: An aircraft that could probably only have come from 1930s Soviet Russia, the ANT-20 was of great propaganda value, until it met its fate in somewhat embarrassing circumstances.

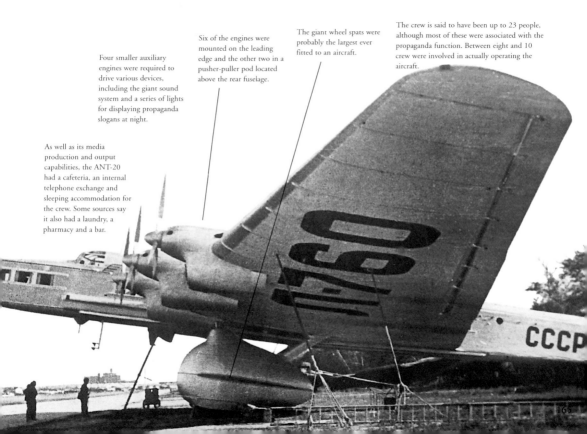

Four smaller auxiliary engines were required to drive various devices, including the giant sound system and a series of lights for displaying propaganda slogans at night.

Six of the engines were mounted on the leading edge and the other two in a pusher-puller pod located above the rear fuselage.

The giant wheel spats were probably the largest ever fitted to an aircraft.

The crew is said to have been up to 23 people, although most of these were associated with the propaganda function. Between eight and 10 crew were involved in actually operating the aircraft.

As well as its media production and output capabilities, the ANT-20 had a cafeteria, an internal telephone exchange and sleeping accommodation for the crew. Some sources say it also had a laundry, a pharmacy and a bar.

TUPOLEV TU-144 (1968)

The USSR beat Concorde into the civil supersonic era with the Tupolev 144, which was inevitably dubbed Conkordski. The original Tu-144 design needed extensive modifications, including a new wing before it was ready for airline service. A production Tu-144 broke up and crashed at the 1973 Paris Air Show, killing 14 people.

Due to its turbofan engines the noise produced outside was less than that made by Concorde, but it was louder inside the cabin. The Tu-144 began operations with Aeroflot in 1975, but carrying mail rather than passengers from Moscow to Alma-Ata. The twice-weekly service fell to once a week and was cancelled in late 1977. A passenger service on the same route made only 102 flights, with one crash. Mechanical problems made it hard to maintain even one flight per week and services ended in June 1978.

SPECIFICATIONS

CREW:	3 and 140 passengers
POWERPLANT:	four 20,000kg (44,000lb) thrust Kuzmetsov NK-144 turbofans
CRUISING SPEED:	Mach 2.0 with afterburners
SPAN:	27.00m (88ft 7in)
LENGTH:	65.70m (215ft 7in)
HEIGHT:	12.90m (42ft 4in)
WEIGHT:	180,363kg (396,800lb)

Left: The Tu-144 was bigger and faster than Concorde, but was so mechanically unreliable and inefficient that even the Soviet Union couldn't sustain it in service.

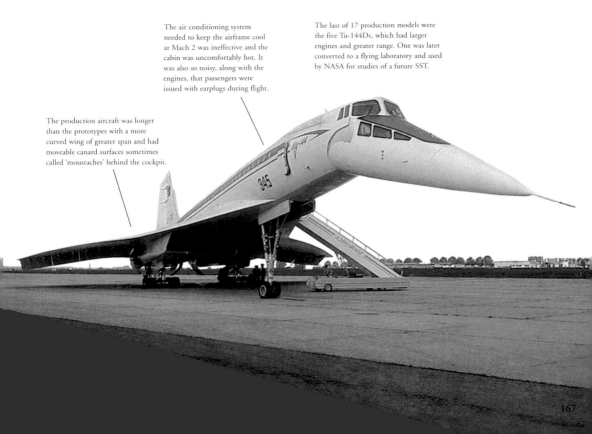

The air conditioning system needed to keep the airframe cool at Mach 2 was ineffective and the cabin was uncomfortably hot. It was also so noisy, along with the engines, that passengers were issued with earplugs during flight.

The last of 17 production models were the five Tu-144Ds, which had larger engines and greater range. One was later converted to a flying laboratory and used by NASA for studies of a future SST.

The production aircraft was longer than the prototypes with a more curved wing of greater span and had moveable canard surfaces sometimes called 'moustaches' behind the cockpit.

WIGHT QUADRUPLANE (1917)

oward Wright designed various aircraft for Isle of Wight boat builders
White & Co. To avoid (or cause) confusion, these were known as
Wight aircraft. After several seaplanes and some undistinguished landplanes,
White/Wight and Wright moved on to a fighter inspired by Sopwith designs,
notably the Triplane, but going one better with a fourth set of wings.
Unusually, the ailerons were only on the upper wings, unlike the successful
Sopwith and Fokker triplanes that had them on each surface. Early testing
showed some problems, including a reluctance to take off due to the shallow
wing incidence. The design was rebuilt at least twice with new sets of wings.
The fuselage was also modified, but instead of a useful lengthening, it was
widened and reprofiled. None of this made the Royal Flying Corps any
keener to order this oddball and it remained a one-off.

SPECIFICATIONS

CREW:	1
POWERPLANT:	one 82kW (110hp)
	Clerget 9Z rotary piston
	engine
MAX SPEED:	unknown
SPAN:	5.79m (19ft)
LENGTH:	6.25m (20ft 6in)
HEIGHT:	3.20m (10ft 6in)
WEIGHT:	unknown

*Left: One of the few aeroplanes that was
longer than it was wide (in span), the
Quadruplane almost appeared to be taller as
well. Predictably, it ended its days with a final
accident.*

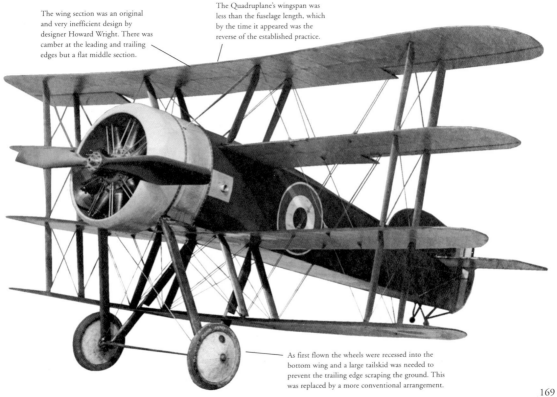

The wing section was an original and very inefficient design by designer Howard Wright. There was camber at the leading and trailing edges but a flat middle section.

The Quadruplane's wingspan was less than the fuselage length, which by the time it appeared was the reverse of the established practice.

As first flown the wheels were recessed into the bottom wing and a large tailskid was needed to prevent the trailing edge scraping the ground. This was replaced by a more conventional arrangement.

YOKOSUKA OHKA (1944)

In 1944 a lowly ranked Japanese transport pilot proposed the idea of a rocket-powered aircraft for suicide missions against Allied naval forces. In record time, the Yokosuka MXY7 Ohka (Cherry Blossom) was developed and accepted for service.

Carried aloft by G4M 'Betty' bombers, the Ohkas remained attached until 32km (20 miles) off the target, well within range of the carrier group's combat air patrols. On their combat debut, all 16 carrier aircraft were shot down before launching their Ohkas. Of the 750 or so Okhas built, the vast majority were never launched, being shot down while attached to their carrier aircraft or destroyed or captured on the ground. It is thought that they sank about 15 Allied ships, having minimal effect on the Allied advance on Japan.

SPECIFICATIONS (Type 11)

CREW:	1
POWERPLANT:	three Type 4 Model 1 Mark 20 solid-fuel rockets with a total thrust of 7.85kN (1764lb)
MAX SPEED:	649km/h (403mph)
SPAN:	5.15m (16ft 10in)
LENGTH:	6.01m (19ft 11in)
HEIGHT:	1.19m (3ft 10in)
WEIGHT:	loaded 1895kg (4178lb)

Left: Known disparagingly by the Allies as the Baka (Fool), the MXY7 was one of the few aircraft actually designed to kill its pilot. Judged against this requirement, it could be considered a success.

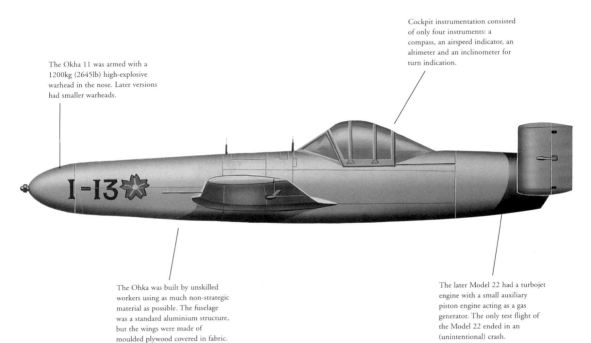

The Okha 11 was armed with a 1200kg (2645lb) high-explosive warhead in the nose. Later versions had smaller warheads.

Cockpit instrumentation consisted of only four instruments: a compass, an airspeed indicator, an altimeter and an inclinometer for turn indication.

The Ohka was built by unskilled workers using as much non-strategic material as possible. The fuselage was a standard aluminium structure, but the wings were made of moulded plywood covered in fabric.

The later Model 22 had a turbojet engine with a small auxiliary piston engine acting as a gas generator. The only test flight of the Model 22 ended in an (unintentional) crash.

I-13

POWER PROBLEMS

The engines have been the downfall of many an aircraft. The low output of early powerplants meant that designers often had to choose between leaving off all excess weight or using as many engines as they could fit aboard – which also multiplied the chance of failures, and every aviator's greatest fear – fires. Many failed projects were sound designs that couldn't wait for the arrival of the right powerplant. Some were redeemed by application of good engines (and in the case of the Avro Manchester – doubling their number for good measure).

Caproni's experiments into forms of ducted fan piston engines in the 1930s appeared to presage the jet, but produced inferior performance to the equivalent engines in a conventional installation. As such they remained historical curiosities.

Even when the turbine powerplant began to establish its dominance after World War II, performance was often disappointing. The US Navy was particularly unlucky with the engines it commissioned in the late 1940s and 1950s and wound up with such turkeys as the Westinghouse J34 and J46 turbojets. Of the latter, one Vought Cutlass pilot said that 'it put out about as much heat as the same manufacturer's toasters'.

Left: Despite its outward similarity to a jet, the Caproni Campini N.1 had poor performance and proved a technological dead end.

AVRO MANCHESTER (1939)

B uilt to a medium bomber specification that called for a catapult launch at maximum load and the capability for dive-bombing, the Manchester was extremely strong but had a very high wing loading. Its poor Vulture engines (one of Rolls-Royce's few outright failures) had a worrying tendency to burst into flames or fall apart with fatigue. Single-engined characteristics were poor and various tail configurations were tried to improve stability.

Few squadrons were equipped with Manchesters and the type suffered appalling losses as well as frequent groundings for modification. In 1941 the sound basic design was married to a longer wing with four Merlin engines and became the Manchester II. Two large fins replaced the triple fins on most early Manchesters and the type was renamed the Lancaster, going on to be one of the most successful bombers of the war.

SPECIFICATIONS

CREW:	7
POWERPLANT:	two 1312kW (1760hp) Rolls-Royce Vulture piston engines
MAX SPEED:	426km/h (265mph)
SPAN:	27.46m (90ft 1in)
LENGTH:	20.98m (68ft 10in)
HEIGHT:	5.94m (19ft 6in)
WEIGHT:	loaded 22,680kg (50,000lb)

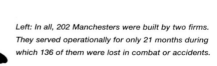

Left: In all, 202 Manchesters were built by two firms.
They served operationally for only 21 months during
which 136 of them were lost in combat or accidents.

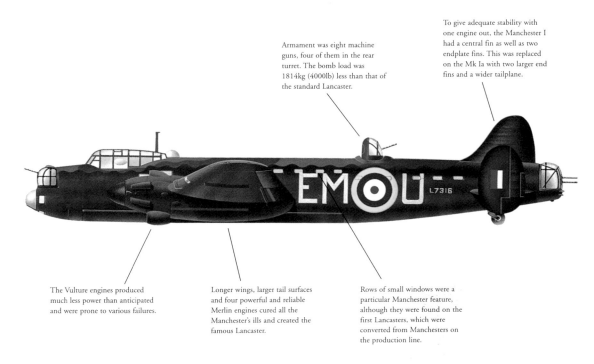

Armament was eight machine guns, four of them in the rear turret. The bomb load was 1814kg (4000lb) less than that of the standard Lancaster.

To give adequate stability with one engine out, the Manchester I had a central fin as well as two endplate fins. This was replaced on the Mk Ia with two larger end fins and a wider tailplane.

The Vulture engines produced much less power than anticipated and were prone to various failures.

Longer wings, larger tail surfaces and four powerful and reliable Merlin engines cured all the Manchester's ills and created the famous Lancaster.

Rows of small windows were a particular Manchester feature, although they were found on the first Lancasters, which were converted from Manchesters on the production line.

BAADE (VEB) 152 (1958)

The VEB 152 was unofficially named after Brunolf Baade, who had a previous career designing landing gear for Junkers jet bombers. After involuntarily spending time helping the USSR with their own aircraft programmes, Baade's team returned to East Germany to create a civil aircraft industry based around a development of the Alekseyev 150 bomber, a fairly satisfactory but one-off design.

The VEB 152 airliner made one successful flight but crashed on the second. The cause was undetermined (or hushed up) but may have been due to air in the fuel system, which had not been tested at glidepath angles. The revised second prototype made two flights but was way behind western designs such as the 707. The East German Politburo ordered the dismantling of the entire industry in 1961 and almost succeeded in erasing it from history.

SPECIFICATIONS

CREW:	unknown and up to 72 passengers
POWERPLANT:	four 25.5kN (5732lb) thrust Mikulin RD-9B turbojets
CRUISING SPEED:	800km/h (497mph)
SPAN:	27.00m (88ft 7in)
LENGTH:	31.40m (103ft)
HEIGHT:	9.40m (30ft 9in)
WEIGHT:	44,500kg (98,105lb)

Left: East Germany's failed attempt to build a civil aircraft industry was based on Communist economics and a bomber's aerodynamics. Even the State-owned airline only wanted 15 and the whole programme cost 2 billion East German Marks by the time it was cancelled and the aircraft under construction cut up.

The lack of space, poor engines and the bomber's wing meant small payloads and short ranges as well as a low speed for a jetliner.

The Model 150 bomber had two large Lyul'ka engines, but the VEB 152 had four much weaker engines (a version of that used in the MiG-19), which gave poor thrust for their weight and high fuel consumption.

The potential baggage space was reduced by the main landing gear wells and the cabin ceiling was obstructed by the large wing box.

With its bicycle main gear and outrigger wheels the 152 needed to be landed very precisely.

177

BARLING XNBL-1 (1923)

World War I showed the potential of large aircraft for strategic bombing, but postwar budgets allowed little money for development. The US Army put much of what it had in one giant aeroplane, the Barling XNBL-1 (Experimental Night Bomber Long Range No. 1), usually known as the 'Barling Bomber', for there was only ever one.

Although it had six engines and eight propellers, the Barling Bomber's power output was barely adequate to overcome the weight and drag of this massive triplane with its two pilots and five gunners. Theoretically able to carry a 2268kg (5000lb) bombload, the XNBL-1 on one occasion failed to get over the Appalachian Mountains between Dayton and Washington D.C. and had to turn back. Funding for an improved version was not forthcoming, but the Barling Bomber carried on to 'show the flag' for air power for a number of years.

SPECIFICATIONS

CREW:	7
POWERPLANT:	six 313kW (420hp) Liberty 12A piston engines
MAX SPEED:	154km/h (96mph)
SPAN:	36.58m (120ft)
LENGTH:	19.81m (65ft)
HEIGHT:	8.23m (27ft)
WEIGHT:	loaded 19,309kg (42,569lb)

Left: Designed by Walter Barling, who was responsible for the Tarrant Tabor, and promoted by the controversial General Billy Mitchell, the XNBL-1 redefined the word cumbersome. At least by this time some lessons of balance had been learned and the Barling had a relatively long and safe, if totally undistinguished, career.

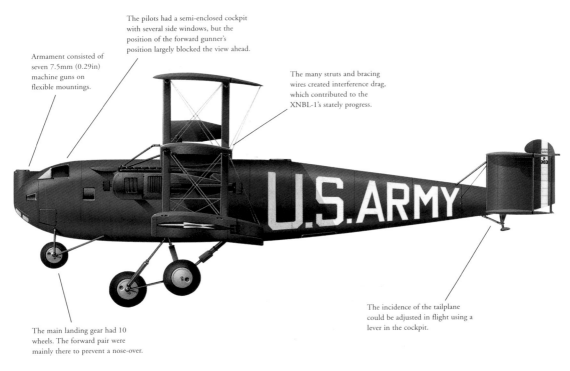

The pilots had a semi-enclosed cockpit with several side windows, but the position of the forward gunner's position largely blocked the view ahead.

Armament consisted of seven 7.5mm (0.29in) machine guns on flexible mountings.

The many struts and bracing wires created interference drag, which contributed to the XNBL-1's stately progress.

The main landing gear had 10 wheels. The forward pair were mainly there to prevent a nose-over.

The incidence of the tailplane could be adjusted in flight using a lever in the cockpit.

BEARDMORE INFLEXIBLE (1928)

The Beardmore Company (mainly shipbuilders by the 1920s) developed the Inflexible to demonstrate the then-innovative stressed-skin metal construction. Unusually for 1928 it was also a mid-wing monoplane at a time when most large aircraft were still wood and fabric biplanes. The Inflexible's maiden flight proved what many had expected – that the aircraft was too heavy for its three Condor engines. As author Bill Gunston put it, 'although it was incapable of serving any useful role it could at least fly'.

Within two years its flying career was over and it was dismantled to save space, ending its days in experiments to investigate airframe corrosion. A related design was the Beardmore Inverness, an all-metal flying boat whose creators had such faith in its airworthiness that it was equipped with two large masts and sails to get it home in the event of a forced water landing.

SPECIFICATIONS

CREW:	2
POWERPLANT:	three 485kW (650hp) Rolls-Royce Condor inline piston engines
MAX SPEED:	175km/h (109mph)
SPAN:	48.01m (157ft 6in)
LENGTH:	23.01m (75ft 6in)
HEIGHT:	6.40m (21ft 2in)
WEIGHT:	loaded 16,783kg (37,000lb)

Left: The Inflexible impressed the crowds at a couple of RAF air displays but achieved little else. Its great size made it difficult to house and the weight of its steel structure ruled out any sort of useful load.

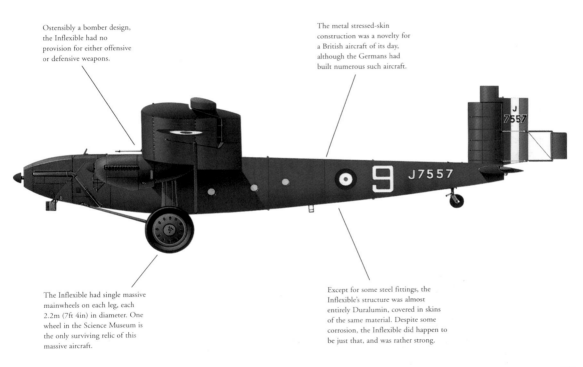

Ostensibly a bomber design, the Inflexible had no provision for either offensive or defensive weapons.

The metal stressed-skin construction was a novelty for a British aircraft of its day, although the Germans had built numerous such aircraft.

The Inflexible had single massive mainwheels on each leg, each 2.2m (7ft 4in) in diameter. One wheel in the Science Museum is the only surviving relic of this massive aircraft.

Except for some steel fittings, the Inflexible's structure was almost entirely Duralumin, covered in skins of the same material. Despite some corrosion, the Inflexible did happen to be just that, and was rather strong.

BELL HSL-1 (1953)

Bell's only twin-rotor helicopter, and one of the few not built by Piasecki (later Boeing-Vertol), the HSL-1 was the largest US helicopter of the day and was intended to hunt submarines and kill them with the Fairchild Petrel air-to-underwater missile.

The Navy would have rather had a twin-engined design instead of the single large radial they got. They would also have preferred a helicopter that fitted onto the elevators of their aircraft carriers, but the HSL was too large even with its rotors folded. Vibration problems caused protracted delays to the development. The piston engine proved so noisy that accurate readings from the sonar equipment were impossible and they saw little service in that role. A few HSLs found use as minesweepers and trainers, or for spare parts.

SPECIFICATIONS

CREW:	4
POWERPLANT:	one 1790kW (2400hp) Pratt & Whitney R-2800-50 radial piston engine
MAX SPEED:	161km/h (100mph)
ROTOR DIAMETER:	15.70m (51ft 6in)
LENGTH:	11.90m (39ft 1in)
HEIGHT:	4.40m (14ft 3in)
WEIGHT:	12,020kg (26,500lb)

Left: The US Navy wanted considerable numbers of HSL anti-sub helicopters, and the Royal Navy ordered more for use in Korea, but the war ended before the test programme did and in the end only 50 were built, all for the US.

The HSL was powered by a more powerful engine than contemporary helicopters. This gave plenty of power but also lots of noise and vibration.

Large fins were added to the tail to correct some stability problems found on the prototype.

An autopilot system allowed the HSL to hover over a suspected submarine for prolonged periods while dipping its sonar in the water, even if the operators could not hear the signals.

NAVY

183

BELL X-1 AND X-2 *(1951)*

The original 'X-plane', the Bell X-1 (or XS-1) was the first Mach 1 aircraft and a great experimental success. However, the X-1 series and the X-2 concealed a fatal flaw. In August 1951, the X-1D exploded under its B-50 carrier aircraft and had to be jettisoned over the desert. A few weeks later the No.3 X-1 blew up on the ground and took its B-50 with it. The No.2 X-2 did the same in flight. The B-50 escaped, but the X-2 pilot and an engineer were vaporized. Investigators surmised that ignition of pure oxygen was causing the explosions. When the X-1A exploded beneath a B-50 and was dropped like a hot potato, enough remained for the real cause to be established. An organic compound called Ulmer leather was used for gaskets that sealed joints around the liquid oxygen (lox) tanks. Under a moderate impact, the lox-saturated leather would explode violently.

SPECIFICATIONS (X-1D)

CREW:	1
POWERPLANT:	one 26.7kN (6000lb) thrust Reaction Motors XLR-11-RM-5 rocket motor
MAX SPEED:	2655km/h (1650mph) Mach 2.44
SPAN:	8.63m (28ft)
LENGTH:	10.89m (35ft 8in)
HEIGHT:	3.30m (10ft 8in)
WEIGHT:	loaded 7478kg (16,487lb)

Left: The experimental utility of the early X-craft was diminished by their tendency to explode without apparent reason. The cause was traced to some elementary chemistry, but not before aircraft and lives were lost.

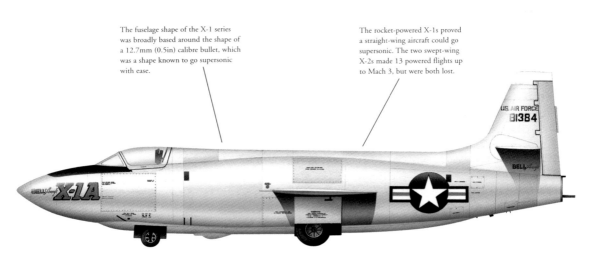

The fuselage shape of the X-1 series was broadly based around the shape of a 12.7mm (0.5in) calibre bullet, which was a shape known to go supersonic with ease.

The rocket-powered X-1s proved a straight-wing aircraft could go supersonic. The two swept-wing X-2s made 13 powered flights up to Mach 3, but were both lost.

High-speed research aircraft were prone to an aerodynamic phenomenon called inertia coupling. This nearly killed Chuck Yeager in the X-1 and caused the loss of the first X-2.

U.S. AIR FORCE
81384

BELL

BELL XP-77 *(1944)*

Bell was the only US manufacturer to produce propeller-driven single-engined fighters with a tricycle landing gear during the war, notably the P-39 Airacobra and P-63 Kingcobra. In between these designs was the diminutive XP-77, which was an early configuration for the P-39 dusted off and redesigned to use non-strategic materials, mainly wood. Six prototypes were ordered and the first was delivered only six months after the contract was signed. Despite its simple construction, project costs rose and delays increased, so orders were reduced to just two prototypes.

The XP-77 proved to have tricky handling characteristics and lower than expected performance. In October 1944 the second prototype went into an inverted spin which the pilot could not recover, so he left it to its own devices. Two months later the project was cancelled.

SPECIFICATIONS

CREW:	1
POWERPLANT:	one 388kW (520hp) Ranger XV-770 piston engine
MAX SPEED:	531km/h (330mph)
SPAN:	8.38m (27ft 6in)
LENGTH:	6.97m (22ft 11in)
HEIGHT:	2.50m (8ft 2in)
WEIGHT:	loaded 1827kg (4028lb)

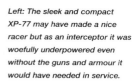

Left: The sleek and compact XP-77 may have made a nice racer but as an interceptor it was woefully underpowered even without the guns and armour it would have needed in service.

186

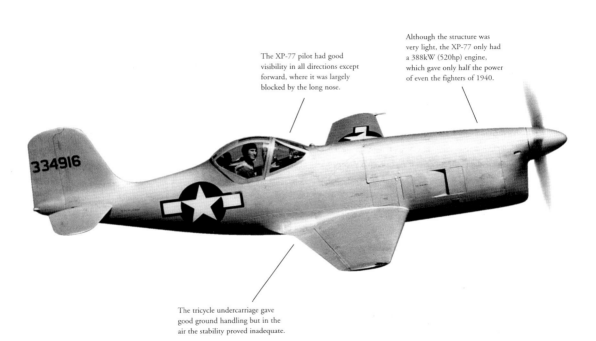

The XP-77 pilot had good
visibility in all directions except
forward, where it was largely
blocked by the long nose.

Although the structure was
very light, the XP-77 only had
a 388kW (520hp) engine,
which gave only half the power
of even the fighters of 1940.

The tricycle undercarriage gave
good ground handling but in the
air the stability proved inadequate.

BLACKBURN BOTHA *(1938)*

This torpedo-bomber, which proved far more dangerous to RAF pilots than it did to German sailors, was designed to compete for the same requirement that produced the Bristol Beaufort and was originally going to be powered by the same 843kW (1130hp) Bristol Taurus engines as the Beaufort. A shortage of these meant that the Perseus X, rated at only 656kW (880hp), was used for the initial versions. The deficiency in power and a series of unexplained accidents in 1940 led to the Botha gaining a very poor reputation. A slightly more powerful version of the Perseus was fitted and a few other changes made, but this did nothing to reduce the accident rate, particularly as the Botha was issued to training units and thus being handled by inexperienced students. Despite its inadequacies, 580 examples of this (deservedly) forgotten bomber were delivered, at least 120 being lost in crashes.

SPECIFICATIONS

CREW:	4
POWERPLANT:	two 694kW (930hp) Bristol Perseus XA radial piston engines
MAX SPEED:	401km/h (249mph)
SPAN:	17.98m (59ft)
LENGTH:	15.58m (51ft 2in)
HEIGHT:	4.46m (14ft 7in)
WEIGHT:	maximum 8369kg (18,450lb)

Left: The Botha never made a bomb or torpedo attack in anger and wound up as a trainer, where it arguably did more harm to the Allied war effort than good.

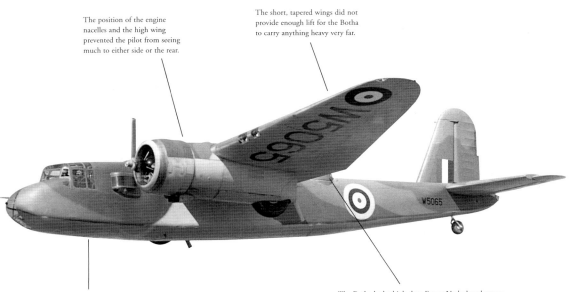

The position of the engine nacelles and the high wing prevented the pilot from seeing much to either side or the rear.

The short, tapered wings did not provide enough lift for the Botha to carry anything heavy very far.

The cockpit was very poorly designed. It was possible for a pilot flying solo to knock the fuel tank switches off but still start the engines, leading to engine failure a short time into the flight.

The Botha had a high-drag Frazer-Nash dorsal turret as seen on many Sunderlands and some Stirlings. As well as the two guns in this turret there was a single forward-firing gun operated by the pilot.

BLACKBURN ROC *(1938)*

Developed from the Skua, a two-seat naval fighter, the Roc was also originally intended to be a fighter, but the heavy Boulton-Paul turret reduced already poor performance to the point where it would have been unable to catch any modern bomber. If the Roc wasn't 'draggy' enough, Blackburn also developed a floatplane version. As well as being incapable of 322km/h (200mph), it proved directionally unstable and making a turn at low altitude could be deadly. The first take-off of a Roc floatplane immediately resulted in the first crash. The Skua itself saw most use as a dive-bomber and had more success than the Roc, which wound up mainly with anti-aircraft training units or dispersed to such combat zones as Bermuda.

SPECIFICATIONS

CREW:	2
POWERPLANT:	one 675kW (905hp) Bristol Perseus XII radial engine
MAX SPEED:	359km/h (223mph)
SPAN:	14.02m (46ft)
LENGTH:	10.85m (35ft 7in)
HEIGHT:	3.68m (12ft 1in)
WEIGHT:	maximum 3606kg (7950lb)

Left: As with the Boulton-Paul Defiant, the basic concept of the Roc was flawed. The 'turret fighter' was no match for a conventional agile fighter with fixed forward guns. Some damaged Rocs found use as fixed machine-gun posts at a Hampshire naval base during the Battle of Britain.

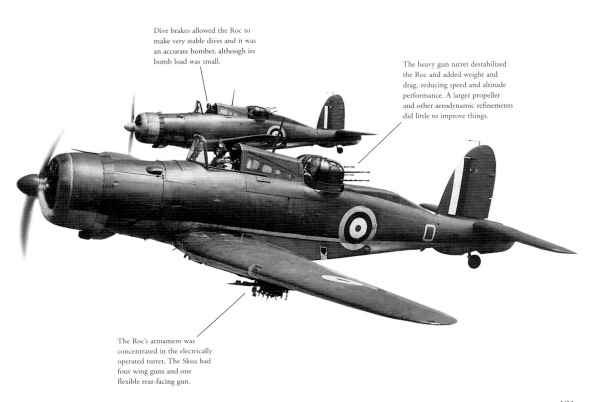

Dive brakes allowed the Roc to make very stable dives and it was an accurate bomber, although its bomb load was small.

The heavy gun turret destabilized the Roc and added weight and drag, reducing speed and altitude performance. A larger propeller and other aerodynamic refinements did little to improve things.

The Roc's armament was concentrated in the electrically operated turret. The Skua had four wing guns and one flexible rear-facing gun.

BOEING MODEL 273 (XF7B-1) *(1933)*

Perhaps a case of too rapid an advance for the conservative admirals of the day, Boeing's XF7B-1 fighter introduced such innovations as all-metal structure, an unbraced monoplane wing and an enclosed cabin. The Navy was unhappy with the (relatively) high landing speed and the poor view compared with biplanes. Boeing modified it with split flaps and later an open cockpit, but the Navy were still unhappy. When the windscreen collapsed during a dive test and the aircraft was overstressed to the point where it had to be written off, the Navy decided it would stick with biplanes for the time being. Boeing did not build another fighter for the Navy until the equally unwanted F8B of 1944 and then the F/A-18E/F Super Hornet, which they inherited from McDonnell Douglas in 1998.

SPECIFICATIONS

CREW:	1
POWERPLANT:	one 410kW (550hp) Pratt & Whitney R-1340 Wasp radial piston engine
MAX SPEED:	375km/h (233mph)
SPAN:	9.73m (31ft 11in)
LENGTH:	8.41m (27ft 7in)
HEIGHT:	2.26m (7ft 5in)
WEIGHT:	maximum 1755kg (3868lb)

Left: Somewhat in advance of the shipboard fighters of the day, Boeing's Model 273 was rejected due to a prejudice against monoplanes. The Navy waited a few more years before ordering its first monoplane fighter – the Buffalo.

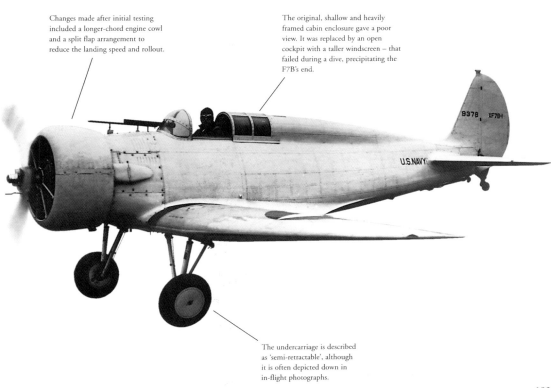

Changes made after initial testing included a longer-chord engine cowl and a split flap arrangement to reduce the landing speed and rollout.

The original, shallow and heavily framed cabin enclosure gave a poor view. It was replaced by an open cockpit with a taller windscreen – that failed during a dive, precipitating the F7B's end.

9378   XF7B-1

U.S.NAVY

The undercarriage is described as 'semi-retractable', although it is often depicted down in in-flight photographs.

BREDA BA.88 LINCE (1936)

This sleek-looking bomber broke two world speed records soon after its first flight, to the delight of Mussolini and his regime. When loaded down with guns, bombs, armour and other military equipment, performance figures plummeted by as much as half. Production models were given twin tails in a partially successful attempt to correct the prototype's instability, but the Lince still had deadly single-engine characteristics.

When fitted for sand filters for use in the Libyan desert, the engines overheated and produced such reduced power that at least one raid had to be cancelled due to an inability to reach bombing altitude or maintain formation. Withdrawn from service in late 1940, a 1943 attempt to revive the design with increased wingspan, new (but lower-powered!) engines and better armament was thwarted by the armistice.

SPECIFICATIONS

CREW:	2
POWERPLANT:	two 746kW (1000hp) Piaggio P.XI RC.40 radial piston engines
MAX SPEED:	485km/h (301mph)
SPAN:	15.60m (51ft 2in)
LENGTH:	10.78m (35ft 5in)
HEIGHT:	3.10m (10ft 2in)
WEIGHT:	6750kg (14,881lb)

Left: Rushed into production on Mussolini's orders, Breda's Lince (Lynx) bombers made their combat debut in June 1940. Reports of these raids were so disappointing that the type was quickly withdrawn except in North Africa. Five months after their introduction they were serving only as airfield decoys.

194

The Ba.88 could carry a
1000kg (2204lb) bomb load
and four machine guns, three
firing forward and a flexible
gun in the rear cockpit.

The modern-looking Lince in fact
had a structure of steel tube with
a light metal outer skin. Most
contemporary light bombers were
of monocoque construction in
which the skin bore the load.

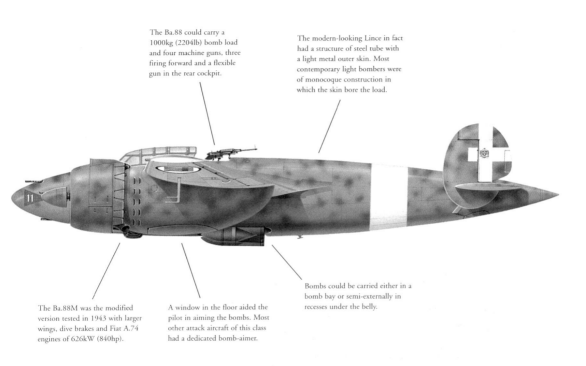

The Ba.88M was the modified
version tested in 1943 with larger
wings, dive brakes and Fiat A.74
engines of 626kW (840hp).

A window in the floor aided the
pilot in aiming the bombs. Most
other attack aircraft of this class
had a dedicated bomb-aimer.

Bombs could be carried either in a
bomb bay or semi-externally in
recesses under the belly.

BREWSTER BUFFALO *(1937)*

The portly Buffalo has gained a reputation as the worst fighter of World War II. In service it was overweight and lightly armed and often outmanoeuvred, but in the right hands could be quite effective. US Marine Buffaloes played a brief part in the Battle of Midway.

RAF and Commonwealth Buffalo pilots scored quite well against the Japanese Nakajima fighters encountered over Singapore, but were greatly outnumbered. Poor organization and no early warning system saw that the Buffaloes were never airborne before the enemy appeared and were always at a lower height when combat was joined. The Buffalo squadrons were cleared from the skies in short order. The Finns, using the lighter-weight F2A-1 and better tactics had great success against the early Soviet fighters they faced in their Winter War with the USSR.

SPECIFICATIONS (Mk 1)

CREW:	1
POWERPLANT:	one 820kW (1100hp) Wright R-1820 Cyclone radial engine
MAX SPEED:	470km/h (292mph)
SPAN:	10.67m (35ft)
LENGTH:	7.92m (26ft)
HEIGHT:	3.68m (12ft 1in)
WEIGHT:	maximum 3101kg (6840lb)

Left: The US Navy's first monoplane fighter, the Buffalo gained fame (or notoriety) with foreign air forces. 'A good aeroplane, but not for fighting' was one British pilot's view, but the many Finnish aces would disagree.

The F2A-1 was only armed with
two machine guns, one 7.62mm
(0.3in) calibre and one 12.7mm
(0.5in). Most export models also
had wing guns, but RAF ones
often flew with half ammunition
to save weight.

Addition of armour plate on
the F2A-2 version reduced
any performance advantage
the basic Buffalo may have
had over Japanese fighters.

The Finns liked the Buffalo enough
to design a version called the Humu
('Reckless') with a wooden wing
and a Russian engine. It proved
unsatisfactory in trials and only a
single example was built.

BRISTOL 188 *(1962)*

The Bristol 188, sometimes called the 'flaming pencil', was designed to research structures for sustained supersonic flight, particularly in support of the Avro 730 reconnaissance aircraft. This required the aircraft to 'soak' at Mach 2.6 for at least 30 minutes. To achieve the required strength the structure was largely stainless steel, which required new techniques and great expense to fabricate into an airframe.

Take-off speed was nearly 483km/h (300mph), but in all other respects the 188's speed was slower than desired, being able to achieve Mach 2.0 for only a couple of minutes. The whole project cost a huge £20 million and failed to achieve its objectives. It was wound down rather than develop the engines further. Test pilot Godfrey Auty was voted the 'man most likely to eject in the coming year' by his peers but thankfully never had to.

SPECIFICATIONS

CREW:	1
POWERPLANT:	two 62.28kN (14,000lb) thrust de Havilland Gyron Junior PS.50 afterburning turbojets
MAX SPEED:	Mach 1.88
SPAN:	10.69m (35ft 1in)
LENGTH:	23.67m (77ft 8in)
HEIGHT:	3.65m (12ft)
WEIGHT:	unknown

Left: The stainless steel 188 certainly looked futuristic. By the time it was completed, the aircraft it was supposed to provide data for had been cancelled. The project lasted from 1953 to 1964 with the two aircraft flying for less than two years.

A new type of stainless steel, joined by a new 'puddle' welding process was needed for the 188. It took over two years to develop the steel before it could even be ordered for construction use.

The PS.50 (modified Gyron Junior) engines had greater diameter than the fuselage but never developed enough thrust to push the 188 to the high speeds required.

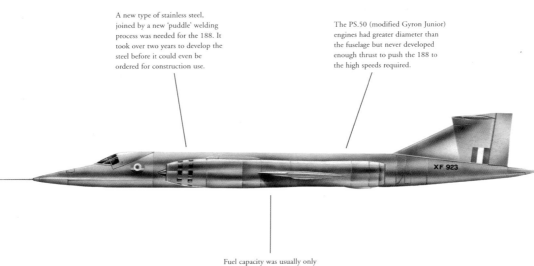

Fuel capacity was usually only enough for 20–25 minutes flight including a high-speed run. By airline standards the 188 was in a fuel emergency situation before take-off.

CAPRONI CAMPINI N.1 *(1940)*

In 1939 inventor Secondo Campini convinced the Caproni company to build an airframe to test his new power unit that he believed would replace the propeller. The Italian aircraft industry had decided that a gas turbine engine was impractical (even as German and British scientists were testing theirs). The Camproni Campini N.1 flew in 1940 and has sometimes been touted as the world's first jet aircraft. It was nothing of the sort – power came from a relatively small piston engine inside the forward fuselage, which turned a variable-pitch compressor in what we would today call a ducted fan. A rudimentary form of afterburner allowed fuel to be burned in a propelling nozzle to give some extra thrust. Despite this, the N.1 would only make 375km/h (233mph), slower than the Fiat CR.42 biplane.

SPECIFICATIONS

CREW:	2
POWERPLANT:	one 671kW (900hp) Isotta-Fraschini radial engine driving a three-stage fan compressor
MAX SPEED:	375km/h (233mph)
SPAN:	15.85m (52ft)
LENGTH:	13.10m (43ft)
HEIGHT:	4.70m (15ft 5in)
WEIGHT:	4195kg (9250lb)

Left: The FAI acknowledged the N.1 as the first jet-propelled aircraft, but were unaware of the secretly flown Heinkel 178. A more powerful supercharged engine might have made a difference to the N.1's pedestrian performance, but wartime pressures brought an end to development.

The low power of the N.1's piston engine kept it below 4000m (13,124ft), where the ducted fan arrangement would have been effective.

The N.1's power system had no hot compressor section. The cold compressed air was ducted and mixed with jet fuel and ignited, giving extra thrust.

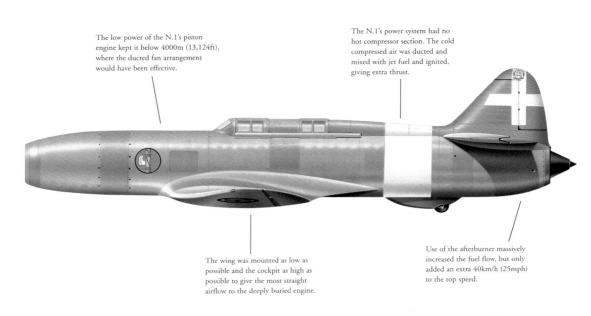

The wing was mounted as low as possible and the cockpit as high as possible to give the most straight airflow to the deeply buried engine.

Use of the afterburner massively increased the fuel flow, but only added an extra 40km/h (25mph) to the top speed.

CAPRONI-STIPA *(1932)*

The principle of ducted fans is well understood now. They require a duct with correct tapering at each end and a low drag but powerful engine at its core. Multiple-bladed propellers, or a fan as on a modern high-bypass turbofan are needed for efficiency. Placing a Tiger Moth engine inside a fat tube doesn't cut it. An Italian government engineer, Luigi Stipa, convinced the Caproni Company to build an aircraft to test his theory that a tubular fuselage gave significant extra thrust to a conventional engine and propeller. The resulting Caproni-Stipa aircraft had a corpulent annular fuselage, which concealed a Gipsy engine and two-bladed propeller. All this achieved was high drag and low noise, although the landing speed was reduced to 68km/h (42mph). Performance was otherwise lower than a conventional airframe with the same powerplant.

SPECIFICATIONS

CREW:	2
POWERPLANT:	one 90kW (120hp) de Havilland Gipsy III inline piston engine
MAX SPEED:	131km/h (81mph)
SPAN:	14.28m (46ft 10in)
LENGTH:	5.88m (19ft 4in)
HEIGHT:	3.00m (9ft 10in)
WEIGHT:	loaded 800kg (1760lb)

Left: The bizarre Caproni-Stipa appeared from some angles to be a jet, but from others it seemed that a de Havilland had fallen down a well. A French company planned a twin-engined version, but this came to nothing.

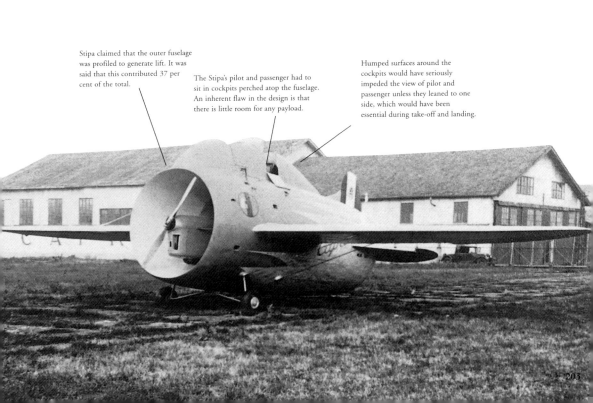

Stipa claimed that the outer fuselage was profiled to generate lift. It was said that this contributed 37 per cent of the total.

The Stipa's pilot and passenger had to sit in cockpits perched atop the fuselage. An inherent flaw in the design is that there is little room for any payload.

Humped surfaces around the cockpits would have seriously impeded the view of pilot and passenger unless they leaned to one side, which would have been essential during take-off and landing.

CONVAIR YF-102 DELTA DAGGER (1953)

Convair's YF-102 was to be the first supersonic delta-winged fighter, but it was discovered that the wind tunnel predictions were wildly optimistic and it stubbornly refused to go supersonic. Panic ensued but salvation came in the form of the newly discovered 'area rule' which stated that minimum drag occurred when the fuselage was narrower adjacent to the wing. A lengthened YF-102 with suitably placed bulges conformed to this principle and easily passed Mach 1 and formed the basis of the successful F-102A fighter. The need to modify the YF-102 completely ruined the novel production plan, which called for series aircraft to be built on the same tooling as the prototype. In all, two-thirds of the 30,000 pieces of tooling purchased had to be discarded.

SPECIFICATIONS (YF-102)

CREW:	1
POWERPLANT:	one 64.5kN (14,500lb) thrust Pratt & Whitney XJ57-P-11 afterburning turbojet
MAX SPEED:	1327km/h (825mph)
SPAN:	11.60m (38ft 2in)
LENGTH:	15.97m (52ft 5in)
HEIGHT:	5.48m (18ft)
WEIGHT:	max loaded 11,975kg (26,400lb)

Left: The YF-102 (top) proved an embarrassing and costly failure, but contributed to the study of aerodynamics. The effect of 'wasp-waisting' the fuselage to reduce drag (bottom) can be seen on most subsequent supersonic aircraft.

To make it supersonic, the original YF-102 was lengthened and given bulges on the rear fuselage to change the cross-section. These protuberances were known as 'Marilyns'.

The YF-102 was a development of the XF-92 research aircraft, which was originally to be the ramjet-powered 'return' component of a large two-part composite attack aircraft.

The canopy of the YF-102 had heavy framing more akin to an early World War II fighter. Convair were probably worried about the stress of supersonic flight on large areas of Perspex.

U.S. AIR FORCE
27994

FC-994

CONVAIR
YF-102

CURTISS XP-62 (1944)

One of several Curtiss fighter prototypes that followed the P-40 but never went into service, the portly XP-62 was at least all new rather than based on P-40 parts.

The largest single-seat fighter of conventional configuration developed during the war, it weighed nearly 850kg (1872lb) more empty than a P-47D Thunderbolt. Although faster than the P-47, it had a much inferior climb rate, ceiling and range figures. Ordered in June 1941 it did not fly until early 1944 and never received the pressurized cabin which was to be its main selling point. Orders for 100 diminished to a single example, which logged very few flying hours. The failure of Curtiss to develop a P-40 successor was a factor in the company's demise and the XP-62 was the last single-seat prop aircraft to bear this famous name.

SPECIFICATIONS

CREW:	1
POWERPLANT:	one 1715kW (2300hp) Wright R-3350 Cyclone radial piston engine
MAX SPEED:	721km/h (448mph)
SPAN:	16.35m (53ft 8in)
LENGTH:	12.04m (39ft 6in)
HEIGHT:	4.95m (16ft 3in)
WEIGHT:	loaded 6650kg (14,660lb)

Left: One of the first fighters with a pressurized cockpit, numerous delays caused the XP-62 to be scrapped before the cabin was ever fitted.

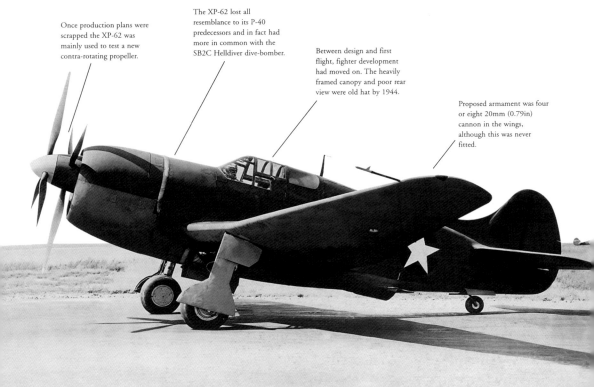

Once production plans were scrapped the XP-62 was mainly used to test a new contra-rotating propeller.

The XP-62 lost all resemblance to its P-40 predecessors and in fact had more in common with the SB2C Helldiver dive-bomber.

Between design and first flight, fighter development had moved on. The heavily framed canopy and poor rear view were old hat by 1944.

Proposed armament was four or eight 20mm (0.79in) cannon in the wings, although this was never fitted.

DASSAULT BALZAC MIRAGE IIIV (1962)

Built to test Dassault's concepts for a 1960s Nato requirement for a Mach 2-capable VTOL fighter, the first Mirage IIIV was rebuilt from the Mirage III prototype, number 001. The name 'Balzac' came from the phone number of a famous advertising firm, 'Balzac 001'. The single Atar turbojet was replaced by a smaller turbofan and no fewer than eight lift jet engines. The Mirage IIIV proved able to take-off and land vertically, and fly supersonically, although not on the same flight. The second IIIV achieved Mach 2, although without the lift engines fitted. It crashed on its 112th flight in January 1964, killing a French test pilot. It was rebuilt but crashed on its 179th flight in September 1965 when it ran out of fuel, killing a USAF exchange pilot.

SPECIFICATIONS
(Mirage IIIV No. 1)

CREW:	1
POWERPLANT:	one 74.5kN (16,750lb) thrust SNECMA/Pratt & Whitney TF-106 turbofan, with eight 15.7kN (3525lb) Rolls-Royce RB162-1 lift engines
MAX SPEED:	Mach 1.32
SPAN:	8.72m (28ft 8in)
LENGTH:	18.00m (59ft)
HEIGHT:	5.55m (18ft 3in)
WEIGHT:	loaded 13,440kg (29,630lb)

Left: The second Mirage IIIV was one of the only aircraft to suffer two fatal crashes. The surfeit of engines led to a deficit of fuel, which contributed to its second, and final, accident.

Although the Mirage IIIV was a flawed concept, the cockpit layout and much of the electronic systems were used in the successful Mirage F1 series.

The fuselage was longer than that of a standard Mirage IIIC, and the wing had increased chord near the root, giving a slightly 'kinked' effect.

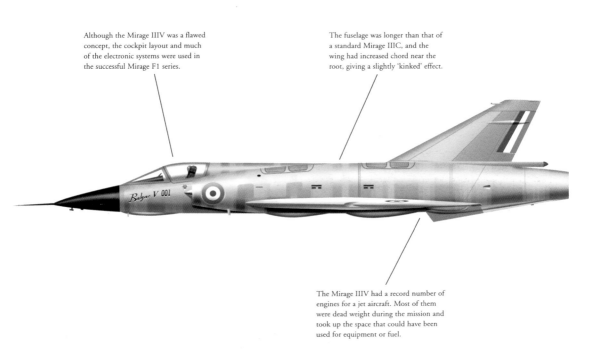

The Mirage IIIV had a record number of engines for a jet aircraft. Most of them were dead weight during the mission and took up the space that could have been used for equipment or fuel.

DORNIER DO X *(1929)*

The impressive but unlucky 12-engined Do X was effectively a flying ocean liner, built to convey 100 passengers in great luxury across the Atlantic. Its single epic flight to the Americas in 1930 was delayed in Lisbon for a month to repair fire damage to the wing, followed by a further three-month delay to repair hull damage in the Canary Islands. Due to these incidents, and being unable to reach its normal operating altitudes, it took nine months to reach New York via South America, but only five days for the more direct return. Total journey time was nearly 19 months, probably slower than walking via the North Pole. Two more Do Xs were built for Italy but proved uneconomic for commercial use. The original Do X was displayed in Berlin but destroyed in a British bombing raid.

SPECIFICATIONS

CREW:	10
POWERPLANT:	twelve 477kW (640hp) Curtiss V-1570 Conqueror piston engines
MAX SPEED:	210km/h (130mph)
SPAN:	48.00m (157ft 6in)
LENGTH:	40.00m (131ft 4in)
HEIGHT:	10.10m (33ft 2in)
WEIGHT:	maximum 56,000lb (123,459kg)

Left: The Do X was the largest aircraft in the world in its day. Having proved it could cross the Atlantic despite the odds, it failed to find a buyer in the US and its last notable flight was the return to Depression-era Germany.

The three decks included a lounge, smoking room, bathroom, kitchen and dining room as well as individual sleeping cabins.

Fuel consumption was 1818 litres (400 gallons) per hour. Returning from South America, the Do X had to land on the water and taxi the last 10km (6 miles) to Portugal.

Fully loaded, the maximum speed was only 160km/h (100mph).

The initial Siemens-built Bristol Jupiter engines proved inadequate, so Curtiss Conquerors were substituted. In all cases the rear-facing engines tended to overheat.

DO-X

DORNIER

D-1929

P 63

DOUGLAS XA2D SKYSHARK (1951)

The turboprop engine offered to provide the power that early jets lacked. However, no manufacturer really achieved a successful turboprop combat aircraft before jet engines improved. A notable failure was the Skyshark, which was a satisfactory airframe design that suffered terribly from problems with the XT-40 engine. In particular, making the gearbox work reliably proved impossible. Other problems included bearing failures and overheated skin around the exhausts. When fighting intensified in Korea, the Navy and Douglas switched their priorities to the proven Skyraider. Development continued, marred by the loss of gearboxes or props on three of the five Douglas test aircraft. Twelve Skysharks were built, but only eight ever received engines. Meanwhile, jets had overtaken the turboprop and by 1954 Douglas was testing the XA4D Skyhawk, destined for over 50 years of service.

SPECIFICATIONS

CREW:	1
POWERPLANT:	one 3805kW (5100hp) Allison XT40-A-2 turboprop
MAX SPEED:	806km/h (501mph)
SPAN:	15.53m (50ft 3in)
LENGTH:	12.66m (41ft 3in)
HEIGHT:	5.24m (17ft 1in)
WEIGHT:	maximum 10,414kg (22,960lb)

Left: The troublesome Skyshark was intended to bridge the gap between pistons and jets, but its development was protracted to the point where jets caught up and it never saw service.

The Skyshark's canopy gave a poorer view than the Skyraider's, but the pilot was at least equipped with an ejection seat.

The propeller control mechanism consisted of 25 unreliable vacuum tubes in a black box about the size of a suitcase and gave constant trouble.

On one test flight the propellers flew completely off. The pilot skilfully made a successful landing, having engine power but no propulsive force.

213

DOUGLAS X-3 STILETTO (1952)

The US Air Force, Navy and NACA (predecessor to NASA) all invested in this extraordinary research craft that looked like it was going supersonic while sitting on the ground, but barely achieved it in the air. Many new construction techniques and materials were needed to build the X-3 to withstand its anticipated flight regime, and large amounts of expensive titanium were used. Unfortunately, engine choice was the Westinghouse J34, one of several turbojets built by this company that failed to perform as advertised.

Although the airframe was designed to reach Mach 2.2, the best it ever achieved was Mach 1.21, in a dive. This meant it achieved little towards its objective of studying kinetic heating research. The USAF only flew the X-3 six times before handing it to NACA, who made but 20 more flights before it wound up in a museum.

SPECIFICATIONS

CREW:	1
POWERPLANT:	two 18.68kN (4200lb) thrust Westinghouse J34 turbojets
MAX SPEED:	1136km/h (706mph)
SPAN:	6.91m (21ft 8in)
LENGTH:	20.35m (66ft 9in)
HEIGHT:	3.81m (12ft 6in)
WEIGHT:	loaded 10,160kg (22,400lb)

Left: Intended to explore high-speed high-altitude flight, the X-3 was one of many 1950s aircraft crippled by useless Westinghouse engines and only one of the intended three prototypes was built.

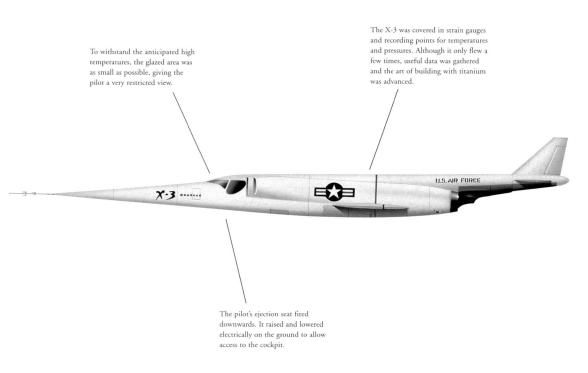

To withstand the anticipated high temperatures, the glazed area was as small as possible, giving the pilot a very restricted view.

The X-3 was covered in strain gauges and recording points for temperatures and pressures. Although it only flew a few times, useful data was gathered and the art of building with titanium was advanced.

The pilot's ejection seat fired downwards. It raised and lowered electrically on the ground to allow access to the cockpit.

HANDLEY PAGE HEREFORD (1938)

The Hereford bomber was a Napier Dagger-engined version of the Hampden 'Flying Suitcase', ordered as a back-up at the same time as the first Hampden production contracts. The noisy new inline engines overheated on the ground and cooled too quickly and seized in the air. Even routine maintenance was more complicated than that required for the Hampden's Pegasus radials. There were no performance advantages from the new engines. On daylight raids in 1940–41 the Hampdens and Herefords were shot to bits by faster and better-armed German fighters, so were quickly relegated to night missions. Only a very small number of Herefords saw action (in Hampden squadrons). The rest were relegated to training units, soon followed by their (marginally) better brethren.

SPECIFICATIONS

CREW:	4
POWERPLANT:	two 712kW (955hp) Napier Dagger VII inline piston engines
MAX SPEED:	(Hampden) 409km/h (254mph)
SPAN:	21.08m (69ft 2in)
LENGTH:	16.33m (53ft 7in)
HEIGHT:	4.56m (14ft 11in)
WEIGHT:	(Hampden) maximum 8508kg (18,756kg)

Left: The antiquated Hampden bomber can hardly be described as a great success, but the Hereford derivative was a total failure. It was such a flop that many were converted back to Hampdens.

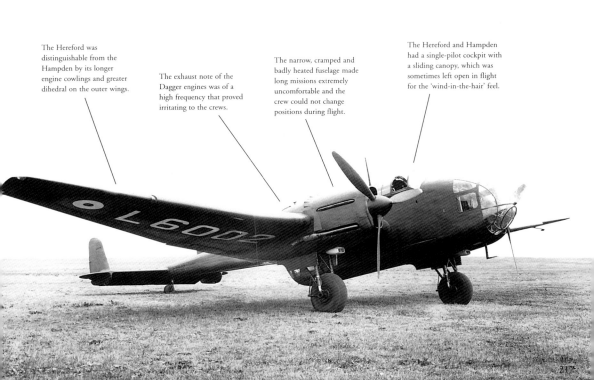

The Hereford was distinguishable from the Hampden by its longer engine cowlings and greater dihedral on the outer wings.

The exhaust note of the Dagger engines was of a high frequency that proved irritating to the crews.

The narrow, cramped and badly heated fuselage made long missions extremely uncomfortable and the crew could not change positions during flight.

The Hereford and Hampden had a single-pilot cockpit with a sliding canopy, which was sometimes left open in flight for the 'wind-in-the-hair' feel.

HEINKEL HE 177 'GREIF' (1939–1945)

The He 177 'Greif' (Griffon) was the closest Germany came to developing a strategic bomber during the war. Due to its faults and Luftwaffe doctrine, it never appeared in the numbers needed to strike a decisive blow on any target. As with the Manchester, dive-bombing was one of the intended roles, which should have made the 'Greif' stronger than otherwise, but several early aircraft suffered structural failure in flight.

To achieve high performance through low drag, the He 177 was fitted with its four engines mounted in pairs one behind the other driving a common crankshaft. The surface evaporation radiator system proved inadequate and the rear engines often overheated and caught fire. The enormous torque from these powerful motors coupled with the long fuselage could cause the aircraft to swing on take-off or landing and crash or collapse. Many hundreds of detail faults were found, only some of which were corrected.

SPECIFICATIONS
(He 177A-5)

CREW:	5
POWERPLANT:	two 2200kW (2950hp) DB 606 piston engines
MAX SPEED:	488km/h (303mph)
SPAN:	31.44m (103ft 1in)
LENGTH:	22.00m (72ft 1in)
HEIGHT:	6.39m (21ft)
WEIGHT:	loaded 31,000kg (68,342lb)

Left: Over 1700 He 177s were built, but rarely did more than a dozen fly a mission together. Fires and failures meant that fewer actually reached or returned from the target.

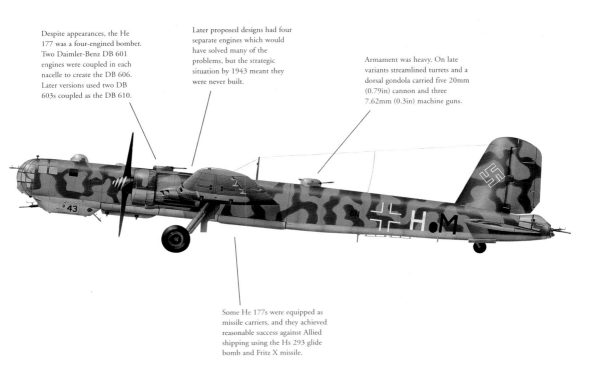

Despite appearances, the He 177 was a four-engined bomber. Two Daimler-Benz DB 601 engines were coupled in each nacelle to create the DB 606. Later versions used two DB 603s coupled as the DB 610.

Later proposed designs had four separate engines which would have solved many of the problems, but the strategic situation by 1943 meant they were never built.

Armament was heavy. On late variants streamlined turrets and a dorsal gondola carried five 20mm (0.79in) cannon and three 7.62mm (0.3in) machine guns.

Some He 177s were equipped as missile carriers, and they achieved reasonable success against Allied shipping using the Hs 293 glide bomb and Fritz X missile.

HILLER HJ-1 HORNET (1950)

Originally intended for the civil market with a price as little as $5,000, the Hiller Hornet was a tiny helicopter powered by ramjet engines mounted on the rotor tips. It was tested in 1956 as the HOE-1 or H-32 for the US Army for use as an artillery spotter or forward observation platform. For this role the Hornet lacked what we now call 'stealth', as it could usually be heard by the enemy and the glowing engines could be seen from a long distance. Hiller once claimed 'the Hornet's sound range compares favourably with that of a conventional-powered helicopter' but without an intercom system the pilots had to scream at each other to communicate. The museum owning the only remaining flyable example of the 17 Hornets built received complaints from neighbours a mile and a half away when they last flew it.

The high drag of the ramjets meant the blade angle had to be set to a very negative angle when power was cut, and this led to the Hornet plummeting at 15mps (49fps) during auto rotation. Only a very skilled pilot could arrest this descent just before the ground.

SPECIFICATIONS

CREW:	2
POWERPLANT:	two 33.6kW (45hp) Hiller 8RJ2B ramjets
SPEED:	130km/h (81mph)
ROTOR DIAMETER:	7.00m (23ft)
HEIGHT:	2.10m (7ft)
WEIGHT:	490kg (1080lb)

Left: The Hornet was rejected by the Army due largely to its poor autorotation characteristics and only 17 were built. Hiller's plan for a lifting crane version with a 100m (320ft) four-turbojet rotor never came to fruition.

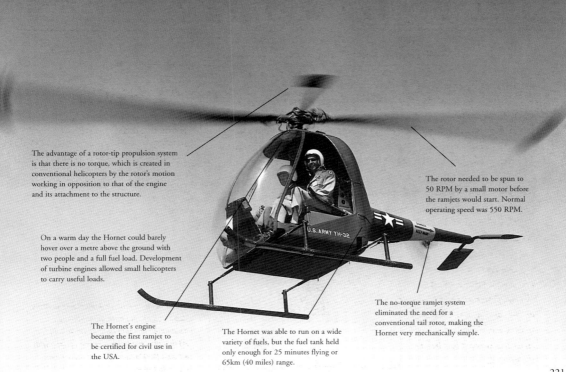

The advantage of a rotor-tip propulsion system is that there is no torque, which is created in conventional helicopters by the rotor's motion working in opposition to that of the engine and its attachment to the structure.

The rotor needed to be spun to 50 RPM by a small motor before the ramjets would start. Normal operating speed was 550 RPM.

On a warm day the Hornet could barely hover over a metre above the ground with two people and a full fuel load. Development of turbine engines allowed small helicopters to carry useful loads.

The Hornet's engine became the first ramjet to be certified for civil use in the USA.

The Hornet was able to run on a wide variety of fuels, but the fuel tank held only enough for 25 minutes flying or 65km (40 miles) range.

The no-torque ramjet system eliminated the need for a conventional tail rotor, making the Hornet very mechanically simple.

U.S. ARMY YH-32

HUGHES XF-11 *(1946)*

Designed to meet the same specification as the Republic XF-12, the XF-11 was said to be scaled up from the mysterious D-2 fighter that Howard Hughes flew in secret in 1943. Resembling an enlarged P-38 Lightning, the XF-11 was optimized for the high-altitude photo-reconnaissance role. Under pressure from Congress to deliver on this project and the equally late 'Spruce Goose', Howard Hughes himself made the XF-11's first flight. Unwisely for a maiden flight, Hughes stayed up much longer than planned – until one propeller went into reverse pitch and the XF-11 crashed into an unoccupied house in Beverly Hills. Hughes survived with head injuries, but some say he never really recovered. The second aircraft was evaluated by the USAF, who, after deciding it was twice as expensive, harder to operate and inferior to the XR-12 Rainbow, terminated the programme.

SPECIFICATIONS

CREW:	2
POWERPLANT:	two 2238kW (3000hp) Pratt & Whitney R-4360-37 radial piston engines
MAX SPEED:	unknown
SPAN:	30.78m (101ft)
LENGTH:	20.15m (65ft 5in)
HEIGHT:	unknown
WEIGHT:	maximum 26,444kg (58,300lb)

Left: Howard Hughes' XF-11 nearly cost him his life. Some say it cost him his sanity. It certainly had its faults, but the USAF could have used a purpose-built aircraft in its class in the 1950s.

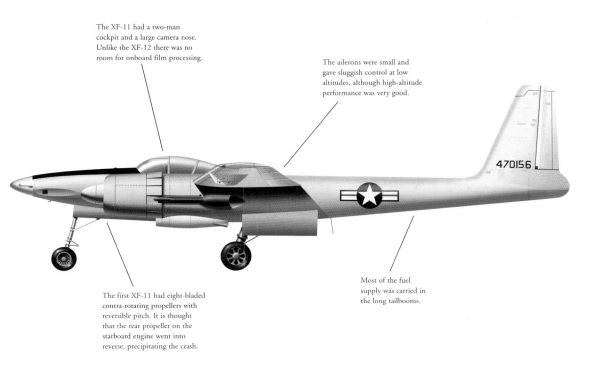

The XF-11 had a two-man cockpit and a large camera nose. Unlike the XF-12 there was no room for onboard film processing.

The ailerons were small and gave sluggish control at low altitudes, although high-altitude performance was very good.

470156

The first XF-11 had eight-bladed contra-rotating propellers with reversible pitch. It is thought that the rear propeller on the starboard engine went into reverse, precipitating the crash.

Most of the fuel supply was carried in the long tailbooms.

MCDONNELL F3H DEMON (1950)

The prototype of the Demon naval fighter proved to have poor stability, poor forward visibility and a low roll rate. These faults were corrected on the initial production model, but the poor reliability and performance of the J40 engine meant that most of the 58 built never flew. Many were barged directly from the factory to shore bases for use as ground trainers. The J40 was replaced by the J71, which still gave limited power. A modified afterburner system gave power in the range needed to make safe carrier landings, although the accident rate was horrendous by modern standards.

The later versions weren't too bad, apart from persistent hydraulic leaks, but by the time they were in service the Demon had gained a reputation that was hard to shake off.

SPECIFICATIONS

CREW:	1
POWERPLANT:	one 43.16kN (9700lb) Allison J71-A-2E turbojet
MAX SPEED:	1116km/h (693mph)
SPAN:	10.77m (35ft 4in)
LENGTH:	17.96m (58ft 11in)
HEIGHT:	4.44m (14ft 7in)
WEIGHT:	15,377kg (33,900lb)

Left: Designed as a shipboard interceptor, the early F3H Demon had a performance described as 'farcical'. Most saw no service. Many of the lessons of the Demon were incorporated in McDonnell's F-4 Phantom II.

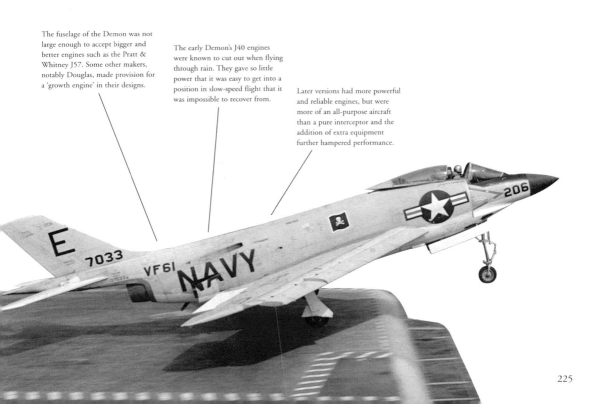

The fuselage of the Demon was not large enough to accept bigger and better engines such as the Pratt & Whitney J57. Some other makers, notably Douglas, made provision for a 'growth engine' in their designs.

The early Demon's J40 engines were known to cut out when flying through rain. They gave so little power that it was easy to get into a position in slow-speed flight that it was impossible to recover from.

Later versions had more powerful and reliable engines, but were more of an all-purpose aircraft than a pure interceptor and the addition of extra equipment further hampered performance.

MESSERSCHMITT ME 163 KOMET (1941)

The Komet was the world's first (and so far only) operational rocket-powered fighter. Although the prototype Me 163A first flew in August 1941, it was not until February 1944 that production Me 163Bs entered service in any number, official disinterest playing a part in the slow progress of development. Although its performance was fantastic, the Komet carried only enough fuel for four minutes powered flying. The fuel was an extremely volatile cocktail mixed in flight, which would in the wrong proportions readily explode. Unlike some other Luftwaffe 'last ditch' aircraft, the Komet required exceptional piloting skills, particularly on landing, and a shortage of trained pilots restricted deployment as much as did fuel supplies or production delays. Destruction of the fuel plant by bombing added to the Me 163 squadrons' woes in the last months of the war. Each mission, however, saw the available aircraft and pilot numbers reduced by fighters, off-field landings and landing crashes.

SPECIFICATIONS
(Me 163B-1a)

CREW:	1
POWERPLANT:	one 16.67kN (3748lb) thrust Walter rocket motor
MAX SPEED:	960km/h (597mph)
SPAN:	9.40m (30ft 7in)
LENGTH:	5.85m (19ft 2in)
HEIGHT:	2.76m (9ft)
WEIGHT:	loaded 4310kg (9502lb)

Left: With a range of only 40km (25 miles), the Komet was only good for point defence. Once combat was over, the pilot faced the most dangerous part of the mission – a safe landing.

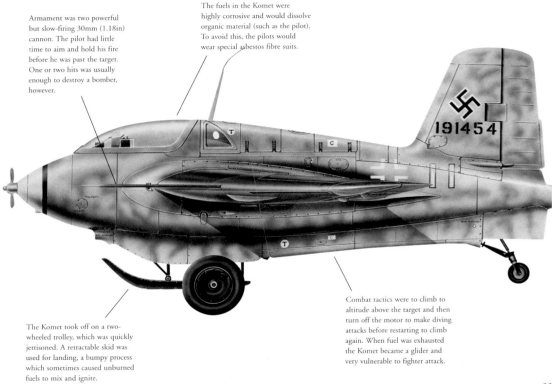

Armament was two powerful but slow-firing 30mm (1.18in) cannon. The pilot had little time to aim and hold his fire before he was past the target. One or two hits was usually enough to destroy a bomber, however.

The fuels in the Komet were highly corrosive and would dissolve organic material (such as the pilot). To avoid this, the pilots would wear special asbestos fibre suits.

The Komet took off on a two-wheeled trolley, which was quickly jettisoned. A retractable skid was used for landing, a bumpy process which sometimes caused unburned fuels to mix and ignite.

Combat tactics were to climb to altitude above the target and then turn off the motor to make diving attacks before restarting to climb again. When fuel was exhausted the Komet became a glider and very vulnerable to fighter attack.

MESSERSCHMITT ME 321/323 GIGANT (1941)

Drawn up in only 14 days, the massive Messerschmitt Gigant was designed as an assault glider for the invasion of Russia. The original Me 321 version needed rocket boost and three Me 110 tow planes to get airborne and dropped its take-off dolly to save weight and drag. This complicated arrangement led to many accidents, including one where all four crew and 120 troops were killed. To simplify things, a powered version, the Me 323, was developed using the cheapest and puniest engines available and adding an 8-wheeled undercarriage. This reduced the carrying capacity greatly but improved practicality. Used on several fronts, the Me 323 Gigant (Giant) proved vulnerable to attack from fighters and even medium bombers, and several 'massacres' occurred with whole fleets of the lumbering transports shot down with heavy loss of life.

SPECIFICATIONS (Me 323E)

CREW:	10
POWERPLANT:	six 850kW (1140hp) Gnome-Rhône 14N piston engines
MAX SPEED:	253km/h (157mph)
SPAN:	55.00m (180ft 5in)
LENGTH:	28.50m (93ft 6in)
HEIGHT:	9.60m (31ft 6in)
WEIGHT:	45,000kg (99,210lb)

Left: In some ways ahead of its time, the Gigant was only useful where the Luftwaffe had air superiority. When this was lost, the Me 323s became lumbering whales and were destroyed in large numbers.

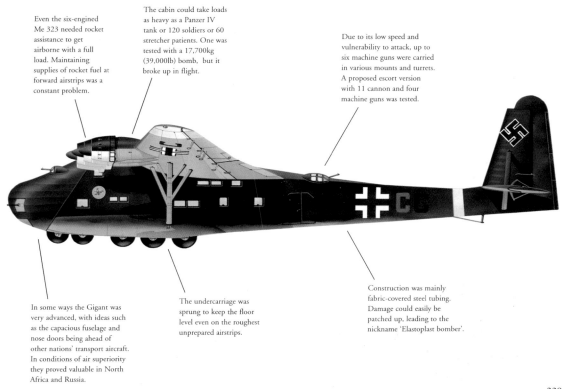

Even the six-engined Me 323 needed rocket assistance to get airborne with a full load. Maintaining supplies of rocket fuel at forward airstrips was a constant problem.

The cabin could take loads as heavy as a Panzer IV tank or 120 soldiers or 60 stretcher patients. One was tested with a 17,700kg (39,000lb) bomb, but it broke up in flight.

Due to its low speed and vulnerability to attack, up to six machine guns were carried in various mounts and turrets. A proposed escort version with 11 cannon and four machine guns was tested.

In some ways the Gigant was very advanced, with ideas such as the capacious fuselage and nose doors being ahead of other nations' transport aircraft. In conditions of air superiority they proved valuable in North Africa and Russia.

The undercarriage was sprung to keep the floor level even on the roughest unprepared airstrips.

Construction was mainly fabric-covered steel tubing. Damage could easily be patched up, leading to the nickname 'Elastoplast bomber'.

PERCIVAL P.74 (1956)

The P.74 was intended as a demonstrator for a new type of helicopter. It worked on the tip-jet principle, but unlike the Hiller Hornet with its individual ramjets, the P.74 had a gas generator under the cabin floor which fed compressed air through triple ducts to the three-bladed rotor, each blade of which had triple ejector ducts.

Months of testing in a static rig showed up many problems with the power system, which refused to develop full power and maximum gas flow. Finally these problems were fixed and a first flight attempted. Despite the efforts of two pilots on the very stiff controls, the P.74 resolutely refused to fly. One engineer associated with the project says that a consultant designer used the wrong formula for calculating lift. All the figures added up but the P.74 went nowhere. Actually it was ordered to be towed across the airfield out of sight, and that is about the last anyone heard of it.

SPECIFICATIONS

CREW:	2 and 8 passengers
POWERPLANT:	two 563kW (754hp) Napier Oryx No.1 gas generators
CRUISING SPEED:	(estimated) 177km/h (110mph)
ROTOR DIAMETER:	16.76m (55ft)
HEIGHT:	unknown
WEIGHT:	loaded 3515kg (7750lb)

Left: The egg-shaped P.74 was the subject of various miscalculations and failed to rise from the ground at all. Percival didn't attempt any more helicopters.

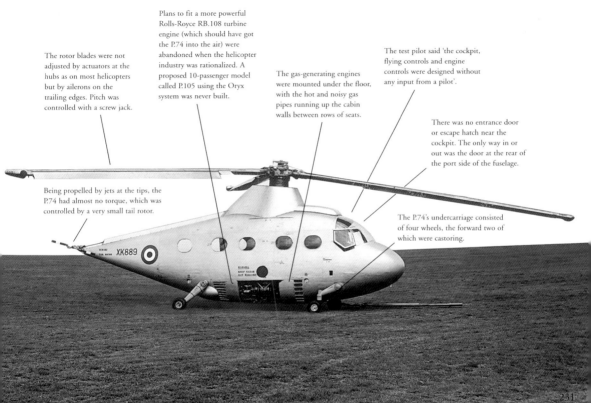

The rotor blades were not adjusted by actuators at the hubs as on most helicopters but by ailerons on the trailing edges. Pitch was controlled with a screw jack.

Plans to fit a more powerful Rolls-Royce RB.108 turbine engine (which should have got the P.74 into the air) were abandoned when the helicopter industry was rationalized. A proposed 10-passenger model called P.105 using the Oryx system was never built.

The gas-generating engines were mounted under the floor, with the hot and noisy gas pipes running up the cabin walls between rows of seats.

The test pilot said 'the cockpit, flying controls and engine controls were designed without any input from a pilot'.

There was no entrance door or escape hatch near the cockpit. The only way in or out was the door at the rear of the port side of the fuselage.

Being propelled by jets at the tips, the P.74 had almost no torque, which was controlled by a very small tail rotor.

The P.74's undercarriage consisted of four wheels, the forward two of which were castoring.

XK889

REPUBLIC XF-84H (1955)

Even in the mid-1950s the superiority of the jet powerplant for combat aircraft was questioned by some. A modern technology propeller driven by a turbine (a turboprop) offered high speeds, long endurance and low landing speeds. To test this concept the USAF commissioned two XF-84Hs from Republic. Powered by the troublesome T-40 turboprop, the noise the F-84H made has been described as an 'unholy shriek', leading to the nickname 'Thunderscreech'. Resonance off the ground made groundcrew physically sick. The two aircraft only made a dozen test flights, all but two of which resulted in emergency landings and the USAF refused to accept it for their own tests, cancelling the programme in 1956.

The first XF-84H spent 40 years on a pole at Bakersfield Airport, California, its propeller slowly (and quietly) rotated by an electric motor.

SPECIFICATIONS

CREW:	1
POWERPLANT:	one 4364kW (5850hp) Allison XT40-A-1 turboprop
MAX SPEED:	837km/h (520mph)
SPAN:	10.18m (33ft 5in)
LENGTH:	15.67m (51ft 5in)
HEIGHT:	4.67m (15ft 4in)
WEIGHT:	8123kg (17,892lb)

Left: Ostensibly modified from F-84Fs, the two XF-84Hs were essentially all-new aircraft and were much heavier than their forebears. Achieving much lower speeds than hoped for, they still managed to break records for propeller aircraft.

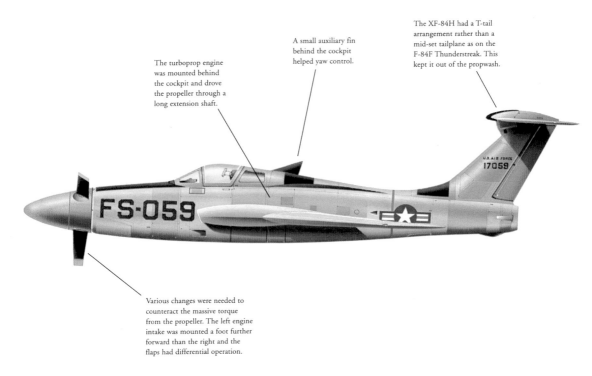

The XF-84H had a T-tail arrangement rather than a mid-set tailplane as on the F-84F Thunderstreak. This kept it out of the propwash.

A small auxiliary fin behind the cockpit helped yaw control.

The turboprop engine was mounted behind the cockpit and drove the propeller through a long extension shaft.

U.S. AIR FORCE
17059

FS-059

Various changes were needed to counteract the massive torque from the propeller. The left engine intake was mounted a foot further forward than the right and the flaps had differential operation.

REPUBLIC XF-91 THUNDERCEPTOR (1949)

L ooking as if it was a plastic kit built without reference to the instructions, the XF-91 combined a unique wing design with a mixed jet and rocket powerplant. Conceived as a point defence interceptor, the airframe was completed long before the XLR-11 rocket (which had an unnerving tendency to blow up, whether on a test-stand or in the aircraft). By 1952 when everything was ready, the requirement for a rocket fighter had been abandoned. Test flights with the rocket showed the XF-91 was unlikely to reach its planned top speed of Mach 1.4 without being shaken to pieces. On the very first flight the jet quit just after take-off and the rocket was needed to avert a disaster. Flight endurance was only 25 minutes, meaning that only a very small area could be defended by such a fighter, particularly one armed only with cannon or rockets.

SPECIFICATIONS

CREW:	1
POWERPLANT:	one 23.13kN (5200lb) thrust General Electric J47-GE-3 turbojet and four 6.67kN (1500lb) thrust Reaction Motors XLR11-RM-9 rocket engines
MAX SPEED:	1812km/h (1126mph)
SPAN:	9.52m (31ft 3in)
LENGTH:	13.18m (43ft 3in)
HEIGHT:	5.51m (18ft)
WEIGHT:	maximum 12,935kg (28,300lb)

Left: Republic aircraft were never known for their looks, but the Thunderceptor (even the name was ugly) was perfectly hideous and cost 5 million dollars, needless to say a lot of money in the early 1950s.

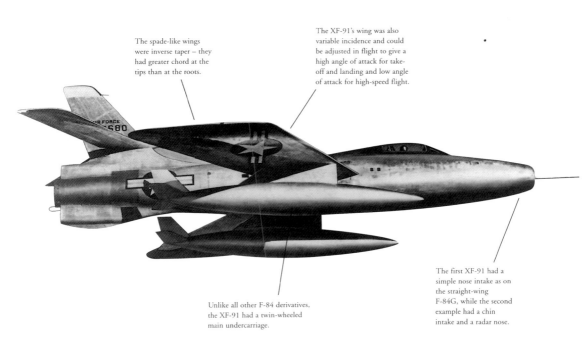

The spade-like wings were inverse taper – they had greater chord at the tips than at the roots.

The XF-91's wing was also variable incidence and could be adjusted in flight to give a high angle of attack for take-off and landing and low angle of attack for high-speed flight.

Unlike all other F-84 derivatives, the XF-91 had a twin-wheeled main undercarriage.

The first XF-91 had a simple nose intake as on the straight-wing F-84G, while the second example had a chin intake and a radar nose.

RYAN FR-1 FIREBALL *(1944)*

Essentially a conventional wartime fighter with a small jet engine stuffed in the back, the unfortunately named Fireball was the US Navy's toe-in-the-water approach to putting jets on their aircraft carriers. The General Electric J31 engine was intended to boost performance at altitude rather than power the Fireball throughout its flight. Following early tests, the FR-1 required a substantial redesign of its tail surfaces, which initially looked quite jet-like but were soon replaced with larger, more conventional units.

Improved FR-2 and FR-3 versions with different engine combinations were ordered in large quantities and then cancelled with the war's end. One example of the XFR-4 with a 15.1kN (3400lb) thrust J34 was tested. For once a Westinghouse engine provided too much thrust and worked poorly in conjunction with the piston engine.

SPECIFICATIONS

CREW:	1
POWERPLANT:	one 1063kW (1425hp) Wright R-1820-72W Cyclone piston engine and one 7.1kN (1600lb) thrust General Electric J31 turbojet
MAX SPEED:	686km/h (426mph)
SPAN:	12.19m (40ft)
LENGTH:	9.86m (32ft 4in)
HEIGHT:	4.15m (13ft 7in)
WEIGHT:	loaded 4806kg (10,595lb)

Left: In some ways neither fish nor fowl, the FR-1 was a very conservative method of introducing jet engines into the Navy. Only 17 of the 66 built saw squadron service, which lasted just over two years.

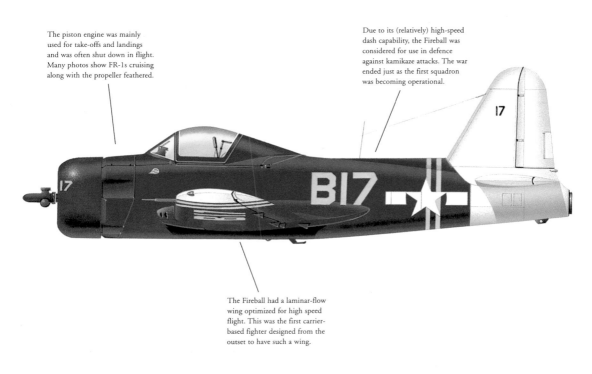

The piston engine was mainly used for take-offs and landings and was often shut down in flight. Many photos show FR-1s cruising along with the propeller feathered.

Due to its (relatively) high-speed dash capability, the Fireball was considered for use in defence against kamikaze attacks. The war ended just as the first squadron was becoming operational.

The Fireball had a laminar-flow wing optimized for high speed flight. This was the first carrier-based fighter designed from the outset to have such a wing.

VOUGHT F6U-1 PIRATE (1946)

Responding to a US Navy request for an aircraft powered by the Westinghouse J34 engine, Vought aircraft made its first tentative step into the jet era with the pedestrian F6U Pirate.

The Pirate was powered by the unimpressive Westinghouse J34. Even when the engine was fitted with an afterburner the F6U's performance was described as 'sub marginal'. Lengthening the fuselage to accommodate the afterburner caused lateral stability problems. In all there were five major modifications needed to correct poor handling. The wood/metal laminate used in large parts of the airframe proved hard to manufacture and prone to damage. By the time it entered service the F6U was obsolete.

Sixty-five Pirates were ordered, but in the end only 30 were built and these were used mostly for ground training tasks such as battle damage repair practice.

SPECIFICATIONS

CREW:	1
POWERPLANT:	one 1916kg (4224lb) thrust Westinghouse J34-WE-30 turbojet
MAX SPEED:	959km/h (596mph)
SPAN:	10.14m (32ft 10in)
LENGTH:	11.61m (37ft 8in)
HEIGHT:	3.97m (12ft 11in)
WEIGHT:	maximum 5851kg (12,900lb)

Left: The F6U was essentially a piston-engined design powered by a jet. After four years of testing, the US Navy decided it would never make a useful combat aircraft and never issued it to a fleet squadron.

The Pirate never received radar or other mission avionics. The aerodynamics were equally unsophisticated.

Extra fins were added on the tailplane to reduce the lateral instability caused by the extended rear fuselage.

The wing and tailfin were skinned with Metalite, a material composed of a sandwich of Duralumin and balsa wood. Other parts were Fabrilite, a laminate of balsa and glass fibre.

534

VOUGHT F7U CUTLASS (1948)

Seeing that the lead in fighter development was falling to the Air Force, the traditionally conservative US Navy ordered the radical swept-wing, twin-tailed Cutlass in 1946. It was an extremely aerodynamically advanced and mechanically complicated aircraft for its day. All three of the initial XF7U-1 prototypes crashed. The Cutlass failed its carrier suitability tests and the initial model was retrospectively designated an 'experimental' type. A complete redesign produced the production F7U-3, which proved short-ranged and maintenance intensive. The Cutlass had a complicated hydraulic system, temperamental engines, weak landing gear, and to top it off, unreliable ejection seats. The Cutlass is usually remembered for its poor safety record, with over a quarter of the 300 F7Us built being lost or involved in serious accidents.

SPECIFICATIONS (F7U-3)

CREW:	1
POWERPLANT:	two 20.5kN (4600lb) thrust Westinghouse J46-WE-8A afterburning turbojets
MAX SPEED:	1095km/h (680mph)
SPAN:	11.70m (38ft 8in)
LENGTH:	13.40m (44ft 3in)
HEIGHT:	4.40m (14ft 7in)
WEIGHT:	loaded 14,350kg (31,642lb)

Left: The Cutlass has been called 'the least safe US Navy fighter ever flown'.

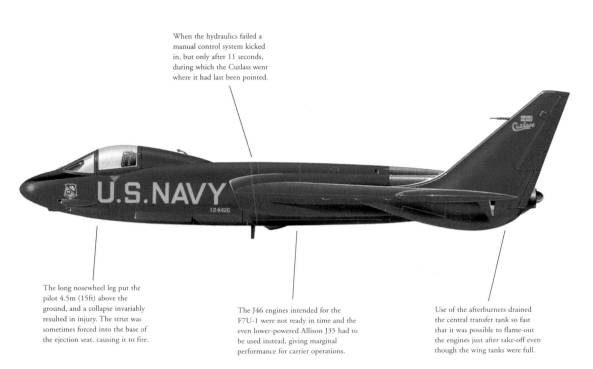

When the hydraulics failed a manual control system kicked in, but only after 11 seconds, during which the Cutlass went where it had last been pointed.

U.S.NAVY

124426

The long nosewheel leg put the pilot 4.5m (15ft) above the ground, and a collapse invariably resulted in injury. The strut was sometimes forced into the base of the ejection seat, causing it to fire.

The J46 engines intended for the F7U-1 were not ready in time and the even lower-powered Allison J35 had to be used instead, giving marginal performance for carrier operations.

Use of the afterburners drained the central transfer tank so fast that it was possible to flame-out the engines just after take-off even though the wing tanks were full.

YAKOVLEV YAK-38 'FORGER' (1971)

Preceded by the Yak-36 'Freehand' and the barely related Yak-36M, the USSR's first operational VTOL aircraft was the Yak-38 'Forger'. Superficially similar to the early Harrier, the 'Forger' was burdened with two extra lift engines, which increased the basic weight and reduced the fuel capacity. Payload was about one-third that of the Mk 1 Sea Harrier and endurance in hot weather about 15 minutes. A constant problem was ingestion of exhaust gases back into the engine, which caused power loss. Failure of one lift jet (which had an operating life of only about 22 hours) would cause an immediate uncontrollable roll. The 'solution' to this was to fit a system which automatically ejected the pilot in the event of an engine failure. Unsurprisingly, as many as a third of Russia's 'Forgers' were lost in accidents.

SPECIFICATIONS

CREW:	1
POWERPLANT:	one 66.7kN (15,000lb) thrust Tumansky R27-B-300 turbofan and two 31.9kN (7170lb) RD38 lift jets
MAX SPEED:	1125km/h (700mph)
SPAN:	7.50m (24ft 7in)
LENGTH:	16.00m (52ft 6in)
HEIGHT:	4.40m (14ft 5in)
WEIGHT:	11,700kg (25,795lb)

Left: The 'Forger' gave the USSR its first carrier-based combat aircraft, but it was poorly equipped and of limited utility, not to say somewhat dangerous to its pilots.

The 'Forger' had a system to automatically eject the pilot if the engine stopped while the thrust was angled below the horizontal. On one occasion this occurred in full view of a British carrier, who rescued the pilot.

A hinged door opened behind the cockpit to feed air to the lift jets, which exhausted out of a hatch at the bottom.

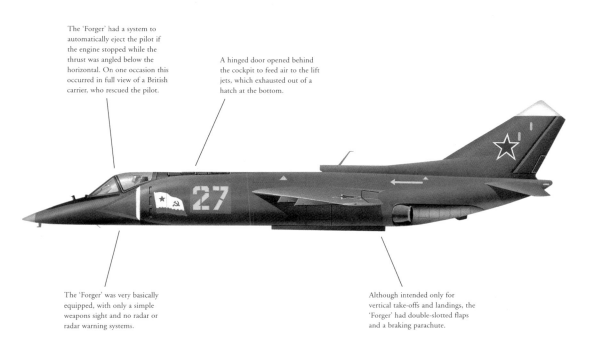

The 'Forger' was very basically equipped, with only a simple weapons sight and no radar or radar warning systems.

Although intended only for vertical take-offs and landings, the 'Forger' had double-slotted flaps and a braking parachute.

CONSTRUCTION DISASTERS

Early aviation development was not always conducted with the same scientific rigour applied by the Wright Brothers. Fellow pioneer Samuel Langley knew something about aerodynamics, but not enough about stressing an airframe. His 'Aerodrome' couldn't survive the force of its catapult launch system. He also neglected to address the question of landing, but never actually had to. Anthony Fokker had no formal engineering qualifications, rejected the need for stress calculations and used the cheapest materials he could find. Almost all his early designs were periodically grounded due to serious structural defects.

Materials science made great strides in the twentieth century, and aviation played a great part in its advancement. Alternatively, the 'solution' to a structural failure problem can be to just nail on more sheets of wood, as was done with the Polish Zubr bomber. In this case it just made the aircraft far too heavy.

Metals and composites in turn presented new problems. It can be argued that the reluctance of the FAA to certify the carbon-fibre Beech Starship can be traced to the Comet disasters of the 1950s. The Comet experience led to the sound airliners that followed, which make increasing use of tried and tested composites.

Left: Extensive use of composite materials along with a protracted development made the RAH-66 Comanche prohibitively expensive.

ALBATROS D.III *(1916)*

Just after its combat debut, one of the sleek new Albatros D.III fighters experienced a cracked wing spar, forcing the pilot to land in open country. Manfred von Richthofen, the 'Red Baron' himself, was lucky to avoid complete structural failure, unlike several other experienced German airmen. As a result of numerous wing failures, restrictions were put on the diving speed of the D.III, which was hardly satisfactory for a high-performance combat aircraft. The cause was the weakness of the V-strut supporting the lower wing, which permitted twisting under load. Another serious fault was that the radiator was located under the centre of the top wing where any battle damage would cause the pilot to be sprayed with boiling water. The radiator was moved to one side for this reason, but still presented some hazard.

SPECIFICATIONS

CREW:	1
POWERPLANT:	one 119kW (160hp) Mercedes D.IIIa piston engine
MAX SPEED:	175km/h (109mph)
SPAN:	9.05m (29ft 8in)
LENGTH:	7.33m (24ft)
HEIGHT:	2.98m (9ft 9in)
WEIGHT:	maximum 886kg (1953lb)

Left: Aerodynamically, the D.III was very advanced for its day, but its streamlining masked serious structural weaknesses, which led to severe restrictions on its operation.

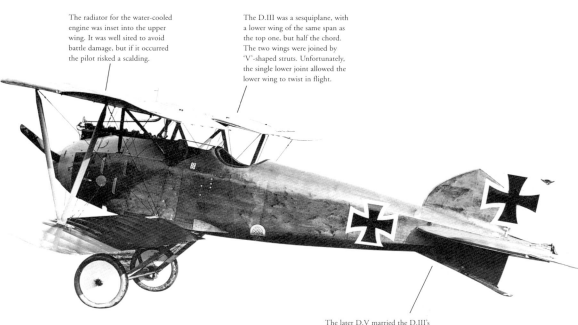

The radiator for the water-cooled engine was inset into the upper wing. It was well sited to avoid battle damage, but if it occurred the pilot risked a scalding.

The D.III was a sesquiplane, with a lower wing of the same span as the top one, but half the chord. The two wings were joined by 'V'-shaped struts. Unfortunately, the single lower joint allowed the lower wing to twist in flight.

The later D.V married the D.III's wing and tailplane to a new fuselage and fin. Of course this just transferred the structural problems to the new type. These were not corrected until the strengthened D.Va model.

BEECHCRAFT STARSHIP 2000A (1986)

To prove the concept of an all-composite replacement for the King Air, Beechcraft commissioned Burt Rutan's Scaled Composites company to build an 85 per cent size proof-of-concept aircraft. When it first appeared at a business aircraft exhibition it caused a sensation, but this was little more than a 'flying wind-tunnel model' and was very far from a certificated aircraft. Beech announced an ambitious schedule for certification, but subcontractors let them down and they had to develop the techniques for fabricating and moulding high-tech materials themselves. As with the LearFan, the FAA insisted on a very rigorous testing programme, including subjecting a test airframe to two simulated lifetimes (40,000 hours) of stress and insisting on extra lightning protection. After a five-and-a-half year development programme that cost over $300 million, only 53 production aircraft were built, and many were never sold, in part due to economic recession.

SPECIFICATIONS

CREW:	2
POWERPLANT:	two 895kW (1200hp) Pratt & Whitney Canada PT6A-67A turboprops
MAX SPEED:	620km/h (385mph)
SPAN:	16.60m (54ft 5in)
LENGTH:	14.05m (46ft 1in)
HEIGHT:	3.94m (12ft 11in)
WEIGHT:	loaded 6758kg (14,900lb)

Left: The first all-composite business aircraft actually certified in the USA, the Starship was one of the most thoroughly tested aircraft ever. To avoid product liability issues and to stop manufacturing unprofitable spare parts, Beech has tried to buy back all the Starships in use and scrap them, but many of the owners have resisted the offer.

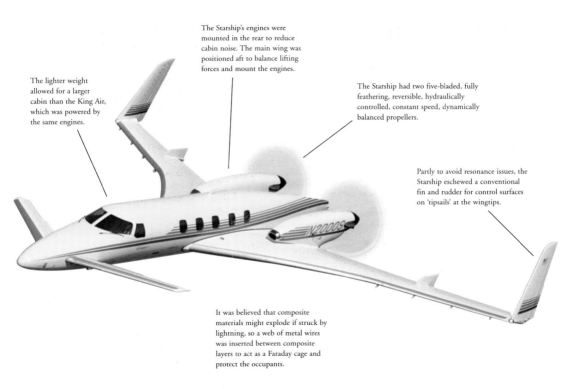

The lighter weight allowed for a larger cabin than the King Air, which was powered by the same engines.

The Starship's engines were mounted in the rear to reduce cabin noise. The main wing was positioned aft to balance lifting forces and mount the engines.

The Starship had two five-bladed, fully feathering, reversible, hydraulically controlled, constant speed, dynamically balanced propellers.

Partly to avoid resonance issues, the Starship eschewed a conventional fin and rudder for control surfaces on 'tipsails' at the wingtips.

It was believed that composite materials might explode if struck by lightning, so a web of metal wires was inserted between composite layers to act as a Faraday cage and protect the occupants.

BLÉRIOT BIPLANES (1917–1925)

Pioneer Louis Blériot established the basic form for the aeroplane with his Model XI of 1909. The large aircraft his company created during and after World War I were anything but classics of form and function.

Most of the big Blériots suffered from a surfeit of struts and wheels, and had their engines mounted very close together near the centreline. The Blériot 67 bomber prototype was underpowered and slow, even by 1917 standards. The 1919 Type 74 was no better, but added especially bad handling qualities. The Type 73 which succeeded it was a truly bizarre creature with eight wheels and a highly swept rear fuselage. It lasted only two or three flights before breaking up in the air. One of the two Type 115 airliners also crashed, and the other could barely cruise at 100km/h (62mph) when loaded.

**SPECIFICATIONS
(Blériot 115)**

CREW:	2–3 and 8 passengers
POWERPLANT:	four 134kW (180hp) Hispano Suiza 8Ac inline piston engines
MAX SPEED:	180km/h (112mph)
SPAN:	25.01m (82ft 1in)
LENGTH:	14.45m (47ft 5in)
HEIGHT:	unknown
WEIGHT:	loaded 5100kg (11,243lb)

Left: Louis Blériot somewhat lost the plot in the interwar years with a series of ugly, overcomplicated and unsuccessful bombers and airliners. Despite few sales, the company traded largely on its founder's name until 1935 when it finally folded.

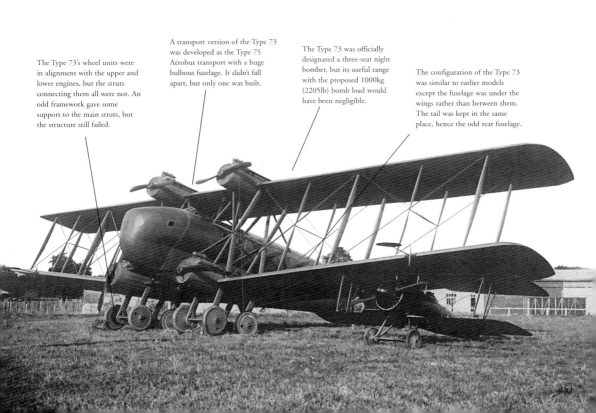

The Type 73's wheel units were in alignment with the upper and lower engines, but the struts connecting them all were not. An odd framework gave some support to the main struts, but the structure still failed.

A transport version of the Type 73 was developed as the Type 75 Aérobus transport with a huge bulbous fuselage. It didn't fall apart, but only one was built.

The Type 73 was officially designated a three-seat night bomber, but its useful range with the proposed 1000kg (2205lb) bomb load would have been negligible.

The configuration of the Type 73 was similar to earlier models except the fuselage was under the wings rather than between them. The tail was kept in the same place, hence the odd rear fuselage.

BOEING/SIKORSKY RAH-66 COMANCHE (1996)

The Comanche was intended to replace the US Army's relatively unsophisticated OH-58D Kiowa Warrior and AH-1 Cobra with a stealthy multi-sensor platform able to carry out scouting and attack missions, shoot down enemy helicopters and pass data directly to the Longbow Apache attack helicopter. Slow funding of the programme encouraged more roles and capabilities to be added, increasing the weight and cost. An early plan envisaged procurement of as many as 5023 Comanches, later reduced to 1400, then 1213 and finally 650. As the numbers fell, the per-unit cost rose from $12.1 million to $58.9 million. In the end, 16 years and the expenditure of $8 billion only achieved little more than two flying prototypes and a partially completed test programme.

SPECIFICATIONS

CREW:	2
POWERPLANT:	two 1069kW (1432hp) T800-LHTEC-801 turboshafts
MAX SPEED:	328km/h (204mph)
ROTOR DIAMETER:	11.90m (39ft 1in)
LENGTH:	14.28m (46ft 10in)
HEIGHT:	3.39m (11ft 2in)
WEIGHT:	maximum 7790kg (17,174lb)

Left: Initiated in 1988, the RAH-66's first flight did not take place until 1996 and the whole thing was cancelled in February 2004. The US Army will put the money into buying 800 new helicopters and modernizing another 1400.

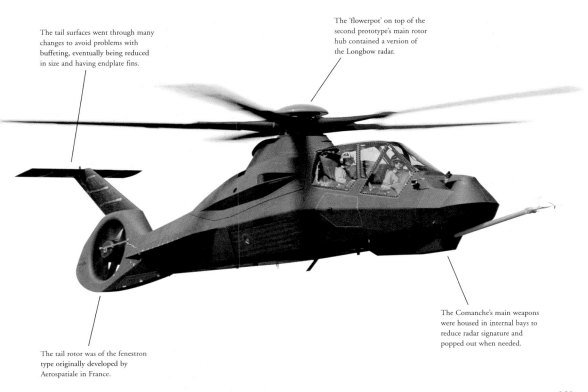

The tail surfaces went through many changes to avoid problems with buffeting, eventually being reduced in size and having endplate fins.

The 'flowerpot' on top of the second prototype's main rotor hub contained a version of the Longbow radar.

The tail rotor was of the fenestron type originally developed by Aerospatiale in France.

The Comanche's main weapons were housed in internal bays to reduce radar signature and popped out when needed.

BREWSTER BERMUDA/BUCCANEER (1941)

Development of the SB2A Buccaneer dive-bomber was protracted and by the time it was ready the US Navy had no need for more aircraft of this type. Used mainly for training, none saw combat and many were scrapped straight from the production line after orders were cancelled in 1943. Company publicity even before the first flight convinced several customers, including the British and Dutch, that the SB2A was a potent dive-bomber, but when evaluated by Boscombe Down, the Bermuda Mk 1 (as it was known in the UK) proved 'entirely unsuitable for combat operations'. The naval section of the UK's main aircraft test centre found it too heavy, underpowered and lacking manoeuvrability. Most of the 740 British examples became target tugs or were used only to train mechanics.

SPECIFICATIONS

CREW:	2
POWERPLANT:	one 1268kW (1700hp) Wright R-2600-A5B-5 Cyclone radial piston engine
MAX SPEED:	457km/h (284mph)
SPAN:	14.33m (47ft)
LENGTH:	11.94m (39ft 4in)
HEIGHT:	4.70m (15ft 5in)
WEIGHT:	maximum 6481kg (14,289lb)

Left: The Brewster Company never quite got the hang of aircraft manufacturing. All their production aircraft are regarded as failures, the SB2A the more so as it saw no operational service at all, despite production of over 1000 examples.

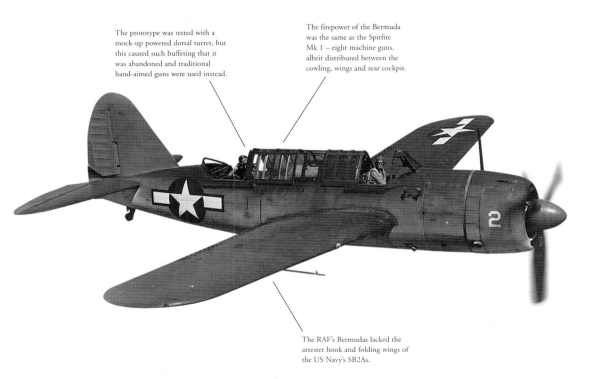

The prototype was tested with a mock-up powered dorsal turret, but this caused such buffeting that it was abandoned and traditional hand-aimed guns were used instead.

The firepower of the Bermuda was the same as the Spitfire Mk 1 – eight machine guns, albeit distributed between the cowling, wings and rear cockpit.

The RAF's Bermudas lacked the arrester hook and folding wings of the US Navy's SB2As.

CHRISTMAS BULLET (1918)

D octor William Christmas believed that struts were unnecessary and that an aeroplane's wings should be free to flap like a bird's. Unfortunately, on the first flight of his 'Bullet' fighter, also known as the Christmas Strutless Biplane and by other names, the wings did exactly that and then came adrift. The pilot was killed instantly. A second Bullet did exactly the same thing a few months later. Christmas claimed all sorts of things, among them that he had 'hundreds' of aeronautical patents and that he was swamped by orders for Bullets from Europe and by million-dollar offers to rebuild Germany's air forces. None of them were true, but he did get the US Army to pay him handsomely for his wing design. Or so he said.

SPECIFICATIONS
(first Bullet)

CREW:	1
POWERPLANT:	one 138kW (185hp) Liberty Six piston engine
MAX SPEED:	n/a
SPAN:	8.63m (28ft)
LENGTH:	6.40m (21ft)
HEIGHT:	unknown
WEIGHT:	unknown

Left: The Bullet is perhaps unique in that both its flights resulted in fatal crashes. Inventor William Christmas was unrepentant, but fortunately built no more flyable aircraft.

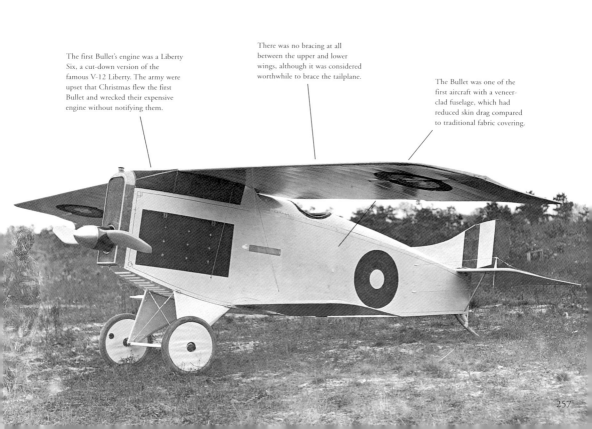

The first Bullet's engine was a Liberty Six, a cut-down version of the famous V-12 Liberty. The army were upset that Christmas flew the first Bullet and wrecked their expensive engine without notifying them.

There was no bracing at all between the upper and lower wings, although it was considered worthwhile to brace the tailplane.

The Bullet was one of the first aircraft with a veneer-clad fuselage, which had reduced skin drag compared to traditional fabric covering.

DASSAULT MERCURE (1971)

Combat aircraft maker Dassault moved into the civil airliner field with the Mercure, a twin-engined 737-lookalike. Its main competitors were the DC-9 and 727, which they exceeded in most performance parameters except range. It was joked that it would not succeed in export markets because it didn't have the range to leave France. Designed to fly short sectors quickly, the Mercure was built without structural provision for extra fuel tankage to save weight. In contrast, Boeing built the 737 with maximum growth potential and it is still in production over 35 years later. Launched during the 1973 oil crisis and devaluation of the US dollar, the commercial timing of the Mercure could hardly have been worse. Air France declared they wouldn't order any and Sabena chose the 737-200, essentially dooming the project.

SPECIFICATIONS
(Mercure 100)

CREW:	3 and 108–150 passengers
POWERPLANT:	two 69.0kN (15,500lb) thrust Pratt & Whitney JT8D-15 turbojets
MAX SPEED:	926km/h (575mph)
SPAN:	34.84m (114ft 4in)
LENGTH:	30.55m (100ft 1in)
HEIGHT:	11.36m (37ft 3in)
WEIGHT:	maximum 56,518kg (124,600lb)

Left: Dassault hoped the Mercure would get a substantial share of a market estimated at 1500 aircraft by 1980, but in the end only sold 11, all for French domestic airline Air Inter.

The Mercure was slightly wider and longer than the Boeing 737-200, which was under development at the same time.

The Mercure 100 had the same engines as later Boeing 727s. A proposed Mercure 200 would have had CFM-56 engines and carried up to 184 passengers.

The maximum range of a Mercure with maximum payload was only about 1100km (683 miles).

259

DE HAVILLAND COMET I *(1949)*

The first flight of the Comet jetliner in 1949 put Britain five years ahead of the USA in civil aviation development. Two Comet 1 crashes caused mainly by pilot error were followed by two mysterious disappearances over the Mediterranean. Public confidence plummeted and a Comet airframe was tested to destruction to establish the cause, proving that inflight break up had been caused by metal fatigue springing from window corners and other angular apertures.

Before these tests were done a further Comet disintegrated, dooming future sales of the Comet 1. Only a few Comet 2s were built for the RAF. The Comet 4 (with round windows) was a bigger, better product, but by the time it appeared the USA, France and the USSR had stolen a march on the UK, from which it never quite recovered.

SPECIFICATIONS

CREW:	7 and 36 passengers
POWERPLANT:	four 22.3kN (5013lb) thrust de Havilland Ghost 50-Mk1 turbojets
CRUISING SPEED:	724km/h (450mph)
SPAN:	35m (114ft 10in)
LENGTH:	34m (111ft 6in)
HEIGHT:	9.1m (29ft 6in)
WEIGHT:	73,482kg (162,000lb)

Left: Knowledge of metal fatigue and the effects of repeated pressurization on airframes was limited when the Comet was built. The findings of the investigation improved the design of future aircraft.

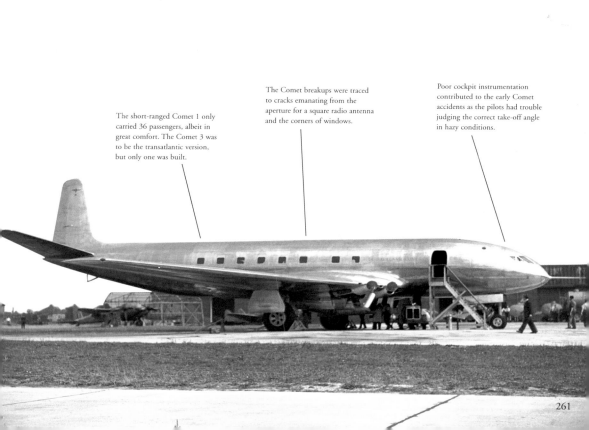

The short-ranged Comet 1 only carried 36 passengers, albeit in great comfort. The Comet 3 was to be the transatlantic version, but only one was built.

The Comet breakups were traced to cracks emanating from the aperture for a square radio antenna and the corners of windows.

Poor cockpit instrumentation contributed to the early Comet accidents as the pilots had trouble judging the correct take-off angle in hazy conditions.

DE HAVILLAND D.H.91 ALBATROSS (1937)

Originally built as a fast mailplane for the transatlantic run, the beautiful Albatross was beset with structural and mechanical problems and just plain bad luck. The wooden monocoque fuselage tapered smoothly to the tail, but it wasn't very strong. On the second aircraft's third landing the rear fuselage broke in two. The Albatros's landing gear gave endless problems – not lowering, collapsing and suffering brake failures. Two mailplanes and five airliners for Imperial Airways were built. The former were impressed into RAF service in 1940 for use on the Iceland run. Both were written off after landing accidents. Fires, accidents and enemy action befell the Imperial aircraft. The final two D.H.91s were scrapped in 1943, it having been discovered that the spars had rotted.

SPECIFICATIONS

CREW:	4
POWERPLANT:	four 391kW (525hp) de Havilland Gypsy 12 piston engines
MAX SPEED:	362km/h (225mph)
SPAN:	32.00m (105ft)
LENGTH:	21.79m (71ft 6in)
HEIGHT:	6.78m (22ft 8in)
WEIGHT:	maximum 13,381kg (29,500lb)

Left: The shapely lines of the Albatross concealed serious structural weaknesses. Only seven were built, one of the lowest totals of any de Havilland production aircraft.

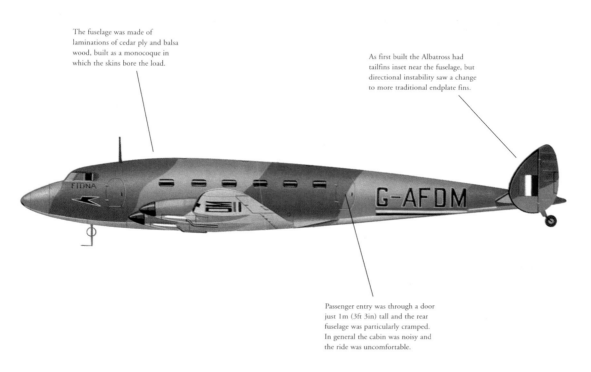

The fuselage was made of laminations of cedar ply and balsa wood, built as a monocoque in which the skins bore the load.

As first built the Albatross had tailfins inset near the fuselage, but directional instability saw a change to more traditional endplate fins.

Passenger entry was through a door just 1m (3ft 3in) tall and the rear fuselage was particularly cramped. In general the cabin was noisy and the ride was uncomfortable.

FOCKE-WULF FW 200 CONDOR (1937)

Gaining the reputation as the 'scourge of the Atlantic' when it appeared, the Condor maritime patrol bomber was an overloaded lash-up of a long-range airliner design. Designed to operate at weights and stresses expected in civil transport use, the design was not up to pulling *g* and carrying bombs, guns and armour. More than half of the aircraft delivered in 1940 suffered structural failure. In particular, the rear fuselage was weak and prone to fracture.

By the time the improved models entered service in 1941, they faced greatly improved convoy defences, including ship-based fighters and well-armed patrol aircraft like Sunderlands and Liberators. Serviceability fell and many aircraft were called away to the Eastern Front where they were used as transports for the supply of encircled Stalingrad, a role to which they were poorly suited.

SPECIFICATIONS (200C-3/U4)

CREW:	7
POWERPLANT:	four 895kW (1200hp) BMW-Bramo 323R-2 Fafnir piston engines
MAX SPEED:	360km/h (224mph)
SPAN:	32.85m (107ft 9in)
LENGTH:	23.45m (76ft 11in)
HEIGHT:	6.30m (20ft 8in)
WEIGHT:	maximum 24,520kg (50,057lb)

Left: A sight common on the Luftwaffe airfields along the Bay of Biscay was that of a Condor that had literally 'cracked up' on landing when its weak rear fuselage was overstressed.

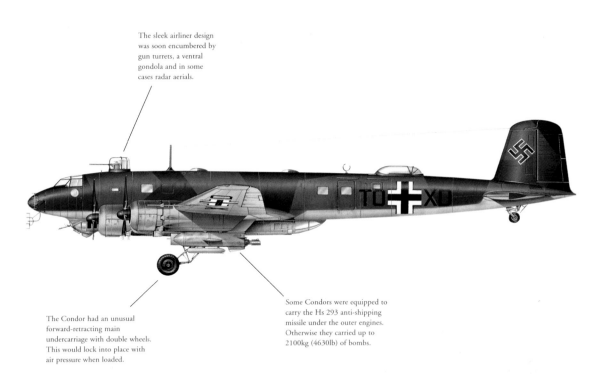

The sleek airliner design was soon encumbered by gun turrets, a ventral gondola and in some cases radar aerials.

The Condor had an unusual forward-retracting main undercarriage with double wheels. This would lock into place with air pressure when loaded.

Some Condors were equipped to carry the Hs 293 anti-shipping missile under the outer engines. Otherwise they carried up to 2100kg (4630lb) of bombs.

KALININ K-7 *(1933)*

Designed by World War I aviator Konstantin Kalinin with a wingspan greater than a B-52's and a much greater wing area, the K-7 was one of the biggest aircraft built before the jet age. It was only one engine short of the B-52 as well, having the curious arrangement of six pulling on the wing leading edge and one pushing at the rear.

The K-7's very brief first flight showed up instability and serious vibration caused by the airframe resonating with the engine frequency. The solution to this 'flutter' was thought to be to shorten and strengthen the tail booms, little being known then about the natural frequencies of structures and their response to vibration. On the 11th flight, during a speed test, the port tailboom vibrated, fractured, jammed the elevator and caused the giant aircraft to plough into the ground, killing 15.

Undaunted by this disaster, Kalinin's team began construction of two further K-7s in a new factory, but the vicissitudes of Stalin's Russia saw the project abandoned, and in 1938 the arrest and execution of Kalinin on trumped up espionage and sabotage charges.

SPECIFICATIONS

CREW:	19
POWERPLANT:	seven 560kW (750hp) Mikulin AM-34 inline piston engines
MAX SPEED:	234km/h (145mph)
SPAN:	53.00m (173ft 10in)
LENGTH:	28.00m (91ft 9in)
HEIGHT:	unknown
WEIGHT:	40,000kg (88,185lb)

Left: The monster (in every sense) K-7 was planned in several versions, including a luxurious VIP transport, a bomber and a military transport able to lift up to 112 paratroopers and cargo or even a light tank suspended between the landing gear sponsons.

The K-7 was one of the first metal aircraft with a twin-boom layout.

As originally designed the K-7 was to have engines in the undercarriage sponsons. As completed the bomber had gun positions, the bomb load and an internal staircase as well as two large wheels in each massive sponson.

The K-7's control surfaces were all deflected by the use of large trim tab surfaces mounted on struts.

The K-7 was said to have had a pilot, 18 crew members and one passenger when it crashed, killing all but five crew. It is not clear what they all did, but no doubt tending to the engines was a full-time task.

PZL LWS.6 ZUBR *(1936)*

Built as a low-risk back-up to the advanced PZL P.37 Los, the LWS Zubr (Bison) bomber had its origin in a design for an airliner that the Polish national airline had rejected as too old-fashioned. Unlike the all-metal Los, the Zubr was built of all sorts of materials. As production began, engines were changed from 336kW (450hp) Twin Wasps to 507kW (680hp) Bristol Pegasuses, which caused different stresses on the airframe. Many weaknesses soon became apparent and cracks were dealt with by fixing on wooden patches. Inevitably the prototype fell apart, unfortunately while carrying prospective Romanian purchasers.

The 'improved' LWS.6 with the same engines and a twin tail weighed more because of its extra strengthening – so much more that they were unable to carry bombs. The Luftwaffe put the survivors into use as unarmed trainers.

SPECIFICATIONS (LWS.6)

CREW:	4
POWERPLANT:	two 507kW (680hp) Bristol Pegasus VIII piston engines
MAX SPEED:	380km/h (236mph)
SPAN:	18.52m (60ft 9in)
LENGTH:	15.39m (50ft 6in)
HEIGHT:	4.00m (13ft)
WEIGHT:	maximum 6865kg (15,135lb)

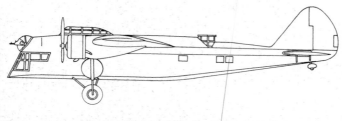

Left: The real failing of the hideous Zubr was under its skin, with its 'multiple media' construction and inadequate stressing. Several basic but serious mathematical errors meant that it was dangerously weak, especially where it was glued together.

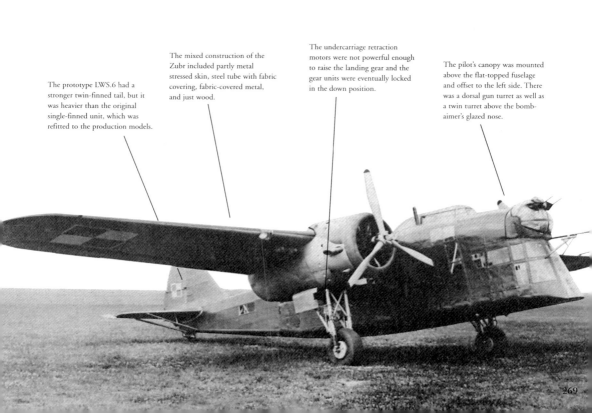

The prototype LWS.6 had a stronger twin-finned tail, but it was heavier than the original single-finned unit, which was refitted to the production models.

The mixed construction of the Zubr included partly metal stressed skin, steel tube with fabric covering, fabric-covered metal, and just wood.

The undercarriage retraction motors were not powerful enough to raise the landing gear and the gear units were eventually locked in the down position.

The pilot's canopy was mounted above the flat-topped fuselage and offset to the left side. There was a dorsal gun turret as well as a twin turret above the bomb-aimer's glazed nose.

LANGLEY AERODROME (1903)

Afghter success with various unmanned rubber, steam and petrol-powered model aircraft, US inventor Samuel Pierpont Langley progressed to a full-size man-carrying machine he called the 'Aerodrome'. Feeling it was safer to fly over water, Langley spent half the project cost (supplied by the War Department) on a houseboat fitted with a catapult launcher. He assembled his Aerodrome on the roof.

His first attempt ended in collapse when the catapult force overstressed the airframe. On 8 December 1903 he tried again. The Aerodrome broke up and fell in the Potomac River. Nine days later the Wright Brothers flew at Kitty Hawk. As secretary of the Smithsonian Institution, Langley did all he could to promote his achievements and belittle the Wrights', leading to a long-lasting feud.

SPECIFICATIONS
(Aerodrome A)

CREW:	1
POWERPLANT:	one 38.8kW (52hp) Manly radial piston engine
MAX SPEED:	(estimated) 100km/h (60mph)
SPAN:	14.60m (48ft)
LENGTH:	16.00m (52ft 5in)
HEIGHT:	3.50m (11ft 4in)
WEIGHT:	loaded 340kg (750lb)

Left: On its two flight attempts, Langley's aircraft (properly called the 'Aerodrome A') proved too weak for the stresses of launch or flight and fell into the Potomac, nearly killing pilot and engine-builder Charles Manly.

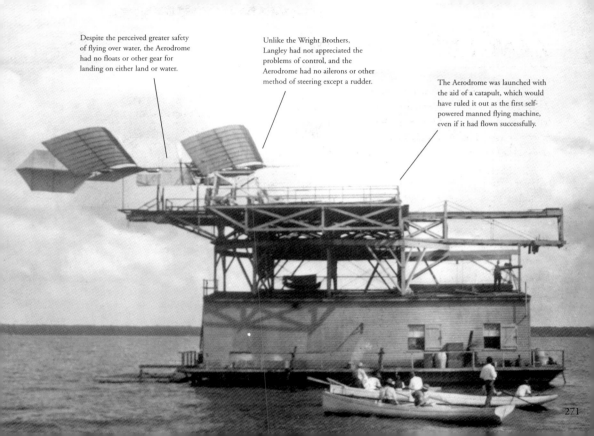

Despite the perceived greater safety of flying over water, the Aerodrome had no floats or other gear for landing on either land or water.

Unlike the Wright Brothers, Langley had not appreciated the problems of control, and the Aerodrome had no ailerons or other method of steering except a rudder.

The Aerodrome was launched with the aid of a catapult, which would have ruled it out as the first self-powered manned flying machine, even if it had flown successfully.

PHILLIPS MULTIPLANES (1893–1907)

B ritish inventor Horatio Phillips advanced the science of aerodynamics in the 1880s with his careful study of airfoil surfaces. Unfortunately, in his aerial experiments he concentrated on airfoils – as many as possible, it would seem – to the exclusion of pretty much everything else. From 1893 he produced a variety of 'multiplanes', beginning with a 50-wing coal-fired machine that predictably failed to become airborne. The slightly more conventional (20-wing) 1904 Multiplane actually achieved one hop of 15m (50ft), but in 1907 he returned to a version of the 1893 machine with a petrol engine. Some sources say this made a straight-line flight of 152m (500ft), which would have been the first powered flight in Britain. If so, it didn't inspire Phillips to greater heights, as he gave up at this point, having spent £4000, mainly on wings.

SPECIFICATIONS (1904)

CREW:	1
POWERPLANT:	one 16.4kW (22hp) Phillips piston engine
MAX SPEED:	(estimated) 55km/h (34mph)
SPAN:	unknown
LENGTH:	4.20m (13ft 9in)
HEIGHT:	3.10m (10ft)
WEIGHT:	272kg (600lb)

Left: Looking like a set of venetian blinds on wheels, this is just one of Horiatio Phillips' designs, none of which achieved true controlled flight.

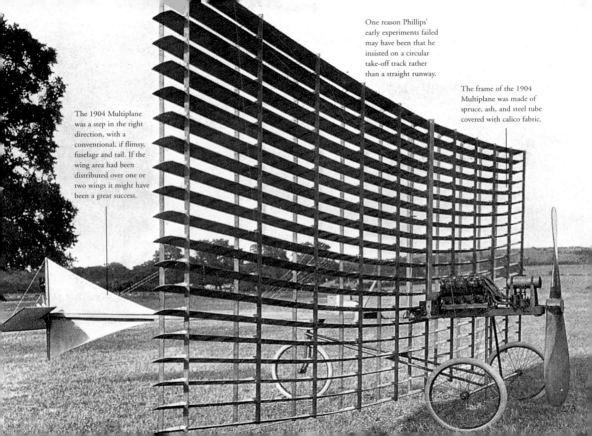

The 1904 Multiplane was a step in the right direction, with a conventional, if flimsy, fuselage and tail. If the wing area had been distributed over one or two wings it might have been a great success.

One reason Phillips' early experiments failed may have been that he insisted on a circular take-off track rather than a straight runway.

The frame of the 1904 Multiplane was made of spruce, ash, and steel tube covered with calico fabric.

273

ROYAL AIRCRAFT FACTORY RE.8 *(1916)*

Astately and stable observation and photo-reconnaissance platform, the RAF RE.8 was designed to replace the slow and vulnerable BE.2 with an aircraft of superior performance and armament. The actual improvements were marginal, but at least the observer was now located in the seat with a view. The RE.8 rarely achieved anything like its stated top speed. The difference between the actual combat speed and the stalling speed was only about 32km/h (20mph). Manoeuvres had to be made carefully so as not to fall into a deadly spin. The high stalling speed also made landings difficult and dangerous. The armament was useless for either offence or defence. RE.8s fell in great numbers to German fighters. Manfred von Richthofen, the 'Red Baron', shot down seven of them, but didn't regard them as much sport.

SPECIFICATIONS

CREW:	2
POWERPLANT:	one 112kW (150hp) Royal Aircraft Factory 4a inline piston engine
MAX SPEED:	166km/h (103mph)
SPAN:	12.98m (42ft 7in)
LENGTH:	8.50m (27ft 11in)
HEIGHT:	3.47m (11ft 5in)
WEIGHT:	loaded 1215kg (2678lb)

Left: Nicknamed the 'Harry Tate' after a popular music hall comedian, aircrews found flying the RE.8 anything but amusing. Despite their pedestrian performance and vulnerability, over 4000 were built.

The RE.8 had a forward-firing machine gun set at an angle so the pilot could fire it, but where the bullets would miss the propeller. This made hitting an opponent almost impossible.

At least on early model RE.8s the observer could not turn around in his seat or fire the rear gun from a standing position, so he had to somehow aim and fire it over his shoulder.

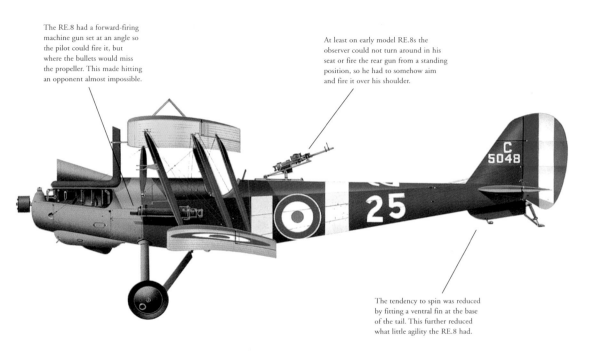

The tendency to spin was reduced by fitting a ventral fin at the base of the tail. This further reduced what little agility the RE.8 had.

SEDDON MAYFLY *(1910)*

In 1908 Lieutenant John W. Seddon of the Royal Navy was inspired by a flying paper model to design a giant tandem biplane, with which he hoped to win a £10,000 prize for the first Manchester to London flight. Convinced that hoops of high-tensile steel tube were much more efficient than conventional wood and wire bracing, he persuaded the Navy to give him leave to work on his project and his mother largely to pay for it. The aircraft, named optimistically (and prophetically) the 'Mayfly', was built in a bicycle factory and used up 610m (2000ft) of steel tubing. On its only high-speed run, a wheel collapsed and the aircraft was damaged. Repairs and modifications were hampered by Seddon's return to duty and the Mayfly never did fly, eventually being dismantled by souvenir hunters.

SPECIFICATIONS

CREW:	1 and 5 passengers
POWERPLANT:	two 48kW (65hp) NEC six-cylinder water-cooled piston engines
MAX SPEED:	unknown
SPAN:	circa 15.20m (50ft)
LENGTH:	circa 15.20m (50ft)
HEIGHT:	unknown
WEIGHT:	loaded 1180kg (2600lb)

Left: The giant Mayfly was an aeronautical dead end. It pioneered a new form of construction, which no one else saw fit to take up, and failed to leave the ground.

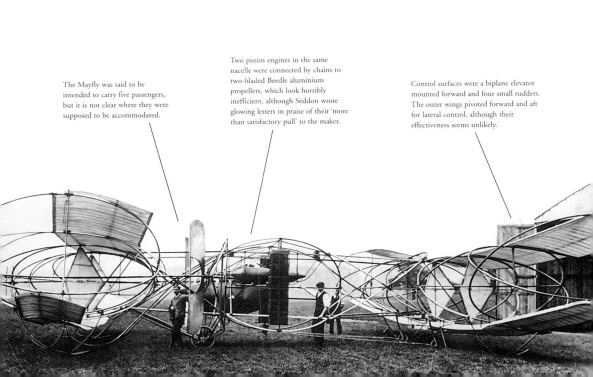

The Mayfly was said to be intended to carry five passengers, but it is not clear where they were supposed to be accommodated.

Two piston engines in the same nacelle were connected by chains to two-bladed Beedle aluminium propellers, which look horribly inefficient, although Seddon wrote glowing letters in praise of their 'more than satisfactory pull' to the maker.

Control surfaces were a biplane elevator mounted forward and four small rudders. The outer wings pivoted forward and aft for lateral control, although their effectiveness seems unlikely.

UNINTENTIONALLY UNSTABLE

Today computers keep the current generation of combat aircraft on the straight and level or under control at the very limits of their physical flight envelopes. Without computerized systems they will not remain in control (or one piece) for a moment. This is often called relaxed stability. Earlier generations of aircraft had examples of this too, but normally unintentionally.

This section contains three World War 1 biplanes that had trouble taking off. Two of these (the De Bruyère C 1 and Tarrant Tabor) were so unstable in pitch or top-heavy that they tipped over on their maiden flight attempts. The Lohner Type AA was so close-coupled that it was impossible to keep straight at take-off speeds – this was a problem even when aerodromes were just big fields.

Instability in yaw (poor directional control) seems to have been the most common problem, particularly with production aircraft, but unwanted pitch movement was more likely to be dangerous, or downright deadly. The Flying Flea and Flying Bedstead shared something more than just similar names – it was terribly easy to tip both of them into a position from which they could not recover, with a crash the inevitable result.

Left: Without the benefit of the computerized control system used in the modern B-2 Spirit, the XB-35 was dangerously unstable.

AVIA S.199 'MULE' (1947)

After the war, Czechoslovakia's aircraft industry was left with a lot of uncompleted Messerschmitt Bf 109 airframes but no Daimler-Benz engines, and a lot of Junkers Jumo engines but no bomber airframes. These parts were combined into the Avia S.199. The bomber engine gave too much torque at high power, as when taking off, and combined with the narrow undercarriage, this meant many accidents. The bigger engine made the S.199 nose heavy, which was a particularly bad way to be during landing. Due to its awful handling characteristics and mismatched parentage, the S.199 was nicknamed the Mezek ('Mule'). Desperate for any sort of fighter, Israel bought 25 in 1948. Although a valuable morale booster, the S.199s were as dangerous to IAF pilots as to the enemy, and three-quarters were written off within a year.

SPECIFICATIONS

CREW:	1
POWERPLANT:	one 1007kW (1350hp) Junkers Jumo 211F inline piston engine
MAX SPEED:	528km/h (328mph)
SPAN:	9.92m (32ft 7in)
LENGTH:	8.94m (29ft 4in)
HEIGHT:	2.59m (8ft 6in)
WEIGHT:	loaded 3736kg (8236lb)

Left: Like the offspring of a donkey and a horse, the Avia 'Mule' proved hard to handle. Many Israeli pilots, even some of the most experienced ones, were killed or injured in operational accidents.

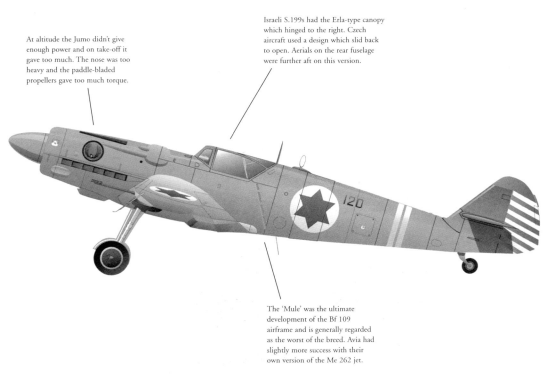

At altitude the Jumo didn't give enough power and on take-off it gave too much. The nose was too heavy and the paddle-bladed propellers gave too much torque.

Israeli S.199s had the Erla-type canopy which hinged to the right. Czech aircraft used a design which slid back to open. Aerials on the rear fuselage were further aft on this version.

The 'Mule' was the ultimate development of the Bf 109 airframe and is generally regarded as the worst of the breed. Avia had slightly more success with their own version of the Me 262 jet.

BLACKBURN FIREBRAND (1942)

Begun as a shipboard interceptor, the Firebrand evolved through different engine fits and several unusable versions into a 'torpedo-fighter'. First flown in 1942, the first marks were too late for World War II and the late ones were unsuitable for Korea. Huge and anything but agile, it was said that the Firebrand was built like a battleship but didn't fly as well. Poor aileron response at low speed and a tendency to float on landing, combined with a terrible view over the nose made the Firebrand a particularly poor carrier-based aircraft, which suffered many landing accidents. The concept of such a specialized aircraft as a high-speed torpedo-bomber was an anachronism in the age of jets and versatile piston-engined aircraft like the Skyraider, and the Firebrand saw little useful service.

SPECIFICATIONS
(Firebrand TF Mk III)

CREW:	1
POWERPLANT:	one 1790kW (2400hp) Bristol Centaurus VII radial piston engine
MAX SPEED:	513km/h (319mph)
SPAN:	15.60m (51ft 4in)
LENGTH:	11.45m (37ft 7in)
HEIGHT:	4.04m (13ft 3in)
WEIGHT:	7152kg (15,753lb)

Left: The specialized Firebrand torpedo-fighter took a long time to get right. Some models never saw service and were delivered straight to storage or ground schools.

The Firebrand had an additional airspeed indicator mounted externally so the pilot could fly the landing approach without having to look into the cockpit.

To compensate for the torque of the Centaurus engine, the later marks had a grotesquely enlarged tail fin. Powered ailerons on the final version also helped.

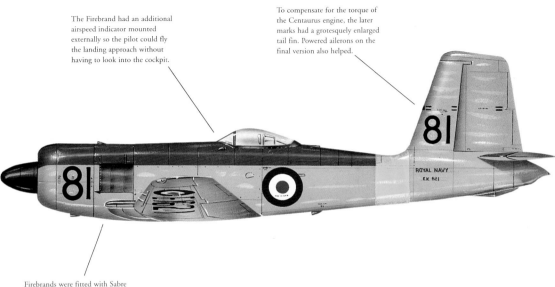

Firebrands were fitted with Sabre inline and Centaurus radial engines. The final TF Mk 5A version was cured of most of the type's fixable faults, but saw limited service.

CURTISS SB2C HELLDIVER (1940)

A successor to the ageing but worthy SBD Dauntless dive-bomber, the Helldiver was built in large numbers but never totally supplanted the 'Slow But Deadly'. Huge orders were made even before the first flight of the XSB2C-1 prototype, which exhibited poor handling and stability and very poor stall characteristics. The prototype crashed but was rebuilt, achieving the feat of having many changes but little visible difference before it crashed again. Sensibly the Royal Navy rejected the Helldiver, but the US committed to mass production from three factories. Production models proved in some ways worse than the prototype and inferior in many to the Dauntless. By 1944 it was in action in the Pacific, suffering many inflight break-ups and deck landing accidents, although slowly proving its worth as a bomber. It had to, as the staggering total of over 7100 were built, making it the most numerous dive-bomber ever.

SPECIFICATIONS

CREW:	2
POWERPLANT:	one 1417kW (1900hp) Wright R-2800-20 Cyclone radial engine
MAX SPEED:	472km/h (293mph)
SPAN:	15.14m (49ft 9in)
LENGTH:	11.18m (36ft 8in)
HEIGHT:	4.49m (14ft 9in)
WEIGHT:	maximum 7598kg (16,750lb)

Left: Affected by a very rigid specification, a weak structure and poor stability, the Helldiver was extremely unpopular with all but the most experienced pilots.

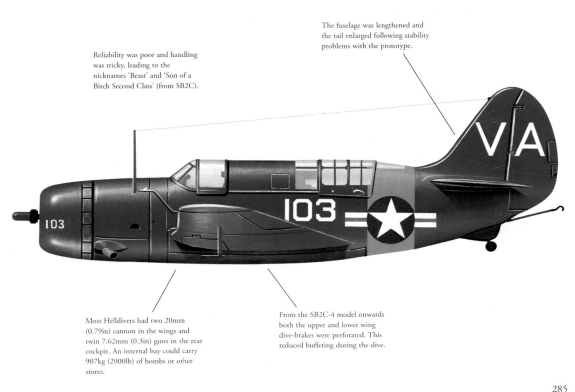

The fuselage was lengthened and the tail enlarged following stability problems with the prototype.

Reliability was poor and handling was tricky, leading to the nicknames 'Beast' and 'Son of a Bitch Second Class' (from SB2C).

Most Helldivers had two 20mm (0.79in) cannon in the wings and twin 7.62mm (0.3in) guns in the rear cockpit. An internal bay could carry 907kg (2000lb) of bombs or other stores.

From the SB2C-4 model onwards both the upper and lower wing dive-brakes were perforated. This reduced buffeting during the dive.

CURTISS SO3C SEAMEW (1939)

Dating from a 1937 proposal to replace Curtiss' own SOC Seagull biplane in the ship-based observation role, the SO3C had all the outward appearance of modernity and efficiency but proved a huge failure, most being withdrawn and replaced by their predecessor.

Right from the outset, the SO3C was unpleasant to fly. To cure its instability various measures were tried, including a ventral fin (rejected in favour of a bigger dorsal fin) and upturned wingtips. The landplane version had unusually tall and narrow track landing gear and a steep ground angle, which made take-off and landing very tricky. The SOC3C was named Seamew by the Royal Navy, who ordered 250 but received 100 and used a few of them only for training. One use they found for the Seamews was as radio-controlled target drones to be shot down by ships' gunners.

SPECIFICATIONS
(SOC3C-2 floatplane)

CREW:	2
POWERPLANT:	one 447kW (600hp) Ranger SGV-770-8 inline piston engine
MAX SPEED:	277km/h (172mph)
SPAN:	11.58m (38ft)
LENGTH:	11.23m (36ft 10in)
HEIGHT:	4.57m (15ft)
WEIGHT:	maximum 2599kg (5729lb)

Left: Despite its inadequacies, nearly 800 examples of Curtiss'
disappointing Seamew were delivered to the US, UK and Canada. Crews
and ship's captains almost all preferred the SOC biplane and many of these earlier
aircraft were brought out of storage to replace the unstable, unreliable Seamews.

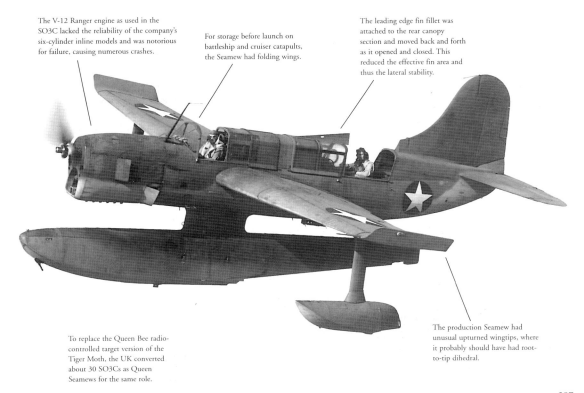

The V-12 Ranger engine as used in the SO3C lacked the reliability of the company's six-cylinder inline models and was notorious for failure, causing numerous crashes.

For storage before launch on battleship and cruiser catapults, the Seamew had folding wings.

The leading edge fin fillet was attached to the rear canopy section and moved back and forth as it opened and closed. This reduced the effective fin area and thus the lateral stability.

To replace the Queen Bee radio-controlled target version of the Tiger Moth, the UK converted about 30 SO3Cs as Queen Seamews for the same role.

The production Seamew had unusual upturned wingtips, where it probably should have had root-to-tip dihedral.

CURTISS XP-55 ASCENDER (1943)

Resulting, like the Vultee XP-54 and Northrop XP-56, from a 1940 competition for 'unconventional' fighter designs, the XP-55 was built with a pusher prop, highly swept wings and a canard foreplane. Named 'Ascender' by Curtiss, this title was often corrupted to 'Ass-ender' due to its backwards-facing appearance. Designed around the Pratt & Whitney X-1800 engine, the cancellation of this project led to the fitting of a standard Allison V-1710. Not surprisingly for such an unusual configuration, the XP-55 suffered stability problems, and all flying surfaces were enlarged at one time or another in an attempt to cure these. Until the canard foreplane was modified the XP-55 showed a marked reluctance to leave the ground at all. Four Ascenders were built, of which two crashed, killing one of the pilots and an unfortunate passerby.

SPECIFICATIONS

CREW:	1
POWERPLANT:	one 1100kW (1475hp) Allison V-1710-95 piston engine
MAX SPEED:	628km/h (390mph)
SPAN:	13.42m (44ft 1in)
LENGTH:	9.02m (29ft 7in)
HEIGHT:	3.07m (10ft 1in)
WEIGHT:	3325kg (7300lb)

Left: Despite its radical looks, the Ascender's performance figures were little better than a conventional aircraft of the same size, and tests showed they were lower than the manufacturer's estimates. The official report declared that the Ascender was 'not desirable as a combat aircraft'.

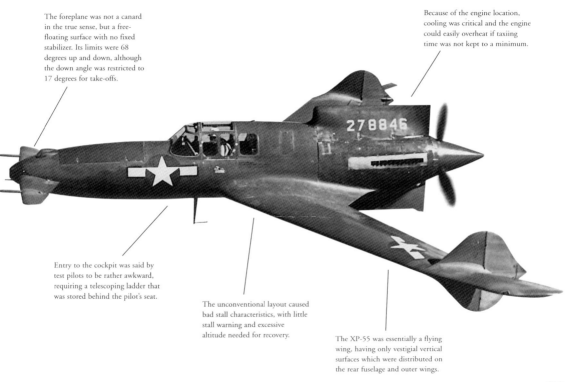

The foreplane was not a canard in the true sense, but a free-floating surface with no fixed stabilizer. Its limits were 68 degrees up and down, although the down angle was restricted to 17 degrees for take-offs.

Because of the engine location, cooling was critical and the engine could easily overheat if taxiing time was not kept to a minimum.

278846

Entry to the cockpit was said by test pilots to be rather awkward, requiring a telescoping ladder that was stored behind the pilot's seat.

The unconventional layout caused bad stall characteristics, with little stall warning and excessive altitude needed for recovery.

The XP-55 was essentially a flying wing, having only vestigial vertical surfaces which were distributed on the rear fuselage and outer wings.

DE BRUYÈRE C 1 *(1917)*

One of the most unorthodox (and obscure) fighter aircraft ever, the C 1 was in some ways ahead of its time, but joined the select band of aircraft to never complete its first flight. Designed by a French engineer called de Bruyère, the C 1 was of pusher configuration, with a long streamlined rear fuselage. The main part of the body was of metal construction and the single nosewheel was semi-recessed in the nose, which was intended to carry a heavy short-barrel Hotchkiss 37mm (1.5in) gun, for which a field of fire unimpeded by a propeller was essential. The one report of its first flight states that it started its run, gathered speed, became airborne and crashed to earth on its back. After that, nothing was heard again of the C 1 or its designer.

SPECIFICATIONS

CREW:	1
POWERPLANT:	probably one 112kW (150hp) Hispano-Suiza 8Aa inline piston engine
MAX SPEED:	unknown
SPAN:	unknown
LENGTH:	unknown
HEIGHT:	unknown
WEIGHT:	unknown

Left: Not only did it appear to be built backwards, but the C 1 wound up upside-down after only seconds of flight.

The C 1 used V struts like those of the Albatros D.III, but characteristically the wrong way round. It is possible that flexing of the upper wing contributed to the crash.

The large ventral fin and tailskid must have scraped the ground early in the take-off run, restricting the angle of attack and thus the lifting ability.

The propeller was driven by an extension shaft from the mid-mounted engine. The strength of this shaft would have been questionable given the technology of the time.

GEE BEE RACERS (1913–1933)

The five Granville Brothers of Springfield, Massachusetts became famous with their high-powered Gee Bee racing planes of the 1920s and 30s. The planes themselves became notorious for crashing, and some developed a reputation as 'unflyable'. The Model Z won several races, but during a record attempt a wing folded up on one Model Z and it crashed fatally. The barrel-like R-1 and R-2 were essentially the largest available engine with the smallest possible airframes behind them. Someone said a Gee Bee was 'a section of sewer pipe which had sprouted stubby wings'. In general the Gee Bees were shorter than their wingspans, made very fast landings and were extremely tricky for all but the most experienced pilots to fly. The Model Rs suffered several crashes. The R-2 killed its pilot and was rebuilt and crashed again not once but twice. Combined with parts of the R-1, the hybrid aircraft crashed fatally on its first test flight.

SPECIFICATIONS
(Model R-1)

CREW:	1
POWERPLANT:	one 544kW (730hp) Pratt & Whitney Wasp T3D1 radial piston engine
MAX SPEED:	476km/h (296mph)
SPAN:	7.62m (25ft)
LENGTH:	5.33m (17ft 6in)
HEIGHT:	unknown
WEIGHT:	loaded 1395kg (3075lb)

Left: During the Depression era air racing was hugely popular. The public got their share of thrills and spills from the Gee Bee racers. They were extremely successful in the right hands, but have not shaken off a reputation as 'death traps'.

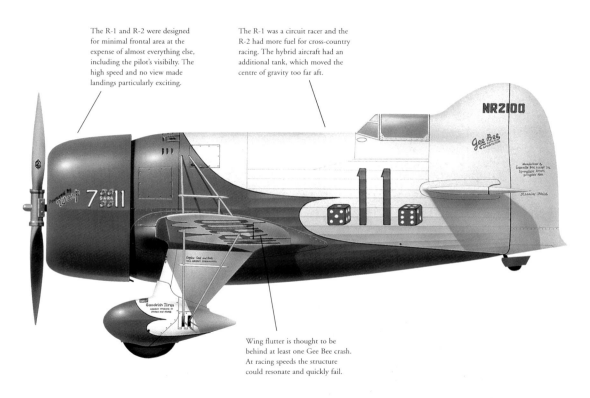

The R-1 and R-2 were designed for minimal frontal area at the expense of almost everything else, including the pilot's visibilty. The high speed and no view made landings particularly exciting.

The R-1 was a circuit racer and the R-2 had more fuel for cross-country racing. The hybrid aircraft had an additional tank, which moved the centre of gravity too far aft.

Wing flutter is thought to be behind at least one Gee Bee crash. At racing speeds the structure could resonate and quickly fail.

GRUMMAN XF10F JAGUAR (1952)

In 40 years of fighter development from the FF biplane to the F-14 Tomcat, the only Grumman fighters not accepted by the US Navy were the XF5F-1 Skyrocket and the XF10F-1 Jaguar.

Created as a redesigned F9F Panther in 1948, the Jaguar evolved into a tubby aircraft sporting the first variable geometry or 'swing wings' to be used on any warplane. This, and its associated system of flaps and spoilers, proved far too complicated, but most of the trouble came from the tiny tailplane and the Jaguar proved almost impossible to keep in balanced flight.

Perhaps uniquely in the annals of naval aviation the cancellation effort was led by the Navy's project officer, usually the person most loyal to any project, whatever its faults. The flying Jaguar was used to test carrier deck crash barriers and the static test airframe became a target for tank guns.

SPECIFICATIONS

CREW:	1
POWERPLANT:	one 30.2kN (6800lb) thrust Westinghouse XJ40-W-8 turbojet
MAX SPEED:	1142km/h (710mph)
SPAN:	unswept spread 15.48m (50ft 7in); swept spread 11.19m (36ft 8in)
LENGTH:	16.46m (54ft)
HEIGHT:	4.95m (16ft 3in)
WEIGHT:	maximum 16,094kg (35,450lb)

Left: Resting on their laurels as the premier designer of US Navy fighters, Grumman achieved large orders for the Jaguar despite not having tested the swing-wing concept on a testbed. The Jaguar only made 32 flights, all of them eventful, before the programme was terminated.

Unlike the variable-geometry wings on later fighters, where only the outer panel moved, the whole wing on the XF10F 'translated', with a complex arrangement of moving panels to fill the gaps.

At maximum wing sweep the directional control was marginal, not helped by the ineffective rudder. The spoiler system was so complicated it was disconnected, leaving only tiny ailerons, which gave a very poor roll response.

At full sweep the wings were only 35 degrees and the performance gains were largely negated by the extra weight of the wing sweep mechanism.

The tailplane was operated by a novel arrangement where the pilot controlled a small delta-wing airfoil at the tip of the tail bullet. This in turn moved the main elevator. Unfortunately, a lag in the response between stick and surface usually resulted in a Pilot Induced Oscillation (PIO) and the Jaguar was virtually uncontrollable much of the time.

The Jaguar was another of those naval aircraft crippled by the Westinghouse J40 engine, which underwent its own development problems and never received the intended afterburner.

LAVOCHKIN LAGG-1 AND -3 *(1940)*

In 1938 the design bureau of Semyon Lavochkin, Vladimir Gorbunov and Mikhail Gudkov (LaGG) began work on a new fighter built of a type of plastic-impregnated wood. The smoothly polished prototype had reasonable speed but exhibited terrible handling, and poorer range, ceiling and manoeuvrability than promised. The roughly finished aircraft delivered to the frontline units were even worse, proving slower than the open-cockpit Polikarpov I-16 they replaced. There was no time for a redesign, so improvements were made progressively during production. The LaGG-3 was essentially the series production LaGG-1, but was still not right. Nicknamed the 'Mortician's Friend', pilots joked that LaGG stood for 'Lakirovannii Garantirovannii Grob' or 'varnished, guaranteed coffin'.

Without Gorbunov or Gudkov, Lavochkin went on to design the La-5FN and La-7, both very successful radial-engined fighters based on diminishing amounts of LaGG, and the all-new La-9 and -11.

SPECIFICATIONS (LaGG-1)

CREW:	1
POWERPLANT:	one 820kW (1100hp) Klimov M-105P piston engine
MAX SPEED:	600km/h (373mph)
SPAN:	9.80m (32ft 2in)
LENGTH:	8.81m (28ft 11in)
HEIGHT:	2.70m (8ft 10in)
WEIGHT:	loaded 3380kg (7451lb)

Left: The LaGG-1 was rushed into production with most of its bugs unfixed, a situation that worsened after the German invasion as Stalin demanded maximum output. The political environment of the time allowed no delays, so improvements were made piecemeal. In the hands of a few skilled pilots, the LaGGs achieved high scores before better fighters emerged.

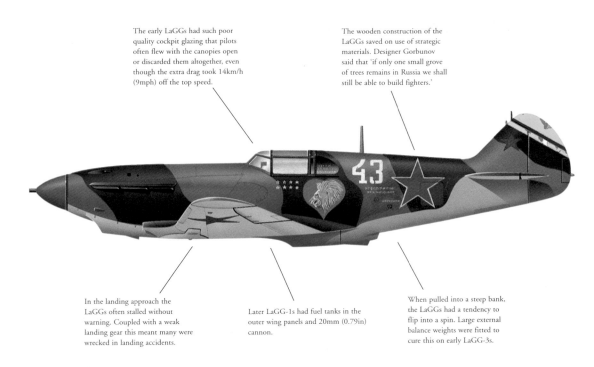

The early LaGGs had such poor quality cockpit glazing that pilots often flew with the canopies open or discarded them altogether, even though the extra drag took 14km/h (9mph) off the top speed.

The wooden construction of the LaGGs saved on use of strategic materials. Designer Gorbunov said that 'if only one small grove of trees remains in Russia we shall still be able to build fighters.'

In the landing approach the LaGGs often stalled without warning. Coupled with a weak landing gear this meant many were wrecked in landing accidents.

Later LaGG-1s had fuel tanks in the outer wing panels and 20mm (0.79in) cannon.

When pulled into a steep bank, the LaGGs had a tendency to flip into a spin. Large external balance weights were fitted to cure this on early LaGG-3s.

LAVOCHKIN LA-250 *(1956)*

The first Soviet aircraft designed as a 'weapons system' combining airframe, radar and missiles, the La-250 suffered from many setbacks and the whole package never quite came together.

In July 1956 the prototype La-250 joined the select ranks of aircraft that crashed on their maiden flight. The La-250's gyrations just after take-off, before it put down again and ran through a fence no doubt contributed to the nickname 'Anaconda' as much as its snake-like fuselage. Extensive ground testing determined the reason for the test pilot's loss of control and the design was revised. In November 1957 the second La-250 crashed on landing, the same fate that befell the third in September 1958. This aircraft was rebuilt and a partial test programme was conducted before the whole project was cancelled in 1959, not long before the death of S. Lavochkin and the dismantling of his design bureau. Once reorganized, it had more success with other missile projects.

SPECIFICATIONS

CREW:	2
POWERPLANT:	two 88.2kN (19,840lb) thrust Lyulka AL-7F afterburning turbojets
MAX SPEED:	2000km/h (1243mph)
SPAN:	13.90m (45ft 7in)
LENGTH:	25.60m (84ft)
HEIGHT:	unknown
WEIGHT:	loaded approximately 30,000kg (66,135lb)

Left: Long-established airframe builder Lavochkin was tasked with designing the missiles and integrating the radar on the huge La-250. The task proved beyond them.

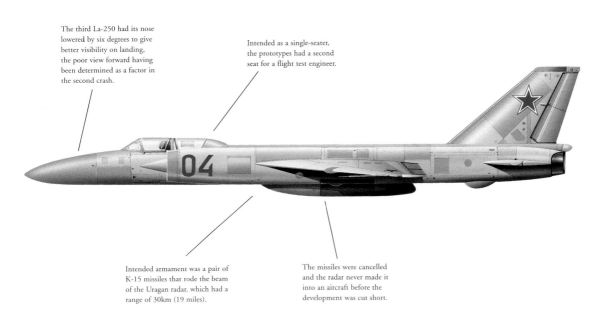

The third La-250 had its nose lowered by six degrees to give better visibility on landing, the poor view forward having been determined as a factor in the second crash.

Intended as a single-seater, the prototypes had a second seat for a flight test engineer.

Intended armament was a pair of K-15 missiles that rode the beam of the Uragan radar, which had a range of 30km (19 miles).

The missiles were cancelled and the radar never made it into an aircraft before the development was cut short.

LOHNER TYPE AA (1916)

In 1916 the Austro-Hungarian Lohner company offered four fighter prototypes for a German Air Service competition. Each confusingly was called the Typ (Type) AA, but was also known by a design number (10.20 or 111.03). The initial 10.20 was an extraordinary-looking slab-sided creation two-thirds as high as it was long. With a feeble rudder and large fuselage keel area, it should not have been a surprise that the 10.20 would not track straight on the ground. The rudder was enlarged several times before the first flight in December 1916. Even then the flight stability was poor and it was damaged in an accident. Rebuilt twice as the 10.20A, in its latter form it was of more or less normal proportions, but fell victim to a final accident in June 1917.

SPECIFICATIONS (10.20)

CREW:	1
POWERPLANT:	one 138kW (185hp) Austro-Daimler inline piston engine
MAX SPEED:	unknown
SPAN:	6.60m (21ft 8in)
LENGTH:	4.65m (15ft 3in)
HEIGHT:	3.05m (10ft)
WEIGHT:	unknown

Left: The Typ AA (10.20) looked like something out of a cartoon or a child's toy box. Even substantially modified it had unsatisfactory handling. Like all Lohner's other fighters it didn't progress past the prototype stage.

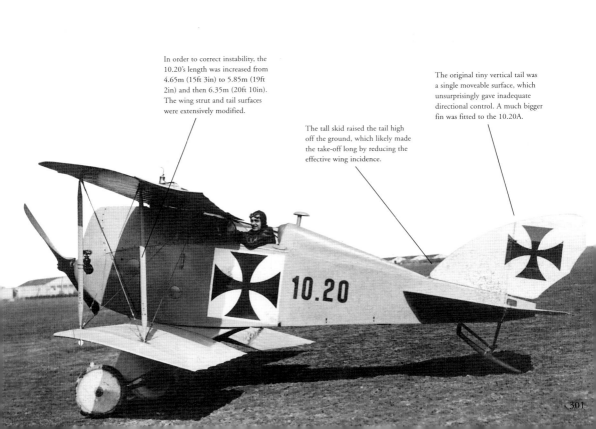

In order to correct instability, the 10.20's length was increased from 4.65m (15ft 3in) to 5.85m (19ft 2in) and then 6.35m (20ft 10in). The wing strut and tail surfaces were extensively modified.

The tall skid raised the tail high off the ground, which likely made the take-off long by reducing the effective wing incidence.

The original tiny vertical tail was a single moveable surface, which unsurprisingly gave inadequate directional control. A much bigger fin was fitted to the 10.20A.

10.20

MESSERSCHMITT ME 210 *(1939)*

The German Air Ministry made plans for a replacement for the Me 110 Zerstörer before the war, and parts were ordered for 1000 Me 210s even before the prototype flew in September 1939. It was then that things started to go wrong. The test pilot reported that the Me 210 prototype was unstable in yaw and pitch and he was lucky to bring it back in one piece. Subsequent test flights found more and more deficiencies. Changing from a twin tail layout to a single fin and lengthening the fuselage failed to cure the handling problems, which included a tendency to spin. There were an unprecedented 16 prototypes and 94 pre-production examples needed to sort out the many problems. Somehow almost every aircraft was found to have differing handling characteristics. Experienced Me 110 pilots suffered many crashes in the 210. Things got so bad that the programme was cancelled in early 1942 and the Me 110 put back into production.

SPECIFICATIONS

CREW:	2
POWERPLANT:	two 1040kW (1395hp) Daimler-Benz DB 601F liquid-cooled piston engines
MAX SPEED:	620km/h (385mph)
SPAN:	16.40m (53ft 8in)
LENGTH:	12.22m (40ft 3in)
HEIGHT:	4.30m (14ft 1in)
WEIGHT:	8100kg (17,857lb)

Left: The Me 210 was a rare failure for the Messerschmitt company. The company's founder was forced to resign over its deficiencies – which were largely rectified in the similar-looking Me 410. Tarnished by its predecessor's reputation, the 410 saw relatively little service.

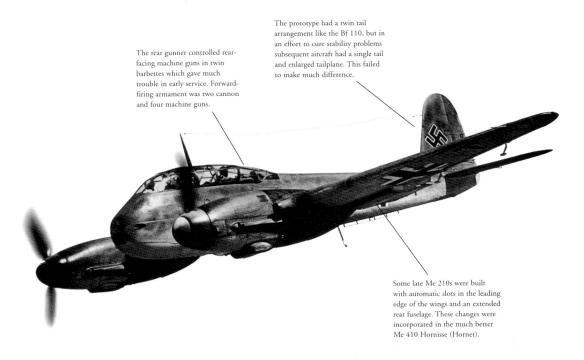

The rear gunner controlled rear-facing machine guns in twin barbettes which gave much trouble in early service. Forward-firing armament was two cannon and four machine guns.

The prototype had a twin tail arrangement like the Bf 110, but in an effort to cure stability problems subsequent aircraft had a single tail and enlarged tailplane. This failed to make much difference.

Some late Me 210s were built with automatic slots in the leading edge of the wings and an extended rear fuselage. These changes were incorporated in the much better Me 410 Hornisse (Hornet).

MIGNET FLYING FLEA *(1933)*

French inventor Henri Mignet created the first craze for home-built aircraft in 1933 when he flew his Pou de Ciel (Flying Flea, or less kindly, Sky Louse) and wrote a best-selling book on how anyone with the skills to make a packing case could build one and then teach himself to fly it. When the book was translated into English, a 'Flea Frenzy' started in many countries. In Britain in particular enthusiastic amateurs across the land started work on machines with a dozen engine types and a variety of wingspans. A series of fatal crashes in 1936 finally warranted a wind-tunnel investigation of the Flea, proving that if the nose was lowered below 15 degrees there was insufficient pitching moment to raise the nose and a crash was inevitable. The Flea was banned in 1939 and never quite regained its reputation.

SPECIFICATIONS (Typical)

CREW:	1
POWERPLANT:	one 22kW (30hp) Carden-Ford piston engine
MAX SPEED:	113km/h (70mph)
SPAN:	7.01m (23ft)
LENGTH:	4.01m (13ft)
HEIGHT:	1.68m (5ft 6in)
WEIGHT:	loaded 250kg (550lb)

Left: In the 1930s the Flying Flea threatened to bring aviation to the man in the street, possibly by falling on him. This is an improved model, built in the USA in the 1970s.

The main feature of the Flea was its tandem wing layout. If the wings were mounted too close together the controls could reverse when the main wing was at high incidence.

The Flea was controlled by a single lever, which moved the whole wing up and down and the rudder from side to side. There was no tailplane, no elevators and no ailerons.

The original Flea, and many of its successors, made use of commonly found components such as motorcycle engines and wheelbarrow wheels.

G-AEBB

NORTHROP B-35/B-49 FLYING WINGS *(1946)*

Although the B-35 was ordered as early as 1941, it was obvious by 1944 that the flying-wing bomber was going to miss World War II and would then be obsolescent. In preparation for the next war, a jet-powered version was begun. The piston-engined XB-35 flew in June 1946, and the jet YB-49 in October 1947. The YB-35 initially had contra-rotating propellers, and had endless trouble with the gearboxes and unwanted yaw, much delaying the programme. The YB-49 performed well, but during pull-out tests the No.2 aircraft tumbled backwards and the outer wings fell off. Edwards Air Force Base was named after the unfortunate test pilot.

All sorts of versions were planned for bombing, reconnaissance and electronic intelligence, but while about a dozen aircraft were under completion, the whole project was cancelled and all were scrapped.

SPECIFICATIONS (XB-35)

CREW:	9
POWERPLANT:	four 2238kW (3000hp) Pratt & Whitney R-4360 radials
MAX SPEED:	629km/h (391mph)
SPAN:	52.42m (172ft)
LENGTH:	16.32m (53ft 1in)
HEIGHT:	6.16m (20ft)
WEIGHT:	81,647kg (180,000lb)

Left: The B-35 (pictured) and B-49 lost out to the more conventional Convair B-36, and the world had to wait until the 1990s for the first flying-wing bomber, the Northrop B-2, to enter service.

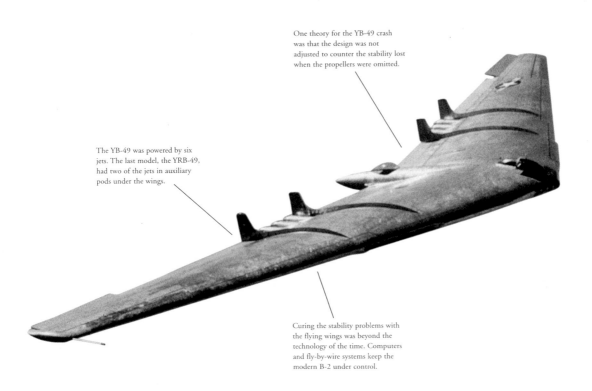

One theory for the YB-49 crash was that the design was not adjusted to counter the stability lost when the propellers were omitted.

The YB-49 was powered by six jets. The last model, the YRB-49, had two of the jets in auxiliary pods under the wings.

Curing the stability problems with the flying wings was beyond the technology of the time. Computers and fly-by-wire systems keep the modern B-2 under control.

NORTHROP XP-56 BLACK BULLET (1943)

For reasons that remain obscure, the Northrop XP-56 (first prototype natural metal, second olive drab) was nicknamed the 'Black Bullet'. It certainly resembled a bullet but lacked the projectile's speed or direction.

The first prototype had no vertical fin, and relied on its underfin more to protect the propeller than to provide stability. This arrangment, of course, was inadequate. Nose heaviness was corrected but became tail heaviness. During a fast taxi run the aircraft blew a tyre, somersaulted and threw test pilot John Myers out. He was saved by his polo helmet and the second prototype was fitted with an upper fin. With a 1492kW (2000hp) engine, one thing the XP-56 was not was underpowered, but it proved slower than expected. The intended X-1800 water-cooled engine had been cancelled and the substituted air-cooled radial was not the most suitable for a pusher layout. Fuel consumption was excessive and while waiting to conduct wind tunnel tests, the project was cancelled.

SPECIFICATIONS

CREW:	1
POWERPLANT:	one 1492kW (2000hp) Pratt & Whitney R-2800-29 radial piston engine
MAX SPEED:	748km/h (465mph)
SPAN:	12.95m (42ft 6in)
LENGTH:	8.38m (27ft 6in)
HEIGHT:	3.35m (11ft)
WEIGHT:	maximum 5509kg (12,145lb)

Left: In original form, the XP-56 was one of a long and diverse series of Northrop flying wings. Modifications to achieve stability made it a slightly more conventional aircraft, but not a viable fighter within the army's budget deadlines.

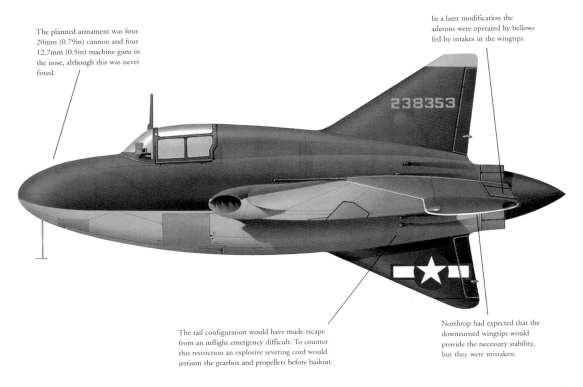

The planned armament was four 20mm (0.79in) cannon and four 12.7mm (0.5in) machine guns in the nose, although this was never fitted.

In a later modification the ailerons were operated by bellows fed by intakes in the wingtips.

238353

The tail configuration would have made escape from an inflight emergency difficult. To counter this restriction an explosive severing cord would jettison the gearbox and propellers before bailout.

Northrop had expected that the downturned wingtips would provide the necessary stability, but they were mistaken.

ROLLS-ROYCE 'FLYING BEDSTEAD' (1954)

The very basic Thrust Measuring Rig or 'Flying Bedstead' was the first British VTOL aircraft and gathered useful data for the P.1127 (Harrier) project. The Bedstead's loaded weight was only about 272kg (600lb) less than the combined thrust of the two engines, and some of that thrust was ducted away for the control ducts. Each control movement reduced the lifting thrust, requiring a bit more throttle and meaning that it could not be controlled at maximum thrust without a height loss. There was little margin for error – and none at all if one engine faltered. The only plus side was that the engine nozzles were arranged to give thrust (lift) on the centreline so that at least it would plunge vertically rather than flip over. Both Bedsteads did crash, one fatally, and the Harrier adopted a quite different lift system.

SPECIFICATIONS

CREW:	1
POWERPLANT:	two 18kN (4050lb) thrust Rolls-Royce Nene turbojets
MAX SPEED:	n/a
LENGTH:	unknown
HEIGHT:	unknown
WEIGHT:	loaded 3400kg (7500lb)

Left: The UK's first vertical take-off aircraft, the Bedstead has been described as the most dangerous flying machine ever tested. Not intended to travel any distance, it had just 10 minutes' fuel and would turn over if landed with any forward speed.

The pilot's control stick opened and closed valves that directed compressed air to the nozzles mounted at front and rear and on the sides.

The pilot was totally exposed in his seat above the rig. Only after the initial test programme was over was a rudimentary rollover cage added to offer some crash protection.

Like all early jet engines, the Nene took a while to spool up to a new power setting, meaning adjustments had to be made before they were needed.

SUPERMARINE SWIFT *(1951)*

The Swift was the first swept-wing fighter in RAF service, designed largely as a backup to the Hawker Hunter. Service entry (with many restrictions on gun firing, top speed and service ceiling) began in February 1954, followed by a spate of accidents and grounding in August. The F.2 version introduced heavier armament, requiring a longer nose and a wingroot change which affected the stability. A tendency to pitch up and flip over without warning was only solved by adding heavy ballast in the nose. The F.2 was also grounded without seeing much service. The F.3s were used only as instructional airframes, and the afterburner of the F.4 would not light at altitude. The low-level reconnaissance FR.5 was actually a good aircraft, as was the missile-armed F.7, but only 14 of these were built, and they never entered squadron service.

SPECIFICATIONS (Swift F.1)

CREW:	1
POWERPLANT:	one 33.36kN (7500lb) thrust Rolls-Royce Avon RA7 turbojet
MAX SPEED:	1062km/h (660mph)
SPAN:	9.85m (32ft 4in)
LENGTH:	12.65m (41ft 6in)
HEIGHT:	3.81m (12ft 6in)
WEIGHT:	loaded 7167kg (15,800lb)

Left: The swept-wing Swift showed much promise, but it was also beset with numerous problems and saw almost no service as a fighter with the RAF.

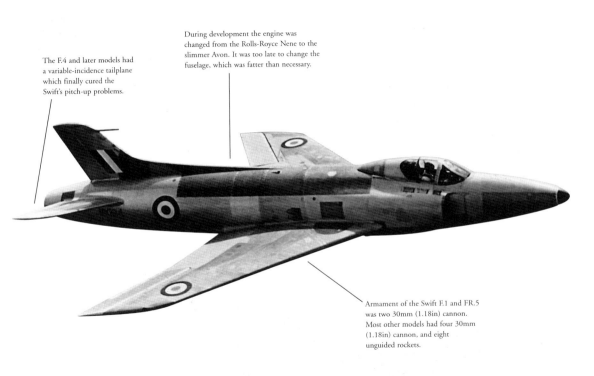

The F.4 and later models had a variable-incidence tailplane which finally cured the Swift's pitch-up problems.

During development the engine was changed from the Rolls-Royce Nene to the slimmer Avon. It was too late to change the fuselage, which was fatter than necessary.

Armament of the Swift F.1 and FR.5 was two 30mm (1.18in) cannon. Most other models had four 30mm (1.18in) cannon, and eight unguided rockets.

313

TARRANT TABOR (1919)

I n 1918, property developer W.G. Tarrant, whose contribution to the war effort to date had been the provision of portable wooden huts to the British Army in France, commissioned Walter Barling to design a giant bomber in response to a call for a 'bloody paralyser' able to bomb Berlin. With its capacious tubular fuselage, the resulting Tabor triplane was designed with one eye on a future civil version perhaps able to carry 100 passengers to India. Its wingspan, at least on the centre wings, was over 10m (32ft) greater than that of a World War II Lancaster. Even before it was ready for flight trials, observers questioned the wisdom of mounting two of the engines high up between the top wings. On the first attempted take-off run the tail was raised using the lower engines, but advancing the throttles on the top pair caused an instant nose-over, killing three of the five on board.

SPECIFICATIONS

CREW:	5
POWERPLANT:	six 336kW (450hp) Napier Lion piston engines
MAX SPEED:	n/a
SPAN:	40.00m (131ft 3in)
LENGTH:	22.30m (73ft 2in)
HEIGHT:	11.36m (37ft 3in)
WEIGHT:	20,263kg (44,672lb)

Left: On the first attempt to fly the giant Tabor, it wound up on its nose, having never left the ground. The RAF gave up on triplanes altogether and the designer went off to America to create the Barling Bomber.

Unlike almost all other triplanes, the centre wings were longest on the Tabor and these mounted the only ailerons.

The Tabor was planned for four Tiger engines, but wound up sporting six Lions. Between each lower wing was a pair of engines mounted back to back.

The tubular fuselage was wider than that of Concorde, and was largely free of wires and internal struts. It was beautifully streamlined, in contrast with the rest of it.

TUPOLEV TU-22 'BLINDER' (1959)

The Tu-22 was the USSR's first supersonic bomber, designed for nuclear strikes against targets in Europe and Asia and (in Tu-22K missile carrier form) against US carrier battle groups. The initial Tu-22B level bomber version saw little active service and the Tu-22K was rushed into use, despite being declared a failure by the official test body. It was dreaded by its crews, and some regarded it as 'unflyable'. This was certainly true on occasions in the 1960s when crews refused to fly it. Among its many faults was a tendency for skin heating at supersonic speeds, distorting the control rods and causing poor handling. The landing speed was about 100km/h (62mph) faster than previous bombers and the 'Blinder' had a tendency to pitch up and strike its tail on landing. The undercarriage was very bouncy and sometimes collapsed – with serious consequences, particularly when carrying a fuelled-up missile. The Tu-22 had downward-firing ejection seats. About 20 per cent of Soviet 'Blinders' were lost in accidents.

SPECIFICATIONS
('Blinder C')

CREW:	3
POWERPLANT:	two 161.7kN (36,376lb) thrust Kolesov RD-7M2 afterburning turbojets
MAX SPEED:	1510km/h (938mph) or Mach 1.4
SPAN:	23.65m (77ft 7in)
LENGTH:	41.6m (136ft 5in)
HEIGHT:	10.67m (35ft)
WEIGHT:	maximum take-off 84,000kg (185,185lb)

Left: The high-performance Tu-22 'Blinder' was forced into service for political reasons, despite failing its acceptance tests. It proved difficult to fly and maintain. Its replacement was the much more successful Tu-22M which, despite its designation, was an all-new aircraft.

Cockpit ergonomics were poor and the aircraft was very tiring to fly, even with autopilot. Even though the pilot's seat was offset, the central windscreen frame blocked the view during crosswind landings.

The Tu-22 carried up to 450 litres (99 gallons) of pure grain alcohol to service its hydraulic and de-icing systems. The ground crews, who predictably drank a lot of it, nicknamed the Tu-22 the 'booze carrier'.

The Tu-22 saw limited Soviet use over Afghanistan, and export customers Libya and Iraq used them in combat, each losing a number to ground fire.

Although faster, the 'Blinder' was shorter-ranged and less reliable than the old Tu-16 'Badger' and could only carry one Kh-22 missile rather than two.

Tu-22s were built with a 23mm (0.9in) cannon in the tail, aimed by a gunner in the forward fuselage using a TV camera. Later this was replaced by an electronic countermeasures system.

Index

Picture Credits